AMERICAN HYBRID POETICS

American Hybrid Poetics

Gender, Mass Culture, and Form

AMY MOORMAN ROBBINS

Rutgers University Press
NEW BRUNSWICK, NEW JERSEY, AND LONDON

LIBRARY OF CONGRESS CATALOGING-IN-PUBLICATION DATA

Robbins, Amy Moorman, 1970–
    American hybrid poetics : gender, mass culture, and form / Amy Moorman Robbins.
        pages   cm. — (American Literatures Initiative)
    Includes bibliographical references and index.
    ISBN 978-0-8135-6465-4 (hardback)
    ISBN 978-0-8135-6464-7 (pbk.)
    ISBN 978-0-8135-6466-1 (e-book)
    1. American poetry—Women authors—History and criticism. 2. Poetics. 3. Aesthetics in literature. 4. Cultural fusion in literature. 5. Women and literature—United States. I. Title.
    PS151.R59   2014
    811.009'9287—dc23

                                                    2013042856

A British Cataloging-in-Publication record for this book is available from the British Library.

Copyright © 2014 by Amy Moorman Robbins

All rights reserved

No part of this book may be reproduced or utilized in any form or by any means, electronic or mechanical, or by any information storage and retrieval system, without written permission from the publisher. Please contact Rutgers University Press, 106 Somerset Street, New Brunswick, NJ 08901. The only exception to this prohibition is "fair use" as defined by US copyright law.

Visit our website: http://rutgerspress.rutgers.edu

Manufactured in the United States of America

A book in the American Literatures Initiative (ALI), a collaborative publishing project of NYU Press, Fordham University Press, Rutgers University Press, Temple University Press, and the University of Virginia Press. The Initiative is supported by The Andrew W. Mellon Foundation. For more information, please visit www.americanliteratures.org.

For Dow
And for our daughters,
Hadley and Daphne

Contents

	Acknowledgments	ix
	Introduction	1
1	Gertrude Stein's *Blood on the Dining-Room Floor*: Hybrid Poetics in Modernist/Mass Culture	20
2	Laura Mullen's *Murmur*: Crime Fiction, Cruel Optimism, and a Hybrid Poetics of Affect	44
3	Alice Notley's *Disobedience*: The Postmodern Subject, Paranoia, and a New Poetics of Noir	71
4	Harryette Mullen's Poetics in Prose: A Return to the Modernist Hybrid	100
5	Claudia Rankine's *Don't Let Me Be Lonely*: A Lyrical Long Poem in a Post-Language Age	124
	Notes	151
	Index	165

Acknowledgments

This book has been a very long time in the making, and many wonderful people have encouraged me along the way. Years ago at the University of Washington I was inspired by the passion and dedication to the field shown by Tom Lockwood, Malcolm Griffith, Ross Posnock, Evan Watkins, and Jack Brenner. At Portland State University I was fortunate to study American feminist literature and Gertrude Stein with the brilliant Francesca Sawaya, and it was at her urging that I embarked on the PhD. Thank you, Francesca. At the University of California, Riverside, I had the greatest good fortune to walk into Steven Gould Axelrod's postmodern American poetry class on the first day of my first semester, and the conversations Steve opened and expertly guided there form the foundation of everything that has followed. Thank you, Steve. Also at UCR, Traise Yamamoto led me through a rigorous education in feminist discourses and modern poetry, always with the highest of intellectual standards and the deep caring of the truest sort of teacher, and the lessons I learned under her tutelage are with me every day. Katherine Kinney and the late, great Emory Elliott offered brilliant courses in American literature and film and were terrific mentors at every step of the way, and Marguerite Waller's course in Third World and feminist cinema was crucial to the development of my thinking about American popular culture. Many thanks also to Rise Axelrod, whose encouragement, generosity, and all around goodwill have made a great difference.

My friends and colleagues in the English Department at Hunter College have supported me in ways I cannot hope to detail in full, but suffice to say that Louise DeSalvo, Jan Heller Levi, and Donna Masini were friends from the first, and our many conversations about writing and teaching have been essential to my professional development but also to my happiness in my department. Marlene Hennessy and Leigh Jones have been faithful and thankfully very funny friends, and Cristina Alfar has provided the strong encouragement and generous support that one hopes for in a department chair but that, sadly, is all too rare in this field. Finally, and not least, the students in my undergraduate and master's classes at Hunter have been remarkable in their willingness to engage the work of little-known poets with seriousness and genuine excitement, and their questions and observations at times have led to important new threads of inquiry. I am fortunate to work with such vibrant and intellectually curious students, who make teaching a rewarding and generative part of my work. My research and writing have been helped along by Shelly Eversley, whose mentorship in the CUNY Faculty Fellowship Publication Program was crucial to the development of my argument in this book. My colleagues in the FFPP during the spring of 2010 were thoughtful readers and engaging interlocutors; sincere thanks to Maria Rice Bellamy, Jason Frydman, Jody Rosen, Charity Scribner, and Vanessa Valdes. Thank you to the City University of New York for that fellowship and for the time off it afforded. I am especially grateful for the two PSC CUNY research grants that allowed me to work at the UC San Diego Archive for New Poetry on two separate occasions. I would also like to thank the curators and staff at the Archive for New Poetry, who were extremely helpful in allowing me access to the archives. Deep thanks to Juliana Spahr and the anonymous reader at Rutgers University Press who offered tremendously helpful comments and raised crucial questions regarding earlier drafts of this manuscript; this book has been shaped by their engagement with my arguments, though of course all faults in the work are my own. Special thanks to Laura Mullen, who graciously granted an interview and who read and commented on an earlier version of the chapter included here. Thank you also to Katie Keeran at Rutgers University Press for her sound advice and guidance.

    This book could not have been written nor even attempted if not for the strong support of my husband, Dow Robbins. For fifteen years I have taken heart from his unending faith in me, faith that has carried me through years of graduate school and many lonely hours as I researched and wrote first a dissertation and now this book. Dow, this book is for you first. And last but also first, I want to thank my patient and long-suffering daughters, Hadley Robbins and Daphne Robbins, who in their brilliant, hilarious, and inimitable ways have kept me thoroughly informed on everything I've been missing while occupied with what follows in these pages. I am fortunate beyond measure to have these giving children who remind me daily of the many other important things in life. This book is for them, too, with love.

Permissions

Charles Baudelaire, excerpts from *The Flowers of Evil*, translated by Keith Waldrop (Middletown, CT: Wesleyan University Press, 2006). Copyright © 2006 by Keith Waldrop. Reprinted with permission of Wesleyan University Press.

Czeslaw Milosz, "The Gift," from *The Collected Poems 1931–1987* (New York: HarperCollins, 1988). Copyright © 1988 by Czeslaw Milosz Royalties, Inc. Reprinted by permission of HarperCollins Publishers.

Harryette Mullen, poems from *Sleeping with the Dictionary* (Berkeley: University of California Press, 2002). Reprinted with permission of the publisher.

Harryette Mullen, S*PeRM**K*T poems, from *Recyclopedia* (St. Paul: Graywolf Press, 2006). Copyright © 2006 by Harryette Mullen. Reprinted with permission of The Permissions Company, Inc., on behalf of Graywolf Press, www.graywolfpress.org.

Laura Mullen, excerpts from *Murmur* (New York: Futurepoem Books, 2007). Copyright © 2007 by Laura Mullen. Reprinted with permission of The Permissions Company, Inc., on behalf of Futurepoem Books, www.futurepoem.com.

Alice Notley, "But He Says I Misunderstood," "January," and "How Spring Comes," from *The Selected Poems of Alice Notley* (Hoboken, NJ: Talisman House, 1993). Used by permission of Alice Notley.

Alice Notley, "I'm Just Rigid Enough," "The Trouble with You Girls," and "Sept 17/Aug 29, '88," from *Mysteries of Small Houses* (New York: Penguin Books, 1998). Copyright © 1998 by Alice Notley. Used by permission of Viking Penguin, a division of Penguin Group (USA) LLC.

Alice Notley, "Change the Forms in Dreams" and "What's Suppressed," from *Disobedience* (New York: Penguin Books, 2001). Copyright © 2001 by Alice Notley. Used by permission of Viking Penguin, a division of Penguin Group (USA) LLC.

Alice Notley, Interview with Brian Kim Stefans, *Publishers Weekly*, August 27, 2001. Copyright © 2001 by Brian Kim Stefans.

Alice Notley, Interview with Claudia Keelan, *American Poetry Review* 33, no. 3 (May–June 2004) Copyright © 2004 by Claudia Keelan.

Alice Notley, "Am Here" (unpublished memoir). Used by permission of Alice Notley.

Claudia Rankine, excerpts from *Don't Let Me Be Lonely: An American Lyric* (St. Paul: Graywolf Press, 2004). Copyright © 2004 by Claudia Rankine. Reprinted with permission of The Permissions Company, Inc., on behalf of Graywolf Press, www.graywolf.org.

Claudia Rankine, interview with Katy Lederer, *The Verse Book of Interviews: 27 Poets on Language, Craft, and Culture*, edited by Brian Henry and Andrew Zawacki (Seattle: Verse Press, 2005). Reprinted with the permission of The Permissions Company, Inc., on behalf of Wave Books.

Claudia Rankine, interview with Jennifer Flescher and Robert Caspar, *Jubilat* 12 (July 2006). Used by permission of the publisher.

Gertrude Stein, passages from *The Making of Americans*, 1925 (Normal, IL: Dalky Archive, 1995). With kind permission of the estate of Gertrude Stein, David Higham Associates Ltd.

Gertrude Stein, passages from *Blood on the Dining-Room Floor*, 1933 (New York: Dover, 1982). With kind permission of the estate of Gertrude Stein, David Higham Associates Ltd.

Gertrude Stein, passages from "Reflection on the Atomic Bomb," in *How Writing Is Written: Previously Uncollected Writings of Gertrude Stein*, vol. 1, edited by Robert Bartlett Haas (Los Angeles: Black Sparrow Press, 1973); "American Crimes and How They Matter" and "Why I Like Detective Stories," in *How Writing Is Written: Previously Uncollected Writings of Gertrude Stein*, vol. 2, edited by Robert Bartlett Haas (Los Angeles: Black Sparrow Press, 1974). With kind permission of the estate of Gertrude Stein, David Higham Associates Ltd.

AMERICAN HYBRID POETICS

Introduction

This book is an analysis of the concept of hybrid poetics as it circulates in the current critical discourse surrounding contemporary American poetry and as it informs innovative work by several American women poets in particular. I argue that, far from being new, hybrid aesthetics—most frequently defined as the playful mixing of disparate formal and aesthetic strategies—have a firm foundation and a distinct history in the work of radical women poets from throughout the past century, poets who have created such mixings as part of a resistance to being fixed in any particular school or camp, sometimes (as in the case of Alice Notley) on the grounds that such camps are most often dominated by male poets. Yet even though many of these important poets are acknowledged and anthologized in the two major venues for hybrid poetics, the Norton anthology *American Hybrid* and *Fence* magazine, repeated claims to the newness of hybrid poetics decontextualizes this work and renders it in a curiously apolitical light. Indeed, I argue that the current debate raging around the politics of hybrid poetics—one part of which comprises the post-Language, "Post-Avant" community claim that hybridity is a watering down of the avant-garde in its appropriation of politically engendered forms for presumably apolitical ends—is provoked if not justified by proponents, enthusiasts, and marketers of hybrid poetics who celebrate what they claim is new on the grounds that it simply *is* new, altogether ignoring the history, context, and political implications of the work itself. That the avant-garde community has not looked more closely at the work assembled under the sign of the hybrid, preferring instead to bicker with editors' often reductive descriptions of the concept, is nevertheless something of a curiosity, suggesting as it does the avant-garde community's anxiety surrounding its legacy and future. And so, with the editors of *American Hybrid* and *Fence* magazine pointing to ostensibly new aesthetics on one side, and the avant-garde community pointing to a perceived erasure of politics on the other, the work that has been labeled hybrid—much of it political, much of it by women writers—goes thoroughly unexamined. The fact that some of these writers have lately received critical attention as experimental writers makes their subsequent erasure as poets creating innovative hybrid works somewhat ironic, but also of a piece with a literary history in which writing by women in any school or movement goes unexamined for far too long.

Throughout this study I explore the ways in which hybrid aesthetics have been the driving force in the work of a historically and culturally diverse group of women poets who are part of a robust tradition in contesting the dominant cultural order—as well as implicitly masculinist avant-garde dogma—in ever-new, innovative, and formally subversive ways. In my discussion of the work of the five poets discussed herein—Gertrude Stein, Laura Mullen, Alice Notley, Harryette Mullen, and Claudia Rankine—I show the ways in which hybridity can be understood as an implicitly political strategy, one that forces encounters between hitherto incompatible literary traditions and that thereby brings to the surface competing ideologies and their implications for lived experience. At the same time, I argue that it is precisely because these poets have mixed forms that entail disparate ideologies (consumer culture with the avant-garde, low culture forms with theory-based poetics, speakerly prose poetry with linguistic experimentation) that their work has largely gone unnoticed by leading members and critics in experimental poetry circles; such mixings of high with the feminized low are rarely treated as serious forays into oppositional art, as the current debate surrounding hybrid poetics reveals. Analyzing this intergenre, interformal work for the ways it crosses aesthetic and ideological boundaries, I show how hybridity can entail a mixing of the high and low in defiance of those highly gendered modernist values that still hold sway (all claims to the contrary); dialogical play with the competing aims of discrete genres; expansion of the limits of established forms; and attempts to complicate the notion of selfhood—and the politics of citizenship—as articulated in the literature of our current moment. Throughout the book, then, the concept of hybridity is explored in terms formal, cultural, historical, and political, as I locate the work of a select group of women writers both in a history of literary experimentation and a current constellation of writing practices that elude the avant-garde's attempts at categorization, even as seeds of their contestations, subversions, and innovations are not new but rather have been germinating for quite some time.

The "New" Movement

The term "hybrid," by now quite familiar to most readers of poetry, scholars, and conference attendees, remains nevertheless vague and curiously underexamined in the critical conversation surrounding poetry, even as it can be seen to function in highly visible mainstream publishing venues as a catchall term for blended aesthetics and generic exotics, newness and fashionability, progress and youth. At first glance, considering one of the primary terms of hybrid poetics currently circulating—a mixing of previously unmixed forms taken from various genres and schools of writing—we might say that so-called hybrid aesthetics have made appearances under other names throughout the twentieth century, evident in the work of Gertrude Stein, William Carlos Williams, Muriel Rukeyser, Gloria Anzaldúa, and Theresa Cha, to name but a few. But this is not the story that is currently being told by critics and anthologists of hybrid works. For, vague descriptions of mixed genres and blended aesthetics aside, the most consistently repeated characteristic attributed to what remains a loosely defined notion of hybrid poetics is its purported *newness*; whatever the formal particulars may be, much if not all of the recent and admired hybrid poetry is—we are told—very, very new.

In the two major publishing venues for the hybrid, the 2009 Norton anthology *American Hybrid* and *Fence* magazine, the editors have claimed that a new, younger generation of poets is actively seeking new ways of innovating in the art form after a long and divisive twentieth century in which poets had to side with one aesthetic camp or another. Stephen Burt, one of the editors of *Fence* and the author of the recent essay, "*Fence*, or, the Happy Return of the Modernist Alligator," describes the sad state of affairs at the end of the last century thus:

> The early 1990s—especially in poetry, but in fiction too—seemed thick with schools and movements, manifestos and charismatic teachers, who mapped out the routes they encouraged young writers to follow. Some of those routes looked far too much like plans of attack: New writing, during those years, defined itself too often,

and too earnestly, by divisions and by taken sides. Who did you represent? Who did you attack?[1]

According to Burt, who places a discussion of context ahead of any descriptions of particular forms, it was young poets' open refusal of their elders' command to choose sides that gave birth to the hybrid—a form that in Burt's essay remains rooted in filial disaffection. Moreover, Burt's choices of descriptors for the hybrid—"fashion forward" and "idiosyncratic"—lend an air of commercialism and superficiality to such poetics, an air that seems somewhat inappropriate when attributed to poets such as Rae Armantrout, Harryette Mullen, and Juliana Spahr, well-known feminist experimentalists who are included in both anthologies.

In their ostensibly more historicist introductions to the Norton *American Hybrid*, coeditors Cole Swensen and David St. John identify hybrid poetic forms as those that cross the line between formerly opposing camps. As such, these new hybrids are formally neither purely lyric nor Language (to name a tired but still functional binary model), neither avant-garde nor New Formalist, neither coherently narrative nor completely epic, neither/nor any single category at all, but instead and in various ways mixings (Swensen rejects the term "blendings") of the features attendant on all of these schools and forms. St. John calls hybrid poetry that which "has ignored and/or defied categorization, poetry that embraces a variety of—even sometimes contradictory—poetic ambitions and aesthetics,"[2] and Swensen says that

> [t]oday's hybrid poem might engage such conventional approaches as narrative that presumes a stable first person, yet complicate it by disrupting the linear temporal path or by scrambling the normal syntactical sequence. Or it might foreground recognizably experimental modes such as illogicality or fragmentation, yet follow the strict formal rules of a sonnet or a villanelle. Or it might be composed entirely of neologisms but based in ancient traditions. Considering the traits associated with "conventional" work, such as coherence, linearity, formal clarity, narrative, firm closure, symbolic resonance, and stable voice, and those generally assumed of "experimental" work, such as non-linearity, juxtaposition, rupture, fragmentation, immanence, multiple perspective, open form, and resistance to closure, hybrid poets access a wealth of tools, each one of which can change dramatically depending on how it is combined with others and the particular role it plays in the composition.[3]

Later I will return to the specifics of Swensen's description, for she does name some writing practices that are to be found in experimental writing by women from across the century, practices that I take up later in this study. But for now, suffice to say that for St. John, Swensen, and Burt, bold new mixings of forms in fact *mean* a rejection of the prohibitions handed down by teachers and elder poets, this last standing as the movement's central claim to oppositional status. Given that this is a primary claim, then, it is somewhat curious that Swensen and St. John chose to include in *American Hybrid* only poets who are established enough to have published at least three books each, both editors averring nonetheless that hybridity is fundamentally new and that the younger poets will have their own anthology soon.[4] And it is even more striking that on inspection of *American Hybrid*'s table of contents, we find Rae Armantrout, Mei-mei Berssenbrugge, Kathleen Fraser, Jorie Graham, Barbara Guest, Lyn Hejinian, Susan Howe, Myung Mi Kim, Ann Lauterbach, Harryette Mullen, Laura Mullen, Juliana Spahr, and other luminaries of various innovative or experimental poetry communities.[5] In fact it would seem that innovative women poets of an earlier generation have played a central role in founding the new movement so designated by Swensen and St. John, and yet they are anthologized under the sign of the hybrid presumably because of their aesthetic innovations in the wake of Language writing, even as the widely acknowledged political dimensions of their work are not taken up in any serious way.

Yet it is important to note that for Swensen and other vocal defenders of hybrid poetics, the hybrid is indeed an oppositional art form, though its opposition is not framed as being against any immediately graspable power structure or social injustice. Rather, for these critics, it is sufficient that hybrid poetics are oppositional to what is perceived to be a long history of factionalism among various poetry schools. Keeping in mind those included in *American Hybrid*, this criteria might recall for some the *HOW(ever)* poets who once occupied a space at times in between and at other times beyond lyric and Language aesthetics; yet this historically specific alternative and feminist space is not mentioned. Instead, and claiming that the hybrid has emerged just now at the beginning of the twenty-first century as a reaction to more than a century of warring camps, Swensen gives a brief account of what she calls a longstanding two-camp "situation" in modern and postmodern American poetry, starting with the split between the neo-Romantic poetics of transcendence and the modernist poetics of the linguistically new as a point of origin on the long road of ideological disagreement and aesthetic discord.[6] Charting the ever-shifting but in her view structurally consistent terrain on which new camps arise out of old ones, Swensen points to the midcentury conflict between New Critical aesthetics of the formally unified text and the "uncooked" aesthetics inspired by Charles Olson's projective verse, the latter reflected in a variety of contemporaneous movements on both coasts and anthologized in Donald Allen's landmark *New American Poetry*. From there, according to Swensen, Language aesthetics took hold as late twentieth-century politically radical poets rejected the use of the post-Romantic expressive lyric and turned instead to avant-garde theories of the materiality of the text, and the lyric-versus-Language divide was thus established, with poets on both sides sticking to their own. In this tidy narrative, the history of poetry in the twentieth century is a history defined by a series of thoroughly intact binary oppositions that have been shored up by the anthology wars and that have forced emerging poets to choose sides. But now, in the presumably utopic present, young poets (Swensen says many of them are under forty[7]) can finally separate from their oppressive "parents" and have it all, aesthetically speaking. Echoing this very sentiment, Laura Mullen very recently has said of her own hybrid poetics, "I don't have to choose Mommy, I don't have to choose Daddy, I can have both."[8] In offering what amounts to a narrative of progress, then, Swensen describes a new trend in poets' recombining of formerly opposed aesthetic strategies taken from any and *all* of these camps, a trend toward creating new work that "has selectively inherited traits" from across the spectrum of twentieth-century poetry and that "honor[s] the avant-garde mandate to renew the forms and expand the boundaries of poetry—thereby increasing the expressive potential of language itself—while also remaining committed to the emotional spectra of lived experience."[9]

Swensen's broad account of a twentieth century of two warring camps notwithstanding, recent debates in public and in print reveal that she in fact views hybridity as a recent reaction to a very recent war. In a published response to critiques of the Norton anthology, Swensen answers critics who say that the anthology is not inclusive of nonwhite poets and does not fully acknowledge the relevance of gender and sexuality in notions of hybridity; against these arguments Swensen claims that the anthology's mission was in fact to publish poets responding to the late twentieth-century poetry wars. Here she backs away from an earlier claim that the poets in *American Hybrid* are responding to a century of discord, now locating the work in the specific context of the lyric-versus-Language division, a two-camp model rife with its own internal divisions, gender politics, and a very important and vocal excluded middle, none of which Swensen addresses.[10] And so, given Swensen's claim that hybridity meets the avant-garde mandate to renew, and her implicit and at times explicit positioning of hybrid poetics as a purely aesthetic movement born out of an unexamined lyric-versus-Language divide, it is not at all surprising that poets identifying with our current avant-garde should express antipathy toward hybrid poetics on the grounds that they are both ornamental and fundamentally apolitical. Indeed, Swensen's and St. John's inclusion of innovative poets, simultaneous with their refusal to speak to politics in any way, makes it possible for the avant-garde to overlook the ways in which some of this work not only can be political, but already has been so.

The Debates

As an example of these strong reactions, Ron Silliman in his blog names the current trend "School of Quietude" poetics, erecting a division between these and "Post-Avant" poetics; as a major point of criticism, he points to the "School of Q" poets' appropriation of historically politicized aesthetics alongside the refusal to claim a mission or a politics of their own.[11] Here Silliman is clearly addressing the editors of these anthologies and missing the table of contents, for one could hardly say that Lyn Hejinian, Susan Howe, and Juliana Spahr participate in any school of quietude; in fact, Silliman's response is directed at Swensen's and St. John's silence on the point of politics. Taking the same tack in a critique of *Fence*, Steve Evans's "The Resistible Rise of *Fence* Enterprises," which appears in his widely read *Third Factory Notes*, is a thoroughgoing assault on the editors of *Fence* that critiques the editors' mission to publish "idiosyncratic" poetry on the grounds that it is silly and commercial; indeed, Evans's choice of "enterprises" as a descriptor of a literary magazine would not seem to indicate any intellectual seriousness therein.[12] In yet another example of this kind of response, at the June 2010 Rethinking Poetics conference held at Columbia University, poet and critic Joshua Clover gave a vehement denunciation of hybrid poetics, implicating the Norton anthology and what he called the "*Fence* manifesto" as evidence of the watering down of the avant-garde. Critic Marjorie Perloff, seated in the audience, chimed in to dismiss hybrid poetics as a simple "A+B formulation," where lyric sensibility is attached to experimental aesthetics, resulting in work that does nothing to advance the political work of the avant-garde. *Fence* editor Rebecca Wolff, also in the audience, responded angrily to Clover's allegations, and the ensuing brouhaha revealed the degree to which hybridity—as defined by Norton and *Fence*—is perceived to be aimed at unseating Language poetry's influence on conceptual poetics as political work, but is also perceived to be avoiding claiming a politics of its own, even as many of the women poets anthologized (some of them in the room when Clover gave his talk) are in fact openly political. Notable about this debate is its effectiveness in shoring up a concept of hybridity as an empty aesthetic response to a political movement; the arguments coming from both sides would seem to indicate that this is in fact the case. Still more striking is the silence surrounding and easy erasure of women's innovative political writing within what amounts to yet another territorial two-camp model.

Moreover, there are other critiques of hybridity taking place in the shadow of this most visible one. In April of 2010—just two months prior to the Rethinking Poetics conference—a panel of five poets and critics at the Association of Writers and Writing Programs (AWP) conference in Denver mounted a multifaceted critique of *American Hybrid*; the five papers have since been published under the heading "Hybrid Aesthetics and Its Discontents" in *The Monkey and the Wrench: Essays into Contemporary Poetics*, edited by Mary Biddinger and John Gallaher.[13] In these papers, Mark Wallace, Michael Theune, Arielle Greenberg, Craig Santos Perez, and Megan Volpert challenge Swensen's creation of a new center with her concept of hybridity (Wallace); the humorlessness of the poetry curated for *American Hybrid* (Theune); the absence of certain other forms of "weirdness" and idiosyncrasy from the relatively heteronormative cast of poets chosen as examples (Greenberg and Volpert); and the utter silence surrounding the origins of theories of hybridity in the poetry and critical race work coming from the Native American, Asian American, and Latina/o communities in the 1970s, 1980s, and 1990s. These last two points of critique add significant dimension to the critique of hybrid poetics as insufficiently political, pushing that critique even further into suggestions of the reactionary. For what are the implications of two predominantly white anthologies claiming "hybridity" as an aesthetically idiosyncratic and playfully insouciant response to thirty years of poetry wars waged by institutionally secure (mostly white, mostly male) teachers while ignoring the centrality of discussions of cultural, racial, gendered, and formal hybridities that informed the literary-critical conversation in other segments of the academy during the exact same time? Pointing to the omission of the hybrid poetics studied and/or written by radical writers of color, including the work of Arnold Krupat, Louis Owens, Lisa Lowe, Gloria Anzaldúa, Alfred Arteaga, and Jose David Saldívar, Craig Santos Perez writes, "Thus it becomes clear that 'American Hybrid' should have been more accurately titled 'White American Hybrid.'"[14] Yet Perez doesn't stop at critiquing what he perceives to be little more than a new marketing ploy for mostly white American writers. For in fact he lays the blame for the emergence of this white version of hybridity at the feet of Ron Silliman and the predominately white avant-garde community who have long presumed to decide what is political—and what is aesthetically relevant—in poetry, effectively provoking responses such as Swensen's, St. John's, and *Fence*'s. In fact it could be argued that one of the legacies of Language writing is a collectively felt fear of being wrong about politics, which seems to have manifested in recent cases as a desire to avoid discussion of politics altogether. Indeed, speaking to the Language writers' dominance in poetry criticism while pointing up the erasure of writers who don't fit within their cultural and aesthetic boundaries—a point that also echoes the sentiments of innovative women writers in the 1980s—Perez says, "Let's face it: it's Silliman's poetry world and we just blog in it."[15]

In what follows I take as a fundamental given that in narratives of literary history where there is presumed to be only staunch opposition between two camps, a tremendous amount of intergenre or politically/aesthetically innovative work from across the century remains invisible, even as the politics of difference as it informs such innovative work is utterly ignored. For in these narratives of the past century, where is mention of Melvin Tolson's hybrid *Harlem Gallery*, Charles Reznikoff's *Testimony* or *Holocaust*, Muriel Rukeyser's *The Book of the Dead*, William Carlos Williams's *Paterson*, or Leslie Marmon Silko's *Storyteller*? Still further, in a discursive model that positions hybridity as an aesthetic response arising out of discord with a territorial late twentieth-century political debate, the politics of later mixed-genre, formally innovative work by poets such as those published by Kathleen Fraser in *HOW(ever)* also remains unexamined. Only by erasing the long history of nonconforming aesthetics and excluded middles in American literary history can Swensen claim that hybrid mixings of genre are new. At the same time, in making these omissions Swensen doesn't have to deal with the politics and unique histories of radical ruptures of poetic form and previous attempts to force material experience into engagement with aesthetics. For his part, Stephen Burt does attempt to claim a legacy for mixed-genre poetics in the work of Williams and Stein, pointing to the resurgence of the "springy, deciduous, gaudy, unscholarly, optimistic immediacies of the New York modernism that Williams and his allies hoped to create," and arguing that "[one] might say that with *Fence* that modernism awoke."[16] Yet here again the politics of the deciduous and gaudy are left unexamined. Indeed, Swensen's and Burt's somewhat bland claims that today's poets are simply feeling free to choose from "a wealth of tools"[17] as they embark on a lot of what John Ashbery referred to as "fence-sitting" suggests not a politically and aesthetically investigative poetics but rather Fredric Jameson's thoroughly pessimistic description of postmodernism, in which aesthetics of formal pastiche produce what he calls "a new depthlessness," a state of affairs marking the end of interested social critique.[18] It is just here that *American Hybrid* can be seen to run afoul of critics of hybrid poetry's most vocal opposition, Language writers and others in the avant-garde community who see opposition to official culture in materialist dialectical terms and who develop aesthetics that are implicitly critical of mainstream American ideology. And so it is at this meeting point of discord between the "purely" aesthetic and the clearly if narrowly defined political, at which so much that has been political in mixed-form poetry is ignored, that I situate my own analysis of some twentieth- and twenty-first-century hybrid poetry by American women.

The Argument

In my analyses of the writings of Gertrude Stein, Laura Mullen, Alice Notley, Harryette Mullen, and Claudia Rankine, I show the ways in which select works by each mix high and low forms and historically distinct literary modes in some degree of shared complicity with American mass culture, and with very clear political implications for gendered subjects in particular. Considered in light of Andreas Huyssen's analysis of mass culture as it has since the advent of modernism played the role of low feminine other to high culture, which Huyssen argues is implicitly masculine, the works chosen for study here each foreground the gendered, classed, and raced associations of their chosen host form, playing with attendant conventions and making "serious" art out of popular culture even as they subvert the traditional workings of gender, class, and race circulating in these forms. Keeping in mind yet departing from Theodor Adorno's assertion that there is no outside to the mass culture that has replaced official culture as the dominant mode of social control in our time, I aim to show how it is precisely through these writers' interrogations and subversions of mass culture or mainstream forms—made possible through development of hybrid high-meets-low, mixed-genre aesthetics—that they foment a feminist, populist avant-gardism. For rather than stand well apart from mass culture in a posture of total rejection, a stance borne out of an avant-gardist dialectical sensibility and one that has been taken up by many in the Language community, the poets studied here take a more complicit attitude, allowing for the pervasive influence of mass culture in shaping public life even as they remain cognizant of the role of the feminine as it has been assigned to all that is low. Thus, their subversions of mass culture forms are both subversions of an outmoded dialectical avant-gardism, in which serious artists must reject forms associated with mainstream culture and bourgeois values, at the same time that these artistic practices are interrogations of the role of the degraded feminine as it continues to inform our official culture.

My argument derives from two somewhat congruent streams, although there is a central division between the two. For on the one hand I am analyzing some hybrid poetries for the ways in which this work is complicit—even celebratory—of mainstream mass culture, while on the other hand I am showing how an art of complicity can also be an art of revolution. As I will show, what connects these two modes of thinking is a feminist drive to imagine new worlds out of familiar ones (and mass culture is nothing if not familiar) together with a sincere doubt about ever finding a secure place therein. As foundation for the first part of my argument I am drawing on the work of feminist experimentalist poet and avant-garde visual art critic Johanna Drucker. In *Sweet Dreams: Contemporary Art and Complicity,* Drucker argues that the avant-garde dialectic in which oppositional art must necessarily stand entirely outside official culture in order to wage effective critique is in fact outmoded and insufficient for showing how much of our contemporary art actually works. She argues that it has become a highly predictable and therefore meaningless rhetorical move to say that such-and-such defamiliarizing art piece is by dint of its form a viable outsider critique of this or that cultural phenomenon, and she points out how this critical position, by now having taken root in academia, is in fact the new official-culture doctrine, one that validates artists for waging alternative critiques even as these artists beg for inclusion in new centers of power.[19] In her view this established pattern of criticism is insufficient for understanding how new art is significant beyond a narrowly formulated dialectic in which what is bad is always the same (capitalism) and what is therefore good is understood in programmatic fashion. Moreover, for Drucker, the valuing of art based almost solely upon its relative degree of separation from mainstream or official culture has resulted in a field of art that "means" to only a select few viewers, a system in which actual relevance to contemporary viewers (many or most of whom turn away) is entirely beside the point. Arguing for attention to new aesthetics that play with the detritus of mass culture in ways not immediately legible as oppositional, Drucker shows how some contemporary visual art finds beauty in the mundane, and she analyzes this work for how aesthetic properties that are not created out of a preformed political doxa can be revelatory of new modes of being and seeing in a post-avant-garde era.[20] Drucker's argument for new ways of understanding the work culturally complicit fine art can do corresponds to my own argument for the cultural value to be found in hybrid poetics that mix previously unmixed forms, making new aesthetics out of material formerly off-limits to would-be serious poets. And precisely because Drucker herself is an experimentalist poet, and also because the poets I am writing about are each and in unique ways engaging visual media, do I feel Drucker's work in the visual arts to be germane to this project.

And yet, although I borrow from Drucker's theory of complicity in contemporary art, I am not arguing that the poetry discussed here is *entirely* complicit or lacking in any oppositional cultural/political value. Quite to the contrary, I argue that its complicity *is* its political value, and that in mixing disparate genres and crossing high aesthetics with low these feminist experimentalist poets are laying groundwork for a new strain of avant-garde literary practice in which mass culture is not to be eschewed or denounced but rather engaged and creatively reinvented. In her groundbreaking *Subversive Intent: Gender, Politics, and the Avant-Garde*, Susan Rubin Suleiman shows that a feminist, avant-gardist challenging of mainstream mass culture in fact has precedence in the visual art of Jenny Holzer and Barbara Kruger. Suleiman points to Holzer's creative use of electric signs in airports and other public spaces to broadcast (or visually blast) critiques of capitalism, and she analyzes Barbara Kruger's often shocking billboards for their similar intent; both artists have launched trenchant metacritiques of advertising media as part of a more sweeping critique of consumer capitalism.[21] Suleiman writes that "[t]he hope expressed in such statements is that it is possible to find openings even in the monolithic mechanism of the culture industry; that it is possible for innovative, critical work to reach a large audience."[22] Whereas the art analyzed by Drucker originates in a search among the commonplace for the beautiful, rather than out of an established politics, the art analyzed by Suleiman shows how avant-garde aesthetic practice can be politically feminist while also being populist. My own argument derives from both of these theorists, in that I consider some women poets' hybrid aesthetics as playful mixings of forms that politics once deemed anathema, even as I argue that the results can be trenchant critiques of consumer mass culture that use its own products against itself.

Thus in what follows I show how we can read the term "hybrid" as both an aesthetics of the mix as well as a politics of the socially constructed in-between, a space from which marginally positioned individuals, through development of innovative and nonconforming art, can wage critique of the totalizing culture within which they find themselves. While there are numerous excellent studies considering the work of contemporary innovative women poets—many of them engaged here—this is the first book-length study of the politics of generic hybridity as it can be seen to function as an innovative and specifically feminist poetics of critical difference. At the same time, this is the first study of recent experimental poetry that treats the role of mass culture in this genre, attending to the significance of women poets engaging forms historically associated derisively with gendered subjects while also reopening the debate surrounding high and low art that was inaugurated with modernism. For undergirding my study of these intergeneric works is the assumption that the high-versus-low divide was not abolished with the dawn of postmodernism—as Andreas Huyssen so optimistically claimed in 1987—but instead remains very much intact, structuring critiques of new poetics via the buried gender politics of avant-gardism.[23]

In my study I am joining a conversation already begun by recent scholars in the field of women's experimental writing, a field within which all or most of these poets have been situated by other critics at one time or another. I build on the critical work of Elisabeth A. Frost, who first theorized a feminist avant-garde that crossed cultural boundaries and who also points to the mixed-genre structure of some of Harryette Mullen's work, as well as the work of Claudia Rankine and Juliana Spahr, who have assembled a landmark anthology of creative and critical work coming from women whose work conforms to neither the lyric nor Language camp, work that has exhibited features we have come to associate with the hybrid well before that term came into wide circulation.[24] At various points in this study I take recourse to Linda Kinnahan's work complicating the lyric and claiming its ongoing vitality as a feminist form, and I borrow from Lynn Keller's theorizing about women's long poems.[25] *American Hybrid Poetics: Gender, Mass Culture, and Form* is in many ways a departure from this body of scholarship in the sense that for the most part, with perhaps the exception of Harryette Mullen, I privilege analysis of the gender politics of competing genres over analysis of the word within the text. For while it goes without saying that what Marjorie Perloff has famously termed "the word as such" remains of interest in relation to experimental writing generally, I show how in attending to formal structures and generic subversions we can discern alternative routes to political critique and new forms of what Joan Retallack has termed "poethical" thinking, or a mode of critical thinking in which the ethics of artistic practice are taken always into account.[26]

The Poets

Like other recent studies of women experimentalists, I begin my own study with the work of Gertrude Stein, a writer whose importance to experimental and innovative poetics continues to grow. Yet I am taking a different direction in analyzing what has been dismissed by critics Ulla Dydo and Richard Bridgman as a failed work, her mystery novel *Blood on the Dining-Room Floor*. Unpublished in Stein's lifetime yet lovingly printed and preserved by Alice B. Toklas, this short novel is perceived as a failure precisely because Stein was writing in the popular genre of detective fiction; indeed, the critical reception of the work once it was published echoes the current view that avant-garde art and popular genres don't mix, a bias in which we hear echoes of the current "post-avant" reception of formally hybrid poetics that are perceived to mix forms in the absence of any political value. I begin the first chapter with an overview of Huyssen's assessment of mass culture as it played the role of feminine other to masculine high culture at the turn of the last century, and I show how this plays out in the critical reception of a popular work coming from the other side of the high/low divide in Stein's time: Dashiell Hammett's hybrid gothic/noir detective novel *The Dain Curse*. Although Hammett was much admired by Stein for being by her own definition a quintessentially modern novelist, Hammett's status as a modernist writer is compromised in the estimation of later critics because he is perceived to have been catering to the mainstream audience's desire for plot resolution. Precisely because the terms of his failure echo the terms by which Stein's *Blood on the Dining-Room Floor* is assumed by critic Ulla Dydo to be mere "audience writing" do I take time in this chapter considering the plotlines and swerves of Hammett's text as compared to Stein's.

Pointing to the gender codes inherent in literary devices as well as the gender politics informing critics' dismissal of mass culture forms, I then turn to Stein's play with the popular form of the Victorian mystery novel in order to show how she both solicits a complicit audience and frustrates desire for the very closure Hammett eventually delivers, thus producing a provocatively experimental work that deserves a more favorable place in the Stein canon. For in its layering of serious play with syntax, repetition, intertextuality, and conventions of narrative realism, Stein's *Blood on the Dining-Room Floor* invites readers into the shared affective space of Victorian propriety in order to mock and subvert those heteronormative middle-class social values that render lesbian sexuality simultaneously invisible and under threat. Just as *Tender Buttons* massages the quotidian normative domestic until it becomes a site of intimate lesbian domesticity, as Elisabeth A. Frost and Rebecca Scherr have argued, Stein's mystery story massages the details of Victorian propriety upheld in mainstream fiction until that propriety is revealed as suffocating. Stein achieves this by placing the reader—through identification with the voyeuristic narrator—in the affective space of surveillance, leading us into a shared desire for illicit secrets, and therefore implicitly toward desire for control over and containment of nonnormative sexualities. Even as structurally the text repeats back on itself in a series of playful undoings, the reader is moved forward by an activated desire for forbidden knowledge, a progress that is interrupted by the suggestively lesbian and outlandishly subversive presence of Lizzie Borden. I argue that it is through this send-up of a vernacular form that Stein makes possible reader identification with conservative social values, a shared identification that she is then able to shatter with textual upheaval. Examining *Blood on the Dining-Room Floor* in this light, as well as for the ways it merges recursive narration and indirection with the popular genre of women's detective fiction, I show how Stein employs gothic conventions of secrecy and the unsayable in an intricate critique of the patriarchal household and the invisibility of lesbian relations in a generic literary framework that functions as metonym for the sociocultural mandate for women to marry and reproduce. Finally, I show how the novel's complex, revisionary narrative structure subverts not only the popular genre of the mystery but also the early twentieth-century culture that consumes these novels, a culture in which Victorian patriarchal values obliterate the potential for lesbian relations within the middle-class family.

In the second chapter, on the work of Laura Mullen, a poet who has received relatively little critical attention, I analyze Mullen's mixed-genre poem/novel *Murmur* for the ways in which it reworks the genre of detective fiction in feminist oppositional terms while foregrounding the politics inherent in women's consumption of mass-market fiction, a politics underscored in Huyssen's analysis of Flaubert's *Madame Bovary*. I show how Mullen follows Stein in parading across the page material fetishes embedded within the popular genre—in Mullen's particular case the fetish of the hypermasculine noir hero and the mutilated female corpse—in order to unpack both their ideological content and their deep functionality in American culture, even as this text is guided by a heavily affective tone of abjection. I show how Mullen develops a lyric/narrative hybrid to articulate the fragmented and minoritized subject position produced by late capitalism's most popular forms of entertainment, bridging the divide between the lyric and the experimental, and commenting upon the changing-same representations of gender—and the politics of consumption—that are at the center of American mass culture. As Caroline Bergvall writes in reference to Kathy Acker's revisions of precursor texts, "Textual plagiarism provides . . . a way out of a societal status quo that must silence or symptomatize the female, minoritarian or differential writer. . . . Thieving denaturizes what it steals."[27] Reading Mullen's narrative "thievings" along these lines, I argue that Mullen's hybrid project is similarly aimed at subverting the mainstream cultural values of her past and present through disruption of our culture's most popular, pervasive, and inherently regressive literary genres. Using rapid shifts in form, major variations in tonal register, and affect-laden signs and distortions of detective fiction, Mullen destabilizes generic conventions and raises questions about the workings of desire in the female consumption of these texts.

Whereas Laura Mullen's work has been marginal to the experimental poetry community, Alice Notley has been singled out already for her early associations with the New York School and for her later creation of a new feminist epic in *The Descent of Alette*. Elsewhere I have argued for Notley's creation of a postmodern poetics of witness in her disjunctively lyric collection *Mysteries of Small Houses*.[28] Yet Notley's more recent work has moved into innovative new forms of cultural critique through her engagements with noir film and fiction, suggesting the renewed potential for story in formally disjunctive poetics. In my third chapter, I show the ways in which Notley's *Disobedience* combines her aesthetics of the feminist epic and her disjunctively flat lyric with these conventions of popular literature and film in a multisited critique of late-capitalist America and its visual manipulation of the gendered and raced subject.

Released on October 1, 2011, *Disobedience* coincides with and in some sense foretells the catastrophe of 9/11 through its sweeping vision of the devastating impact of global multinational capitalism. I explore Notley's development of a post-noir female paranoia as a tool of resistance in this real-time diary of thirteen months she spent as an expatriate in Paris in the mid-nineties. I argue that precisely because hypermasculinist American noir and its ideological premises by now have had such a wide global reach, Notley's deployment of the paranoia associated with noir film and fiction is a powerful means of calling into question the politics of a once-American/now-global popular culture in the immediate historical moment in which Notley's hybrid epic/lyric subject locates herself.

In my fourth chapter, on Harryette Mullen, I show how Mullen revolutionizes the modernist prose poem, an intrinsically hybrid form pioneered (if not entirely invented) by Charles Baudelaire and continued in the modernist poetry of Gertrude Stein. Pointing to the exploitation of the black female body in early prose poetry works, I take recourse to Aldon Lynn Nielsen's discussion of cannibalism and Patricia Hill Collins's notion of containment to show how the African American body—the female body in particular—is imprisoned, consumed, and contained in modernist prose poetry, a form Holly Iglesias has defined in its more contemporary iteration as the poem-as-box.[29] I show the ways in which Mullen's prose poetry can be read as both summoning the presence of the African American body and concealing it from view through a linguistically complex poetics of dis-embodiment, in which the body is not available for consumption or containment. Mullen already has been recognized as a hybrid poet in her *Muse & Drudge*, her blues-inspired, linguistically innovative long poem that complicates and expands the terms of black women's identity formations as they are imposed by the dominant culture or emergent out of a long history of African American culture.[30] Elsewhere, too, Mullen has said her work embodies a mongrel poetics. In my own analysis of the prose poetry in the consumer-oriented *S*PeRM**K*T* and the suggestively titled *Sleeping with the Dictionary*, I show how Mullen turns the form inside out, creating a new version of the flâneur who enjoys the privilege once held by Baudelaire's own, yet who refuses to represent in realist terms the cultural group she is writing about. Using the "box" of the prose poem as a frame for procedural, serial, and intertextual language games that call attention to the regressive and subliminal workings of the languages of our contemporary mainstream culture—the languages of marketing, television, film, and the street—Mullen removes the lyric speaker, and therefore the body, from the text. Eschewing the traditional descriptive and narrative forms of the prose poem in favor of disembodied language machines, then, Mullen mixes a high-art sensibility with the language material of the masses, making palpable through affective tone the underlying racism and regressive ideology saturating popular consumer culture at the same time that she works to skew and derange those languages such that they become sites of play and reinvention.

In my fifth chapter, on the work of Claudia Rankine, I undertake a detailed close reading of her revolutionary long poem, *Don't Let Me Be Lonely: An American Lyric*, showing this work's indebtedness to Aimé Césaire's project of forming a new spiritual/national identity for those of the African Diaspora, and analyzing Rankine's post-Whitmanic, post-Césairian efforts to summon and assemble a new and radically diverse American body politic out of the detritus of our degraded present. Toward this end, I show the ways in which Rankine manufactures a lyric subject that resists enclosure within any particular gendered or raced body, even as the speaker is embodied in a neutral sense as the receptor of pain and register of others' suffering. I argue that Rankine's complex account of a uniquely American loneliness can be usefully read as an account of what the anthropologist Kathleen Stewart calls "floating" in mass-mediated space. Writes Stewart, in language resonant with Rankine's, "Things have started to float. It's as if the solid ground has given way, leaving us hanging like tender cocoons suspended in a dream world. As if the conditions and possibilities of a life have themselves begun to float. We notice our common drifting and the isolation and conformity in it. We know it's fueled as much by circuit overloads and meltdowns as by smooth sailing."[31] In Rankine's lyric replication of the feeling of floating in contemporary American culture—a space that is always mediated by image and technology—*Don't Let Me Be Lonely* activates a tension between two knowledge positions that are simultaneously affective states: a state of loneliness and final resignation to a status quo that is both represented in and produced by the relentless flow of mass media representations of racism and violence, and a movement toward intellectual resistance to such resignation through articulation of communal affective response. Rankine thus places readers in—while challenging us to think our collective way out of—a space that is both intimately personal and broadly public, an affect-laden minefield created out of the regressive and repressive mass media culture that engulfs us all, but also a space in which readers can imagine new communities of shared feeling.

In the current critical climate surrounding American experimental, avant-garde poetry, very little work has been done placing the formally radical in direct conversation with the everyday, and this conversation is long overdue. At the same time, the work of women poets is ever under threat of erasure as new movements come to the fore, making studies that attend to the specifics of writing by women ever important to the field. Even more, as the Language movement wanes in influence, as the concept of "hybrid" is both on the rise and under fire, and as critical interest has been reignited in the burgeoning genre of the prose poem in particular, it is vital that we as critics set down the terms of old debates and look at emergent poetry on its own complicated terms and in a constant awareness of all that the term "American" might entail.

1 / Gertrude Stein's *Blood on the Dining-Room Floor*: Hybrid Poetics in Modernist/Mass Culture

In "Reflection on the Atomic Bomb," one of Gertrude Stein's last writings, Stein begins as follows:

> They asked me what I thought of the atomic bomb. I said I had not been able to take any interest in it.
> I like to read detective and mystery stories, I never get enough of them but whenever one of them is or was about death rays and atomic bombs I never could read them.[1]

Characteristically mixing matters of high importance with the mundane details of daily living, Stein here travels the considerable distance between human mass destruction and the stuff of popular literature with ease, effectively recontextualizing the atomic bomb—along with those death rays—as mere tropes in the mass-market genres of detective and science fiction. Although it is quite possible to read the comment with humor and irony, such a move requires an understanding of Stein's wry and subversive sense of humor, and not all critics are inclined toward such an understanding. In fact it is offhand comments such as these that have fuelled her detractors, writers such as Janet Malcolm and Barbara Will seizing upon similarly quixotic remarks as proof that Stein was unserious about politics generally, concerned only with preserving her comfortably middle-class way of life.[2] Perhaps especially now, at a time when criticism of Stein's politics has reached new heights of vitriol, it does not take much effort to take a hostile reading of this short passage as the flippant musing of a privileged woman who can easily escape the pressing political issues of her time through the simple pleasure of reading, and lowbrow reading at that.[3]

But in an alternative reading, Stein's equation of the atomic bomb with death rays as tropes of mass-market fiction functions not only as a commentary on the deep absurdity of warfare (and, as modern male writers such as Joseph Heller, Kurt Vonnegut, and Thomas Pynchon have repeatedly reminded us, war is fundamentally absurd), but also on the cultural expectations surrounding an elderly woman's response to Big Questions. For in positioning herself as one who would rather read pulp than talk about such matters, Stein is also pointing up while appearing to merit the culture's generally low opinion of the woman reader, who in this particular case is also a writer, though that is easily forgotten in moments such as these. Indeed, there is a noticeably gendered cast to Stein's quick turn away from the sine qua non of the masculinist war machine and toward what critics including Andreas Huyssen have shown to be the implied *female* consumption of mass-market fiction, a rhetorical move that indicates perhaps an ironic sense of her own position in society as a female producer (as opposed to passive consumer) of art, one whose status as an artist was uncertain for much of her lifetime and complicated by her sudden celebrity in the early 1930s.[4]

Stein's placement of modern warfare within the context of detective fiction, wrapping things up with a metareference to "a nice story," may seem at first glance an essay-length exercise in evasion, yet such a reading is complicated by the fact of Stein's previous comments on detective fiction as serious modern literature. In "What Are Master-pieces and Why Are There So Few of Them," written as a lecture to be given on her 1934–35 tour of the United States, Stein says that the detective novel is the pure product of the human mind at work and thus "the only real modern novel form."[5] And in *Everybody's Autobiography*, written just after her return to France, Stein says, "I do like detective stories. I never try to guess who has done the crime and if I did I would be sure to guess wrong but I like somebody being dead and how it moves along and Dashiell Hammett was all that and more."[6] Aside from explaining her explicit request to meet Hammett when she visited Los Angeles, a request that Hammett graciously accommodated, this comment also suggests another, complementary side to Stein's interest in the mystery story: in "someone being dead," the emphasis is formally upon the movement of a narrative radiating outward from an abyss and thematically upon a startling tear in the social fabric, a tear that requires mending. In addition to her comments praising the genre, there are also Stein's provocatively titled short pieces, "Subject-Cases: The Background of a Detective Story" (published in 1923), "American Crimes and How They Matter" (1935), and "Why I Like Detective Stories" (1937), all indicators of Stein's thinking about crime and detection as tied in various ways—literal, aesthetic, and, in the instance, of "Subject-Cases," linguistic—to modernity and to writing.[7] In light of these associations, it is possible to read the opening sentences of "Reflection on the Atomic Bomb" as part of a larger whole, a reflection on what it might mean to produce and consume popular literature in an age of global catastrophe.

Brooks Landon has traced Stein's sincere interest in detective stories and the process of detection to the period between 1933 and 1936, and given her oft-stated interest it is not at all surprising that she should have undertaken in 1933 to write a mystery novel herself, which she titled *Blood on the Dining-Room Floor*.[8] This short roman à clef is based on a set of odd events happening near Stein's home in Bilignin that summer of 1933, including the unexplained death of a local hotelier's wife who fell from a fifth-story window, as well as the arrival of servants "from afar" to the Stein/Toklas household and the subsequent cutting of phone wires, disabling of their car, and vandalism of Stein's writing desk. Also, there was the mysterious suicide or murder of a former houseguest of Stein and Toklas, a death that authorities did little to investigate and that hovers at the margins of *Blood* but never fully materializes as a plotline.[9] In composing her novel, Stein mapped these events through what she later referred to as "just conversation,"[10] offering details and suggestions of perpetrators through the voice of a curiously semidetached narrator, and in a recursive prose that never fully arrives at a solution to the crime. At the same time, Stein layers into the text numerous suggestive references to other of her works relevant to the submerged narrative of *Blood*, a point I elaborate on below. Thus, what arises out of this layered meditation of the events of that summer is a complicated little novel unlike anything Stein wrote previously or after, a textual hybrid merging mass-culture form with experimentalist aesthetics and interspersing historical events with fictional ones taking place in other of Stein's works. As a series of stories within stories, the novel entails crossings of literary forms and historical/fictional incidents that otherwise would never meet, even as its intricate structure finally dismantles the mystery genre by both foregrounding the gender of the genre and concealing within the text that which cannot be revealed in the material world beyond it.

Joan Retallack has pointed out that Stein was an avid reader of popular literature at the same time that she was interested in experimental art, and these two interests merge in *Blood on the Dining-Room Floor*.[11] Nevertheless and at the same time, because of *Blood*'s approximation of a popular narrative form, Stein's creative intertextual, intergeneric plotting has been swept aside by numerous critics and scholars who have dismissed the novel as little more than an exercise designed to bring Stein out of the writer's block she suffered following the success of *The Autobiography of Alice B. Toklas*. Stein herself said at this time, "What happened to me was this. When the success began and it was a success I got lost completely lost . . . I could not write . . . the syrup does not pour."[12] Arguing that the writing of the novel stemmed from Stein's doubt about her own authenticity as an artist in light of her sudden celebrity, Kirk Curnutt writes that Stein "questioned her freedom to pursue abstruse literary experiments without concern for readers' expectations" following her achievement of "la gloire" she had long sought, and Susanne Rohr writes that the novel "brought the words back to her, and . . . reflects both the terror of having lost and the joy of having regained them."[13] As part of Ulla Dydo's claim that the book was mere "audience writing," and in keeping with biographer James R. Mellow's judgment that it is a "meager production" and a "nonbook,"[14] Dydo offers as evidence the book's failure at plotting, arguing that the "crisp logic of the detective story—the engine of discovery—is bent out of sharp shape. We have no culprit, no witnesses. We have only twisting whispers, changing scenarios . . . [a]lways we expect ratiocination, and always it gets cut off."[15]

Indeed, formal innovation and playful rewriting of the detective genre aside, *Blood* has been labeled by most of its critics as a throwaway exercise produced during a difficult period in Stein's life rather than as a serious piece of writing, which I want to suggest arises from an academic bias against popular literature. For the aforementioned critics' pretenses to maintaining the appropriate standards for popular detective fiction aside, the dismissal of Stein's mystery story on the grounds that it tries to be popular and fails is a dubious criticism that derives in no small part from an abiding prejudice against a genre too closely associated with the masses, and one that is by dint of this association unimaginable as serious art. In other words, for these detractors of the novel, Stein shouldn't have tried to cross over in the first place. Of course, this bias is deeply informed by an overarching desire to see modernist high art as entirely distinct from mass culture, as Adorno would have it, rather than as reliant upon mass culture in a dialectical relation, an argument made by Andreas Huyssen in *After the Great Divide: Modernism, Mass Culture, Postmodernism* and one that informs this book. Moreover, and also of central concern throughout what follows, the long-entrenched binary opposition of modernism and mass culture is a deeply and pervasively gendered model, making it the case that when Stein crosses her modernist innovator's sensibility with the stuff of mass culture, she crosses several thresholds at once: thresholds of culture, aesthetics, and gender in artistic production and consumption.

Gendered assumptions inform the overwhelming rejection of *Blood on the Dining-Room Floor* in a couple of ways. In the first place, it is certainly true that if one reads the novel as Ulla Dydo does as an attempt at detective fiction in the highly masculinist Hammett style, it does seem a tremendous failure. Yet in reading it according to such a standard, one is necessarily ignoring the novel's innovative hybrid structure and blended aesthetics in which recursive form and the carefully orchestrated assemblage of other texts work in tension with the strict rules of conventional plotting. Moreover, accepting such a critical judgment requires forgetting all that one knows about Stein's other recursive, subversive, alternative, and frequently-termed feminine aesthetics. Indeed, numerous important critics, including Elisabeth A. Frost, Rebecca Scherr, and Joan Retallack, have traced these aesthetics as they appear throughout the Stein oeuvre, Retallack having theorized the ways in which such subversions of convention and resistances to established logics and forms can be read in terms of what she calls "the experimental feminine."[16] And yet, experimentally feminine texts rarely are met with approbation by the dominant literary culture, which makes it somewhat ironic that Ulla Dydo's final assessment of *Blood on the Dining-Room Floor*'s failure as a masculine text should be consonant with much of the criticism Stein's work has received since its emergence. On the other side of this coin, relating to Hammett's place in the canon, Dydo seems also not to know that Hammett himself did not always display such a sharp engine of discovery in his detective fiction and was therefore by his own critics once considered a failure. Indeed, Hammett's 1929 novel *The Dain Curse* was widely disparaged for its excesses, comprising many forays into what we now might term feminine aesthetics, including those associated with the gothic. And precisely because Stein, a female modernist, links herself to Hammett, a male writer of popular novels, at the same time that Hammett's complicated relationship to modernism resonates and contrasts in important ways with Stein's own, Hammett's hybridizing of his own genre bears some discussion here.

Originally serialized in *Black Mask*, *The Dain Curse* has been critiqued for its uneven pacing, loose plot, and proliferation of characters and scenes nearly independent of each other and randomly imagined.[17] The story centers around a family curse of murky origins that, in the time of the Continental Op's involvement, comes to result in the mysterious death of a family patriarch, the quick-to-follow-suit murder of his wife, the disappearance of the daughter/niece into a religious cult, the Op's battle with a ghost, the ritual murder of a religious figure, the presence of various documents of questionable authenticity, and the apparent suicide of the ingenué's husband, who is found at the bottom of a rocky cliff overhanging a fog-shrouded sea. The text hits all the high notes of a sensational detective story, yet is also noticeably more richly inflected than other of Hammett's novels with gothic elements reminiscent of women's detective fiction of the end of the nineteenth century, a genre that relies on tropes of questionable paternity and the occult as emblematic of threats to middle-class domestic security.[18] As such, *The Dain Curse* limns the border between the Victorian detective story and the modern hard-boiled novel, negotiating between what Stanley Orr has shown to be the central difference between the two genres: the Victorian detective novel's concern with the protection of the borders of the home in response to a growing anxiety—borne out of colonial expansion—surrounding the encroachment of ethnic others onto home territory, as against the hard-boiled novel's concern with the lone alienated individual negotiating a hostile frontier.[19]

In an analysis comparing Stein's work to Hammett's, and including discussion of *The Dain Curse*, Marxian critic Mark McGurl situates Hammett's work at the very point of modernism meeting mass culture, arguing that Hammett's work "shows us both what modernism looks like to mass culture and what mass culture looks like to modernism, without cancelling the relative autonomy of these two discourses."[20] Yet he concludes that although Hammett, like other detective novelists of the 1920s and 1930s, occupies such an intermediate space, he does not finally penetrate the realm of high culture because he plays to the masses in giving narrative closure to otherwise aesthetically radical undertakings. Showing how Hammett fails in his own work to achieve the status of what Stein values as an essentially asocial masterpiece, that is, a purely creative text written without consideration of audience, McGurl implicitly supports Stein's larger assessment of the genre as both asocial and of serious value.[21] Moreover, McGurl accepts Stein's distinction between writing that is for God versus writing that is for Mammon (or audience), and places her work in the former category while locating Hammett's in the latter. The reversal in critical assessment here is striking: in a late-twentieth-century critic's reading, Stein has become the true modernist and the legitimate innovator of detective fiction, and Hammett is now perceived as a pulp writer who couldn't escape the demands of audience. How curious, then, that critics have continued to refuse to take *Blood on the Dining-Room Floor* seriously as literature. But in response to McGurl's argument, I would like to suggest that *The Dain Curse* in fact fails as high literature not because the wildly spinning narrative pretends to resolve under the controlling sign of the alienated male writer—an arrangement that T. S. Eliot's *The Waste Land* could be said to model, albeit in a different formal and aesthetic register, which McGurl himself points out—but rather because the material of those multiple threads is taken from the gendered iteration of the detective tradition. For although Hammett ultimately rescues *The Dain Curse* from a gendered and therefore necessarily ignominious end through recourse to standard devices of narrative closure—these being the criminal's confession and a solution given by the male detective—both his novel and *Blood on the Dining-Room Floor* can effectively be read as texts that foray into a highly gendered materiality, predictably meriting low marks among critics who hold an unexamined bias against the proliferation of generically feminized excesses. It would seem that it was precisely for this popular genre's ability to display and play with excess that Stein undertook to write her own gothic/domestic version of the detective story, one that closely examines social transgression through a floridly gothic sensibility and that refuses in its marked absence of narrative closure to wall those excesses off from the surrounding culture.

Examined in light of *The Dain Curse*, the structure and excesses of *Blood on Dining-Room Floor* take on a different hue, making it possible to read Stein's text as a thoroughly feminized and gloriously outlandish response to the reigning hard-boiled style; and indeed there was precedent for just such a feminine alternative. In *The Web of Iniquity: Early Detective Fiction by American Women*, Catherine Ross Nickerson outlines how gothic-inspired representations of home, family, and outside threats to middle-class order in early detective novels by American women reflect broad cultural anxieties and local domestic insecurities surrounding changing roles for women in a rapidly modernizing society. Citing Eve Sedgwick's theory of the coherence of gothic fiction, Nickerson shows how gothic motifs—including foreign invaders, an obsession with sexuality that manifests in doubts surrounding paternity and suggestions of incest, ambivalence about authority figures, and a preponderance of spinster figures—serve as the repeating tropes in a body of popular fiction written for a mass audience transitioning from Victorian/domestic to modern/marketplace.[22] And, indeed, there are clear correspondences among the tropes of gothic/domestic detective fiction and the details and atmosphere of Stein's novel. But even more interesting is the application of Sedgwick's theory of the structure of the gothic to a new reading of *Blood*. Pointing to Sedgwick's Chinese-box model of the gothic, in which narratives are embedded within other narratives as "the unspeakable" struggles to be told,[23] Nickerson shows how the embedding of multiple themes in these detective novels demands the presence of a detective in the same way that the story-within-a-story model works in the gothic to compel readers' pursuit of some illicit truth.[24] And so, following Nickerson following Sedgwick, if we return in *Blood* to "read the beginning again" (as Stein repeatedly urges us to do) for signs of that which cannot be said but which we as readers are charged nevertheless with uncovering, we come to find that this little novel centers precisely upon what remains unsayable in mainstream Victorian culture, even as the novel occupies a space exactly in between American middle-class values and modernist aesthetics.

In order to fully appreciate Stein's foray into mass-market fiction as a complicated formal and thematic engagement with the gender and sexual mores of her time, we would do well to consider the gendered terrain of artistic production and consumption during Stein's own moment. In *After the Great Divide: Modernism, Mass Culture, Postmodernism*, Huyssen argues that the rise of the European avant-garde at the end of the nineteenth century and on into the early part of the twentieth was founded upon the implicit association of mass culture with the feminine and the corresponding view that the masses themselves were made up of women "knocking at the gate of a male-dominated culture."[25] Huyssen points to Flaubert's infamous claiming of the feminine position of outsider with his "Madame Bovary, c'est moi," which was concurrent with his construction of Madame Bovary as a petty reader/consumer of lowbrow fiction. Elaborating on the point while suggesting the impossible position of the woman modernist, Huyssen writes,

> One aspect of the difference ... about the gender inscriptions in the mass culture debate is that woman (Madame Bovary) is positioned as reader of inferior literature—subjective, emotional and passive—while man (Flaubert) emerges as writer of genuine, authentic literature—objective, ironic, and in control of his aesthetic means. Of course, such positioning of woman as avid consumer of pulp, which

I take to be paradigmatic, also affects the woman writer who has the same kind of ambition as the "great (male) modernist."[26]

In this binary model of the woman as passive reader of pulp versus the male as active producer of "genuine, authentic literature," it is assumed that the latter is always objective and in control, descriptions that certainly don't fit all of the avant-gardist artistic production taking place at the turn of the last century. Laying this point aside, and regarding the very real difficulties and trivializing assumptions facing women artists who worked in the shadow of their male counterparts, Huyssen cites Christa Wolf's sympathetic reading of avant-gardist Ingeborg Bachmann as a "counterexample to Flaubert: '... Bachmann *is* that nameless woman ... who simply cannot get a grip on her life, cannot give it a form; who simply cannot manage to make her experience into a presentable story, cannot produce it out of herself as an artistic product.'"[27] Recent critics and scholars of experimental writing have shown the very real art emergent in the guise of such apparent failures, a whole body of scholarship having grown throughout the past three decades arguing for women's disjunctive forms as dyslogically feminine in a most positive sense; Rachel Blau DuPlessis, Kathleen Fraser, and Joan Retallack all have theorized this terrain as marked by radical formal innovation and socially resistant aesthetics. But thinking back upon the intellectual/artistic terrain in the 1920s and 1930s, it certainly was the case that women artists were considered inferior, if they were considered at all. According to Huyssen and Wolf, then, the woman writer of a certain era who would step out of the role of mere consumer and venture to create serious art faced the threat of total rejection, or worse, inattention, and this was indeed Stein's experience for some time. Moreover, the specific terms of this gendered critique—that the woman writer "cannot give it form ... cannot manage ... cannot produce it out of herself as an artistic product"—can be heard in the anxious lament of Virginia Woolf's Lily Briscoe as well as in the many critical dismissals of Stein's and other women's creative work throughout the twentieth century. In Stein's case, this sort of criticism came early on from her brother Leo, a respected theorist of aesthetics. But also, far more recently and somewhat ironically, important critics have leveled this same criticism at *Blood on the Dining-Room Floor*, the only Stein work for which "the feminine" means not Retallack's theory of experimental form but instead a double failure: a work of low mass culture, and one poorly executed at that.

Considered in light of Flaubert's association of women with mass-market literature and a century of criticism locating women at some remove from the center of avant-garde literary practice, Stein's complicity with mass culture as she merges her uniquely experimentalist aesthetics with this highly gendered genre comes into view as an attempt to rend the fabric of bourgeois ideology and insert a new field of meaning in between reader and text. At the same time, Stein critiques the gendered association of women as passive consumers of mass-market literature, showing herself to be that genre's consumer, producer, and innovator all at the same time. For in its hybridization of modernist innovation in language and narrative structure, together with the mass-market formula of realist detective fiction, *Blood on the Dining-Room Floor* troubles the boundary between the high-art masterpiece and the stuff of popular culture that high modernism has been credited with establishing. It is a uniquely hybrid text comprising multiple literary genres, including those found in the domestic detective story, the gothic novel, and the autobiography, and is infused with a culturally investigative experimentalist sensibility that is underscored by many intertextual references to Stein's works dealing with lesbian domesticity even as the narrative functions within several frames simultaneously. In mixing feminine/feminized genres and styles together with an avant-gardist sensibility of rupture, Stein foregrounds only to subvert several competing strains of popular as well as "high" literary aesthetics dominant in her own moment, while at the same time forming a new composite out of *Three Lives* (1909), *A Long Gay Book* (1912), *Tender Buttons* (1914), "Sacred Emily" (1922), and *The Making of Americans* (1925). As such, *Blood on the Dining-Room Floor* is a polyvalent hybrid that assembles a community of texts that in various ways critique American cultural values surrounding the patriarchal family, domesticity, and female sexuality. At the same time, in constructing this hybrid work, Stein breaks new ground for women poets and writers who understand the relationship of mass culture to regressive American social values, and who further understand the ways in which complicity with mainstream form can quickly turn into pointed critique of same. A pioneer in so many other ways, Stein also led the way in remaking gendered mass culture in critically and creatively oppositional terms.

Adding a fourth dimension to Stein's formally experimental, generically composite, and broadly intertextual critique of the normative patriarchal family, *Blood on the Dining-Room Floor* breaks the narrative frame in making an avant-garde text out of the criminal cause célèbre of Lizzie Borden, the late-nineteenth-century American woman—and subsequent cult figure—believed to have axe-murdered her parents. Elsewhere admiring Borden for what Stein calls her "integrity,"[28] Stein alters Lizzie Borden's signification such that she registers as a stoically honorable victim of patriarchy and a courageous rebel against oppressive social convention; at the same time, Stein uses Borden's notoriety to shore up her critique of the normative family while also attaching her own celebrity status to that of a gendered American outlaw. That is, Lizzie Borden becomes an extratextual catalyst for a new interpretation of the mainstream middle-class family, as well as a catalyst for Stein's own self-fashioning as an American outlaw *and* celebrity. Thus, in Stein's artful reconstruction and rearrangement of these various frames surrounding modernist aesthetics, detective fiction, domestic ideology, and tabloid crime, she produces an altogether new sort of text as well as a new identity for herself within American culture as an innovative modernist, a literary populist, and a social critic, negotiating the shifting boundaries between high and low, gender and genre, literary text and historical context, as a hybrid third term of her own.

Stein reverses the trajectory of noir plotting in *Blood on the Dining-Room Floor* by producing a domestic milieu in which the narrative is comprised not of action but instead is "just conversation," moving ever away from any solution to the puzzle in an ultimate refusal of narrative closure. Stein playfully acknowledges her departure from the genre's norm in "Why I Like Detective Stories":

> I tried to write one well not exactly write one because to try is to cry but I did try to write one. It had a good name it was *Blood on the Dining-Room Floor* and it all had to do with that but there was no corpse and the detecting was general, it was all very clear in my head but it did not get natural. . . . [I]t was such a good detective story but nobody did any detecting except just conversation so after all it was not a detective story. . . . I was sorry about it because it came so near to being a detective story and it did have a good title.[29]

Invoking "to try is to cry," a refrain pervasive in Stein's writing—particularly evident in *Patriarchal Poetry*—which biographer Linda Wagner-Martin and others have interpreted to signify Stein's awareness that women's creative efforts will be met with disdain by the artistic community, Stein here at once acknowledges the difficulty of writing something new at the same time that she suggests that her novel both is and is not like a detective story.[30] Significantly, she couches her departure from masculinist convention in terms obliquely suggestive of a lesbian sensibility, pointing to the fact that the text "did not get natural."[31] This then raises the question of whether, as a failed detective novel, *Blood on the Dining-Room Floor* is not also a success as a counternarrative against the terms structuring the masculine genre and the social realm from and to which it speaks. Making a similar point, though connecting the notion of Stein's generative failure in this text to Wittgenstein's self-proclaimed failure to articulate philosophical thought in a "natural order" in language, Joan Retallack argues that "[a] narrative will fail to meet is generic conditions if the writer is incompetent, yes, but also to the extent that it becomes poethical in its vitality." In Retallack's view, in *Blood*'s demonstration of an investigative poetics it both fails as a particular sort of text and succeeds as a philosophically vital one.[32]

Indeed, Stein's *Blood on the Dining-Room Floor* rewrites the gothic/domestic detective story in a brilliant tour de force that did not get natural precisely because it frames all that is unnatural about heteronormative Victorian family life while offering a lesbian alternative. Through circuitous and palpably intimate storytelling that unfolds as "just conversation," Stein writes a revolutionary novel that layers multiple narrative frames as a means of both courting and suppressing discovery of lesbian sexuality within middle-class society, leading her reader down diverging garden paths and teasing her with clues that are not related to the novel's central crime but rather that return us to the novel's preoccupation with moving lesbian sexuality from the private sphere into its rightful place in the public consciousness—a concern this text shares with other of Stein's early work. For the plot of the text is not one of detection at all but is instead one concerned with making visible the intimacy and mutuality possible in the lesbian home and impossible, in Stein's view, within the repressive structure of the normative family, a distinction slyly reinforced by the novel's voyeuristic narrator's compulsive nontelling of what she sees. Indeed, as opposed to narrative action, it is the movement among suppression, innuendo, and disclosure of sexual knowledge that drives this novel. And so with an ear tuned to the tempo of gothic secrets and revelations and attention to Stein's claim elsewhere that "it takes time to make queer people,"[33] I propose that we return to *Blood on the Dining-Room Floor* as the canny readers and material witnesses Stein was hoping for.

Beginning at "They had a country house" and distinguishing this from a mere "house in the country," the novel immediately establishes an aura of mystery within this emphatically domestic context by referencing the two new servants, man and wife, who arrive "from afar" and who were present in the house when Stein's car was sabotaged, her phone wires cut, and her writing desk vandalized.[34] At the same time that we can acknowledge these events as being historically true (recounted again as fact in Stein's *Everybody's Autobiography*) and yet seemingly unrelated to later events in the narrative, we can also recognize them—given their very oddity, their lack of resolution within a domestic setting, and their prominent place at the beginning of the text—as serving the function of gothic atmospheric device, providing a vague if quickly covered-over domestic unease as the story of the murdered hotelier's wife gets under way. Indeed, the curious set of circumstances surrounding the servants' presence and dismissal calls up the interrelated politics of class and ethnicity in popular mystery and gothic fiction, in which the elimination of a racialized or orientalized other restores order and domestic security within the home, as Stanley Orr has pointed out.[35] Crucially, then, at the outset of the novel Stein's narrator introduces threat and comforting restoration of order to an idealized lesbian domestic sphere, one against which subsequent domestic arrangements will be measured and found wanting.

In inverse relation to the private space of the country house, the village hotel is also domestic in arrangement yet embedded within and beholden to the rules of the public marketplace, including the rules of male power and ownership. If the crime in the Stein/Toklas household resolves under Stein's assertive action, the mysterious death at the hotel remains unsolved throughout the length of the text; one way of reading this death is as evidence of the corrupt domestic arrangements within the hotel itself, which contrast sharply with the domestic economy of the country house. The tension in the hotel between male-dominated marketplace and a feminine domesticity is rendered in the descriptions of man and wife, the father/hotel owner's identity given through reference to his war service as well as his place in a long line of male primogeniture in which he is preceded and followed by men occupying the profession: "Some time ago there was a hotel keeper who had succeeded his father, who had succeeded his father, who had already succeeded his father. In other words if there was a son and there came to be three, there would then have been six generations of hotel keepers" (8). If the chain of succession here is confusing, requiring the reader to read recursively to determine which son or father is in play at any given moment, this chain also suggests that in a genealogical line men are interchangeable in their perpetual role as heads of household; indeed, this transhistorical deep structure of authority and paternity looms as large as the physical hotel itself in Stein's village landscape.

In contrast to her husband's solid origins, the wife—Mme Pernollet—is rendered in terms of both the poverty in her birth family and the femininity that allows her to rise in class status as the suitable wife of the hotel keeper: "He saw a young girl who was also small but rather flat of face, who had a smile and who also later on would be stout but she would be stout and charming and be very steadily moving. She would be occupied with every little thing that she ever saw. She would know about clean linen, about peaches and little cakes, as few as possible of each, and yet always enough. She would oversee the maids at work" (9). This sympathetic and—in Stein's lexicon—eroticized characterization of the hotel keeper's wife is reminiscent of other domestic women in Stein's work, perhaps most especially of the capable Mrs. Lehntman, who is the object of Anna's love in "The Good Anna": "Mrs. Lehntman was a good looking woman. She had a plump well rounded body, clear olive skin, bright dark eyes and crisp black curling hair. She was pleasant, magnetic, efficient and good. She was very attractive, very generous and very amiable."[36] Read in relation to Stein's other domestic women, particularly those circulating in one of Stein's particularly suggestive domestic texts, the hotel keeper's wife stands out as a capable and sensual woman who in this text is undervalued and finally unable to survive within a male-dominant domestic economy. At the same time, the text also resonates with *Three Lives*'s "The Gentle Lena" in its trajectory of the innocent young woman from a poor family who is ultimately destroyed because she is unable to escape a system of arranged marriage and obligatory child bearing. In this double-coding of Mme Pernollet, Stein places an idealized version of the feminine within the body of a socially doomed subject. As a logical extension of and explanation for the doubly-coded wife, the paradoxically private and public space of the hotel represents a perversion of domestic space in which what is private and intimate in the Stein/Toklas household is dominated by a philandering patriarch who owns and operates a corrupt facsimile of home.

At the same time that this opening chapter offers the shadow of a concrete plot for the literal-minded reader of detective fiction—a plot that will unravel in a vague and unsatisfying way—Stein also scatters clues regarding several smaller plots embedded within the main plot. In syntactically straightforward yet temporally circuitous prose, the narrator makes oblique reference to the lesbian couple who will visit Stein/Toklas, one of whom will later be found mysteriously dead with gunshot wounds to the head; claims provocatively that the dead Mme Pernollet had "withered with her mind" (6); alludes to another village family and the members' scandalous removal of its father/patriarch ("but they got rid of the father just the same. At that time it was to everybody's shame so they thought, this that they had wrought" [17]); and suggests that all of these events are taking place in or around a garden, which is rendered in mythical/biblical terms ("Once upon a time there was a garden" [14]). As conclusion to this impacted list of suggestion and innuendo, Stein writes, "Has everybody got it straight. So far we have two families and besides a country house. We have three times crime. Remember there was a country house where everything happened one day, and other things happened the other days. Then there was a funeral. Read the beginning again" (18). The play here is among scandal and discovery, Stein trotting out the conventional preoccupations of gothic fiction even as she challenges her reader to read between the lines of the proliferating narratives.

For in her exhortation to the reader that s/he "read the beginning again," Stein points the reader back to the start of the historically specific story of Mme Pernollet but also farther back to that original story of the garden, where the Fall precipitates the many weighty consequences for women throughout literature, myth, and history, as well as markedly unclear consequences for those women left unimagined—lesbians and unmarried women who will presumably escape the pain of childbirth that is the punishment for Eve's transgression. Significantly, Eve makes an appearance in the novel, referenced in place of Mme Pernollet and alongside mention of the line of male authority, an authority that in the Bible comes with the power to name others and that Stein here seizes for herself: "He had nothing to say of the three wills, the will of the grandfather, the will of the eldest son, the will of the sister of the horticulturalist, Alexander, her name was not Alexandrine, as may be, not any one, can or cannot dream. For which, for sooth, for faith. Eat Eve when inclined. Her name, the name of the one who was dead was not Eve or Eva or just any name she had. Of course she had a name" (67). Stein here wrenches the power of naming away from the male line and assumes it for herself in a languid and eroticized way suggesting both the eating and the naming of Eve at one and the same time. Here the text seems to be asking the reader to "begin again" at the site of the Stein/Toklas household as an alternative site of the original couple, even as that original couple is marked by Stein's image of eating Eve "when inclined" (and one can't miss the suggestion of eating Eve when *reclined*).

Throughout the duration of the text, all action and innuendo points inexorably—if circularly—toward the slow erosion of the integrity of the respectable patriarchal family. Closest to the central event, the son of the dead woman comes under enough suspicion to foreclose his prospects as a lawyer in the town, thereby interrupting his march up the class ladder (8–9). The mysterious death prompts another corrupt male character, the sexually promiscuous son of the local horticulturalist—also possessing his own murky reputation—to suggest sleepwalking as the cause in an image that might have been lifted straight from a gothic novel: a somnambulent woman proceeding steadily toward the precipice over which she will meet her doom (21). If the terms of the scene are gothic, so are the family circumstances surrounding the young man who gives such an explanation, Stein's narrator coyly suggesting and retracting the notion that he might be the father of his own siblings through an incestuous relationship with his mother: "As I said there were eight of them, four brothers and four sisters. The four sisters and three brothers exactly resembled the eldest brother and their mother. But of course this is not possible. It is foolish to think such a thing is possible since there was only two years difference between every brother and sister until the youngest. And he was to be a priest" (14). The narrator's fleeting suggestions of impropriety notably center upon crimes within families that undermine the normative patriarchal order, crimes of incest, parricide, and unbridled sexual promiscuity, neatly filling out Eve Sedgwick's model of the gothic as a genre concerned with dominant patriarchs and anxieties surrounding sexuality.[37] But at the same time that *Blood on the Dining-Room Floor* relies upon conventions of the feminized genre of the gothic, the novel also subverts the social organization that the domestic detective story is invested in restoring; rather than locate criminality as a force outside the family that must be eliminated, this text concerns itself with the moral and ethical corruption circulating within the home and across multiple generations in a family line.

Adding another layer to these conventions of the gothic and the domestic, Stein foregrounds and eroticizes Victorian conventions of propriety by way of the novel's voyeuristic narrator whose urge to tell what she sees is tinged with feigned modesty and a dubious innocence surrounding the illicit motives of the actors. At times meticulous and sincere ("It must not be forgotten that it was a country house and so naturally there were visitors" [5]), direct and pleading in address to the reader ("Do you see what I mean" [7]), self-consciously and greedily fictionalizing ("Listen to this one" [8]), immersed in sensational empathy ("Oh dear. We all cried. When we heard she was dead" [7]), and provocatively gnomic much like Stein herself ("There are so many ways in which there is no crime" [34]), this narrator directly addresses the audience from the perspective of a curious outside observer whose witnessing eye comes with an elaborate performance of modesty—a performance that Stein massages until it comes into sharper view as a disingenuous ruse. As a replacement for the logos-driven male detective of the popular detective novel who paces the reader through the solution to the crime, this narrator plots the text along a trajectory of scandal and what Stein terms, again, "just conversation," leading the reader through the pleasures of uncovering that which any respectable family would wish to conceal. Her independence from the action of these households together with her palpable fascination with the goings-on within them link this narrator to the figure of the spinster in mainstream fiction, the woman whose unmoored or uncertain status in relation to the normative family is itself a site of fascination and cultural anxiety. Indeed, explicitly connecting the figure of the spinster in gothic domestic fiction to the figure of the lesbian in the American public imagination around the turn of the twentieth century, Catherine Ross Nickerson has shown how the unmarried woman of a certain age was viewed in the late nineteenth century as a mildly threatening aberration from the middle-class heterosexual woman, eventually morphing into the "mannish lesbian," the latter incarnation a far more serious threat to the patriarchy in her "unacceptable degree of control over her sexuality . . . finances . . . and . . . civil rights."[38] In this narrator's liminal subject/object status in relation to the plot trajectory of *Blood*, she is both outside the frame of action as teller of the story and, simultaneously, an unmoored female character within the text, a single unmarried woman playing a double role, and one that is doubled again in this narrator's intimate connection to Lizzie Borden.

For even as *Blood*'s narrator gestures provocatively toward the taboo, massaging the surface of domestic respectability until it begins to fray, she also rips a hole in the surface of narrative by turning to address the extratextual person of Lizzie Borden, celebrity murderer and—significantly for Stein—media sensation. In a key connection that we see resonating throughout the novel, Nickerson links the popular fictional trope of the spinster/lesbian explicitly to the widespread public fascination with the Borden case of 1892, a fascination that Stein herself shared. According to Nickerson, Lizzie Borden's achievement of financial independence through her alleged murder of her parents and her lifelong avoidance of marriage placed her publicly in a transitional space between Victorian mores of proper domesticity and the emerging figure of the modern woman.[39] Presaging this shift in perception, in "American Crimes and How They Matter," Stein mentions Lizzie Borden as a fascinating and enviable phenom, a celebrity criminal who lives on in the American imagination long after her own historical moment:

> I know I was perfectly astonished to know that even the present generation knew the name of Lizzie Borden and that she had gone on living. There are the two kinds of crime that keep the imagination, the crime hero and the crime mystery, all the other crimes everybody forgets as soon as they find out who did them . . . in the real crime it is more interesting if you do not know the answer at all. . . . [N]ot telling anything showed the integrity of the American woman and the case of Lizzie Borden is the same, she held back nothing she never lied but she never told anybody anything, that is integrity and is very American.[40]

It is possible to read Stein's figuration of Lizzie Borden here in a dual register—as a celebrity criminal but also as a sexually independent outlaw woman—and in both versions Stein's admiration for her discretion is palpable. Concerned throughout her life with her deeply felt sense of her own American-ness, Stein's allegation that Lizzie Borden's truthfulness coupled with her having "never told anybody anything" constitutes a particular form of American integrity points to Borden's enviable ability to remain true to herself while maintaining a necessary privacy. In fact, this description of Lizzie Borden's integrity, privacy, and selfhood might just as easily apply to Stein's vision of herself, even as Borden's longevity in the American imagination so clearly impressed Stein. With the presence of Lizzie Borden, then, this little novel becomes a domestic mystery text of another order, one that enacts rupture within the family through the transgression of fictional form with tabloid lore, the result being a highlighting of the restrictive terms of women's place in the middle-class heteronormative family and the dire consequences of stepping outside that frame.

Although Stein never gives Lizzie Borden a voice of her own in the novel, the narrator nevertheless draws her into the text as witness and presumptive interlocutor in various sly asides, as in "Lizzie do you mind"; "Lizzie do you understand"; "Of course Lizzie you do understand of course you do." At each appearance, reference to Lizzie provides a distance from the narrative, a place from which the action, as well as the narrator's musings on causes, effects, and moral implications, can be reviewed. For example, in relation to the Stein/Toklas servants: "The garage man said send them away and forget them and this was done. Lizzie do you understand" (6); as confidante for the narrator as she philosophizes about human behavior: "There is no difference between a very old woman and her son nor between the son and the son of some other one. They all live together even as they come and go. Lizzie do you mind" (31); and as witness to speculations regarding the unexplained death of Mme Pernollet: "What, walk in their sleep for example. Which one. Which one oh which one. Walk in their sleep for example. For not at all. Usual is disuse. Lizzie do Lizzie do try to understand" (53).

Yet if in these contexts the Lizzie references mark a gap in the text's structure while also suggesting a pervasive and underlying hostility within the several subnarratives, Lizzie functions in the concluding chapter on a much grander scale, suggesting the possibility for an interpretation of the text as a whole that stretches well beyond the disparate frames of literary genre, narrative, and/or language as medium:

> Once upon a time they began it is begun.
> Once upon a time a mother of six lost her husband and mourned him.
> . . . .
> Lizzie do you understand.
> Of course she does.
> Of course do you.
> You could if you wanted to but you always want something else but not that but not that yes.
> Listen while I tell you all the time.
> There was a country house in which they came to pay, nothing more than the rent. They of course paid servants' wages, sometimes twice, and anything else that fish and flesh and fowl and mushrooms can were needed. Naturally of course they did.
> In case that a hotel should use words. It had no need because in spite of time, they came to please that all which held together was not their tender tie but always which they mean in which they cost. A hotel can all be had with which they want. For living and for leaving and for cost and taught. It is no matter so. Indeed and tall and all and small and well and fed and placed and bed. A bed is always comfortable if it is made so.
> And then there were the rest. It has to be that holding all together, there must be a family whom nobody lost and nobody cost and nobody nobody which is nobody.
> By that time they had not wished cake wished for cake.

Do you really understand, Edith and Lizzie do you do you really understand.

And they may carry meddle Mary Mabel medal. Oh do you see how aided to be by and by. Aided by aided by which they may not die.

. . . .
No one is amiss after servants are changed.
Are they.
Finis. (70–73)

Through arrangement of words that are heavily loaded in other of Stein's texts, this concluding chapter lays out a wide-reaching and highly-charged field of meaning in which Lizzie Borden—as a queer representation of the modern woman—becomes the overseer and patron saint of lesbian domesticity. "Once upon a time" indicates through reference to fairy-tale beginnings that a marriage plot is in the works; quickly, that plot veers from that of the novel in becoming the plot of a lost father, rather than a mother—the term "mourning" thus becoming pleasurable and faintly erotic in this context, as "in the morning there is meaning" indicates a time of female intimacy in *Tender Buttons*.[41] The movement of "Lizzie do you understand. Of course she does. Of course do you. You could if you wanted to" renders Lizzie as an intimate and sympathetic presence, one who "understands" as "you" could "if you wanted to." In other words, the reader is led through a combination of understanding and desire into a relationship with the legendary person of Borden, who at this point is no longer an outsider or transgressor but is now a trusted friend and material witness.

"Listen while I tell you all the time" carries the pleasure of the whisper along with the suggestion of passing time together, and this prompts a review of the "country house" as a site where no commerce is transacted except for that required to pay servants—who perforce symbolize the domestic security of that household. This household is then contrasted with the hotel, where "all which held together was not their tender tie but always which they mean in which they cost"; that is, as opposed to the bliss of the private domestic, the hotel relies upon "no tender tie" but instead the bald economics of "cost." "For living and for leaving and for cost and taught" reprises and revises Stein's provocative refrain from *A Long Gay Book*, in which "living was all loving"; the shift in wording indicates that the utilitarian approach to love characterizing life in the hotel bears absolutely no relation to the kind of loving celebrated elsewhere in Stein's domestic texts.

Stein's inclusion and massaging of favorite terms continues with reference to "[a] bed is always comfortable if it is made so. / And then there were the rest," recalling the first two lines of "Sacred Emily," Stein's poem of lesbian seduction that begins, "Compose compose beds. / Wives of great men rest tranquil."[42] In a telling anticipation of *Blood*'s intertextuality, Lizzie Borden in fact shows up in "Sacred Emily," making a brief appearance in "Lizzie do you mind" in line 95; her presence in this precursor text further suggests Lizzie Borden's proximity for Stein to subversive lesbian sexuality. In the same breath and line, Stein hails Edith Sitwell, Stein's dear friend and contemporary. Elsewhere the subject of Stein's prose poem "Sitwell Edith Sitwell," Sitwell was a strong supporter of Stein who encouraged her to lecture publicly at Cambridge long before the American tour. Significantly, Sitwell was, like Lizzie Borden, also a spinster daughter enduring a difficult relationship to autocratic parents, at the same time that she was one of the only women Stein conversed with in her salon, Toklas usually having been responsible for "sitting with the wives."[43] Considered in this light, Stein's invocation of Lizzie Borden alongside Edith Sitwell constitutes a pairing of two versions of the outlaw against the backdrop of Stein's own lived history.

The conjoined reference "Mary Mabel medal" returns us to "Mary M." and "Mary spoke of Mabel" in chapter 3 while also pointing to *The Making of Americans*, Stein's novel of the progress—or unraveling of—a family across multiple generations. Readers may recall how in that novel, Mary and Mabel are dressmakers and partners for a time before the business fails and Mary becomes pregnant out of wedlock.[44] Against Stein's fluid and admiring description of Mary's character in *The Making of Americans* ("Mary Maxworthing had not any recklessness or wildness in her. She had very little weakness in her . . . [s]he had a certain gayety in her") is the examining doctor's irritated exhortation, "You'd better get him to marry you."[45] Here the Mary/Mabel/Mary M. nexus comes to stand for another of Stein's loving descriptions of women who will succumb to social pressure to marry and reproduce, even as the string of names calls up associations with Stein's early romantic triangle with May Bookstaver and Mabel Haynes, detailed in *Q.E.D.*[46]

In a gesture toward one of her most intimately domestic texts, the "aided by aided by" echoes "This is the dress, Aider" section from *Tender Buttons*, which William Gass and Elisabeth A. Frost have connected to Stein's pet name for Alice (Ada), as well as to the pleasurable doubling of desire and female distress in the domestic setting of that text.[47] With the concluding "No one is amiss after servants are changed," Stein returns the reader to the beginning of *Blood on the Dining-Room Floor*, wherein the central problem of the text is the threat to the lesbian domestic household, but also, when placed in the Victorian domestic detective tradition, the threat represented *by* the lesbian domestic household. The concluding statement "Are they" can thus be read as the statement "They are," an assertion of the permanence of Stein and Toklas as partners in a loving relationship, and a telling return to and revision of the biblical plot originating in the garden.

But, as in gothic fiction, there is a deeper secret layered into this web, for at the center of so much complicated telling is an even greater silence, the unspeakable at the core of this novel. The title of this book refers to a nonevent—there never was any blood on the dining-room floor—it is merely an expression Stein picked up from her cook, who used the phrase to indicate general chaos, as mentioned in *Everybody's Autobiography*.[48] As such, the phrase marks a curious nonpresence, the suggestion of a smear on the carpet of the genteel home and something of a garish recurrence of the "rosy charm" of *Tender Buttons*.[49] But the phrase has a corollary in another strange absence—that of the dead Englishwoman on the path, referenced at the beginning of this essay. One of a broken-up lesbian couple who were former house guests of Stein and Toklas, this woman was found dead that same summer near Stein's home with two gunshot wounds to the head, causing Stein to speculate in *Everybody's Autobiography* on whether this was a murder or a suicide; the manner of her body's disposal distressed Stein, as the woman was taken away by the police without any real investigation.[50] It is a death that is only passingly mentioned in *Blood*, and yet Stein writes in *Everybody's Autobiography* that "every time I want to write I want to write about what happened to her";[51] indeed, for a long while after that summer Stein continued to think about this story of a woman entirely outside mainstream culture's narratives of home, as Eric Haralson also has pointed out.[52] As a palpable absence in the novel, the dead Englishwoman does not come into view in Stein's inside-out revision of the gothic mystery story but rather disappears within its folds—never narrated, a woman entirely lost in history and unlocatable in this fiction, and yet the object of Stein's intense preoccupation for some time. If the work of this novel is to play with and undo mainstream expectations, to unsettle the need for closure by offering provocative alternatives to social norms, we can read this woman's absence from the text as a sign of her illegibility in a culture regulated by patriarchy capitalism; read in the context of Sedgwick's model of gothic fiction, this woman's death functions as the unspeakable center of the gothic narrative that both invites and represses such knowledge.[53] And if we consider, as we are invited to, Stein's dense layering of textual reference as a field of details under which this dead woman lies, Lyn Hejinian's reading of *Blood on the Dining-Room Floor* comes to bear. Writes Hejinian, "Detective stories are not about guilt and innocence, that is, not morality; they are about details ... [t]he nature of [which] ... forces the trivial to become moral, even humanitarian."[54] In just the way Stein turns away from Marinetti's futurist manifesto in "Marry Nettie,"[55] winking at the reader as she radicalizes the feminine household in response to violent, masculinist rhetoric, Stein approaches the very serious threat to lesbian existence through a game of cat and mouse in which the secret is not whodunit and the point is not how, but rather is how we as readers might learn to read against the grain of the dominant culture.

Tellingly, in "American Crimes and How They Matter," Stein places discussion of American crime squarely in the context of home, suggesting that crime in America is directly related to the conventions surrounding privacy. Contrasting the American style of living to that of the French, Stein writes,

> It is true you come to America and the most extraordinary thing in all America is the little wooden houses anywhere, everywhere and no shutters and the blind up and the lights on and anybody passing can see anything that is going on. . . . .It is the way people have in their houses and the kind of houses they have that make their kind of crime and that is what makes the crime of one country so fascinating to the inhabitants of another country.[56]

Stein here establishes a relationship between crime and the domestic sphere, indicating that crime is intimately tied to one's style of living. Whereas Stein and Toklas guarded their privacy very carefully, and whereas Stein develops the pleasures of intimacy and privacy in *Three Lives* and *Tender Buttons*, among other texts, *Blood on the Dining-Room Floor* registers the deep insecurity of life lived in terms of the public and male-dominant American domestic marketplace: that version of home that is run by the controlling father and the laws of primogeniture, which are at root the laws of economics, as opposed to the laws of mutual affection and emotional sustenance. Against that prevailing narrative, the resolution to the wildly unraveling plot of this little novel is offered in the form of lesbian domestic bliss, a safe space outside of the marketplace, a marketplace that is represented within the text as well as imbricated within the text's very form as a would-be mass-market novel.

Blood on the Dining-Room Floor, written during the period of Stein's emergence on the world stage, demands to be read as her serious attempt to bridge in her writing the two realms she straddled in life—the realms of the middle class and of modern art—but also to make visible and to subvert the social codes inherent in the mass-market popular literature of her day. In the coming together of Stein's subversive play with language and form and the mass-market formula of gothic/domestic detective fiction, this novel troubles the boundary between the high-art masterpiece and the stuff of popular culture that high modernism has been credited with establishing, while at the same time functioning as a heavily-coded text tying together Stein's larger body of work concerned with critiquing the Victorian family and opening the possibility of lesbian sexuality for her audience. Coming just after *The Autobiography of Alice B. Toklas* and just before *Everybody's Autobiography*, this roman à clef poses as a playfully serious companion piece to both autobiographies and in important ways to the other texts mentioned here. For, in addition to its qualities as a linguistically experimental text, it is a private, internal, multilayered mediation arising out of Stein's fascination with the composition of family and all that the term "family" must not be allowed to contain. As such, the novel achieves at the level of form the very tear Stein would have liked to see in her material present, a rending made possible through her forcing of disparate genres and fields of reference into a complicated, at times nearly incomprehensible, engagement—an aesthetic strategy that presages more contemporary hybrid works mixing high and low forms that are just now emerging from Stein's inheritors in experimental poetics.

2 / Laura Mullen's *Murmur*: Crime Fiction, Cruel Optimism, and a Hybrid Poetics of Affect

> *"I think that a thought is an old feeling, and a feeling is just a young thought. I don't think they're different . . . they're the same, just at different stages . . . of course it's going to be a subject in my work."*
> —LAURA MULLEN, INTERVIEW, 2012

If Stein's bloodless *Blood on the Dining-Room Floor* turns on the subversive potential but also the palpable absence of lesbian sexuality within patriarchal/capitalist systems of familial and economic control, Laura Mullen's hybrid novel/poem *Murmur* (Futurepoem 2007), which nods frequently to Stein—perhaps most provocatively with her inclusion of Stein's comment "There is no such thing as being good to your wife."[1]—floridly displays multiple images of the mutilated female body as evidence of the lasting impact of patriarchal values in a commodity culture. Even as both formally transgressive texts work against the scripted conventions of the traditional detective story with the aim of exposing the workings of power manifest in patriarchal culture's most popular genre, the interventions are in a sense diametrically opposed: Stein's post-Victorian text performs its work at the boundary separating scripted narrative convention from lived life, using the tropes of the gothic mystery together with the affective aura of tabloid gossip to massage an ultimately fetishized private secret, whereas Mullen's postmodern work posits the schema of mass-market fiction as revelatory of the very structure of capitalist American culture, a culture within which there is constant consumer demand for female corpses. If for Stein the modernist, the protean popular murder genre serves to highlight an unspeakable—yet discoverable—private interior, for Mullen, who came into her own when theorization of postmodernism dominated the critical conversation surrounding literature and culture, mass-market/pulp fiction is legible in semiotic terms as a telling symptom of contemporary existence for the socially-marked subject.

In a recent interview, Mullen distinguishes her view of hybrid poetics from the dominant lyric-meets-Language model that the avant-garde community historically has disavowed, saying that in her own work hybridity entails a kinetic mixing of high and low and visual and textual forms in a constant state of awareness surrounding the class implications of her art. Describing her childhood experience of being poor and on food stamps while visiting the home of her grandmother, a wealthy art collector and dealer, Mullen says that the point where poverty meets high art and visual culture informs the space in which she works, at the same time that she draws upon her rich experience of avid reading to "write into" other texts, including the popular and salacious genres of horror, mystery, and romance that she consumed as an adolescent. In the same interview, Mullen has said that "[t]he hybrid isn't a movement for me: it's a breakdown of boundaries between forms and genres, fact and fiction, criticism and creativity . . . and it's physical."[2]

In light of this complex of artistic influence, genre crossing, and subject position, one way of reading Mullen's hybrid texts is as a set of reenactments of the physically embodied, marginal subject's mediation by the discourses of high art, theory, and mass culture all at once, the gaps, disruptions, and lacunae pervading her hybrid texts marking transitional spaces in which the subject and reader share an affective experience of irresolvable tensions among discourses that historically have been considered in isolation. Mullen describes the mixing of forms within her work as the creation of opportunities for cultural critique, saying, "The thing about hybridity, about crossing the work with a low genre, is that it opened the lyric up to something that was not biographical, and the lens widens to include the cultural and historical." For Mullen, it is in the *crossing* of genres—the emphasis being on the moment of encounter—that the form of the lyric is made public, even as her textual collisions make palpable a shared sensation of the subject's hypermediation by competing discourses in charged environments that are at once linguistic and material, high and low.

I develop in what follows a reading of the ways in which *Murmur*, the middle book of Mullen's planned trilogy of pulp novel/poetic hybrids, produces a series of what Mullen herself has called "activated spaces," moments of surprise and contingency that occur when a stock plot swerves or fails. Says Mullen, in the interview just quoted, "[T]he crucial aspect of the low genre for me, first and foremost, is that it is a framework that has expectations built into it . . . the moment when I don't do the things you're supposed to do in a murder mystery become very glaring.

The mistake is really the thing I am interested in, and you can't feel it immediately unless you know what should happen." Here I examine these activated spaces for their affective content, that is, for the excess of palpable feeling or critical *mood* that emerges as a mode of knowledge in a shifting field in which the lyric subject has been dispersed or emptied out. For, regarding the lyric subject, Mullen claims, "There's the *I* in its function in language which is a double function: incredibly specific and personal and also empty—anyone can slip into it." In offering her own model of the *I* as available for anyone to enter, Mullen sets up a site of fluid exchange between text and reader, an intersubjective process that inflects affective communication with a subversive sense of contingency; this contingency is then further heightened with the crossing of genres. Connecting Mullen's fluid model of reader/subject interaction to moments of generic rupture in *Murmur*, I will show how the series of affective exchanges produced in the text comprise a shared emotional landscape that serves as a guide to the ways in which the culturally-marked subject is mediated by mainstream mass culture, even as the very nature of affective communication makes final, closed readings of the subject and the text impossible. Echoing Alice Notley's construction in *Disobedience* of an I/eye that is "slipping out to see,"[3] Mullen creates spaces between lyric and stock genre, and between reader and text, in which the socially situated subject exists as both consumer and critic of her culture, constructed by what she consumes and yet resistant to the coercive demands of the mainstream. Mullen says, paraphrasing Roland Barthes, "[W]e are a symptom of our culture"; what her hybrid novel/long poem seems to suggest is that our culture has become in many ways synonymous with pulp or mass-market fiction.[4] Against such a closed system of identity formation-by-imposition and mass-market thought control, *Murmur*'s moments of intergeneric collision create spaces of transition and contingency that can serve as sites of resistance to these ubiquitous and totalizing cultural forces.

Noir fiction is a logical site for Mullen's innovative, hybrid rewritings given that the genre's now-clichéd aura of gritty contemporary realism in fact derives from the nouveau cityscapes of an earlier almost-high modernism; in fact, this is a genre with a past far grander than its current status as pulp would seem to indicate, and the genre that Gertrude Stein famously designated "the only really modern novel form."[5] Those psychosocial urban spaces of alienation first limned by Dashiell Hammett and Raymond Chandler have their origins in, for example, Baudelaire's *Fleurs du Mal* and Eliot's "Preludes" and *The Waste Land*, all texts that—it must be noted—carry along with their atmospherics a palpable aura of misogyny, a fact that clearly compels Mullen's affect-laden revisitations. In line with Roland Barthes's claim that we write our reading, *Murmur* embodies and performs this notion through Mullen's engagement with pulp fiction as the derided feminine; indeed, in the character of the reading woman/corpse, we see that Mullen appears to be quite interested in the status of the genre as feminized trash, as Andreas Huyssen has theorized the broad category of mass-market entertainment.[6] Although I will not be discussing the other two texts in Mullen's trilogy here, it bears noting that the first of the series, *The Tales of Horror*, takes up gothic fiction as a genre that is both feminine and paradoxically also misogynist; as in *Murmur*, *The Tales of Horror* returns readers to popular fiction as the starting point for contemporary rewritings. The last book in the trilogy, *Enduring Freedom: A Little Book of Mechanical Brides*, is a departure from fiction even as it stages the bride as a reflective mirror in which mainstream cultural values surrounding femininity appear holographically on the screen that is the bride herself. As such, the bride functions as a compelling visual and linguistic text upon which ideologies of gender and class are screened in multiple dimensions.

Murmur echoes precursor texts in Victorian literature as well as in modernism (Wilkie Collins, Gertrude Stein, William Carlos Williams, and the broad category of noir fiction) and postmodernism (Frank Bidart, Robert Coover, shades of Margaret Atwood's paranoid fictions and Kathy Acker's ruthless revisions, as well as contemporary police procedurals), even as the style of the book wanders across linguistic experimentalism, fragments of pulp fiction, memoir, quotations from other texts, line-based poetry, and dramatic monologue. It is a book that steals from other texts and traditions in the spirit of Kathy Acker's aggressive rewritings, foregrounding American cultural fascination with and consumption of murdered women, a fascination plainly evident in tabloid news as well as the popular fiction that Mullen consumed in quantity as a child. Of Kathy Acker's textual thievings, Caroline Bergvall writes, "[Acker] conceives of writing as a collated and plagiarized multiplicity. Cultural pillaging provides a poetic trajectory that negates the original authorial voice ... and ... provides ... a way out of a social status quo that must silence or symptomatize the female, minoritarian or differential writer.... Thieving denatures what it steals."[7] "Denaturing" noir fiction through formal disruptions and shifts in perspective, voice, and tone, Mullen's composite *Murmur* frustrates readers' desire for the image of the fetishized corpse and the consolation of a clear solution to the case (the nature of which itself remains ambiguous). Rather than offer up these satisfactions, Mullen instead draws the reader into a twisting quest to find the emotional center of a narrative with which we are already quite familiar, that missing piece that will shed light in a decidedly murky and messy textual world in which the vague sense of dis-ease, dissatisfaction, and loss proliferate beyond the bounds of the singular subject.

Reminiscent of Susan Howe's notion of the "stutter," that mode of halting and uncertain articulation coming from a marginal subject who attempts to tell a story hitherto unauthorized by the dominant culture,[8] *Murmur* opens several times before it opens, via a set of clues radiating outward in several directions and across multiple literary conventions, all prior to the book's ostensibly authoritative Table (a word suggesting both table of contents and a table upon which a corpse might lie). Mullen's title page quotes Marcel Duchamp's instruction manual for his *Étant Donné*, "Approximation Demontable," or an "approximation" that can be taken apart. Echoing Duchamp's eerie tableau, there are many pieces to Mullen's own "approximation," here used as an open term absent the "of what" that would link the text to another object, even as the reference to Duchamp carries significant freight for the gendered subject. Next, and still before the Table, the reader encounters an epigraph taken from Wilkie Collins's *The Law and the Lady* (1875), a Victorian detective story in which a woman detective sets out to prove that her husband did not in fact murder his [first] wife: "From the title page to the end, without stopping to rest and without missing a word, I read the Trial of my husband for the murder of his wife."[9] In Mullen's rewriting, Collins's words read like an epitaph on the speaker's own tombstone; the provocative suggestion that a dead woman will investigate her own murder and will speak from beyond the grave thus inaugurates this narrative of many subsequent undoings. Mullen then directs us past the deceptively slight dedication "for my mothers" to The Audience, a sketch of the everywoman/frustrated writer for whom this text is written, here situated in an unremarkable middle-class present recognizable to any contemporary American reader.

Mullen's Audience is in the banal domestic act of mopping up a mess with paper towels while reflecting on the decimation of natural resources and mass production of throwaway products (the towels suggesting the feminine/domestic substitution for writing paper), the general invisibility of women in a world of famous men, and a plethora of print media representations of an apparently emotionless white middle class who are compared to the poor, the raced, the gendered, and the otherwise marginalized, routinely portrayed as feeling clichéd emotions on behalf of everyone else:

> The thus and such review arrived today, full of the usual stories about upper-middle-class white people (in which the deepest emotional experience available to the characters is dismay), and lower-class types, the preference being for Southerners who feel everything, intensely. (Southerners being allowed feeling as women and certain specific ethnicities are—in exchange.) If something does, despite everyone's best efforts, actually happen in these stories, the characters react with—depending on their class, race, gender, sexual orientation, and background—voluble but meaningless shock, sorrow, and possibly horror, or silent but *meaningful* dismay. There are no stories at all about the war or shopping, and few about politicians or the extremely rich. You don't see executives.[10]

In describing her audience as/through one sentient woman's perspective, Mullen calls attention to consumer society and the cheap entertainments that reinforce the most conservative of social values through would-be "authentic" representations of human feeling. Moreover, in placing her Audience in a repressive domestic context, she summons the mood of frustrated domesticity that permeates the work of precursor lyric poets such as Sylvia Plath and Anne Sexton, poets who wrote of women trapped in the Cold War household of objects and consumer ideology, as Marsha Bryant has recently reexamined.[11] But this critique of the dominant culture soon gives way to a broader concern over the state of the relational subject in contemporary American culture:

> Have personal relationships (so called "intersubjectivity") become more difficult, or does it just feel that way? . . . The pictured trees dissolve in her hands; the rising water's flecked with white. In the apartment above, a husband and wife can be overheard arguing . . . their sharp tones and muffled voices, at dawn, a part of the harsh gray light and the unceasing rumble from the street. Of course there's a baby, which sobs and wails and shrieks. So much, sometimes there's a vague uncertain fear—carefully kept vague, kept uncertain—they might be hurting it. . . . But they exist up there, like a story written over and over which there is still an audience, like a story, like a fate. (n.p.)

Like a fate, that is, for the woman/Audience in the apartment below, the listener inside the text who consumes this life of her neighbors, living through them and making stories of them in the same way a reader of pulp mines mysteries and romances for fantasies to replace material existence—notice the careful and moody description of weather and ambient noise, hallmarks of noir fiction. The speaker feels bound to become a member of such a family model, fated to assume the traditional role in a society that reduces difference to painfully reductive clichés. Her response to what she overhears is not laid out in narrative terms; there is no protracted explication of the woman's hopes, dreams, or anxieties. Rather, it is in this flash image loaded with the affective pleasure of listening as well as the disturbing sensation of imagining violence that one is powerless to do anything about that the reader experiences a felt connection to the woman; moreover, in the curious workings of affect, the implied but unexpressed feeling accompanying the woman's contemplation of such a fate touches the reader who becomes then similarly implicated in this narrative. Here as elsewhere in the text, it is this transmission of feeling associated with reading and/as witnessing that is the subtextual action underwriting a text otherwise ostensibly concerned with cheap detectives and gory female corpses; indeed, the question of "or does it just feel that way?" begs the question of *for whom* does it feel, a rhetorical move that opens an intersubjectivity between writer and reader, who comes to share the role of Audience. This section opens the possibility for intersubjective connectivity and then snatches it away, as the woman/Audience is left alone with a constructed "knowledge" of others, her move to make a story of them amounting to the inability to relate to them. Her self-involvement is thus a commentary on the isolating forces of American culture, the way in which people live together in proximity but remain remote by dint of cultural norms of domesticity as well as the bad habit of story making about others, who then become mere objects in one's own narrative.

Speaking to the radical political potential of affect as instigator of ethical action, Gregory J. Seigworth and Melissa Gregg identify affect as that which "arises in the midst of *in-between-ness*" and as "those forces—visceral forces beneath, alongside, or generally other than conscious knowing, vital forces insisting beyond emotion—that can serve to drive us toward movement, toward thought and extension, that can likewise suspend us (as if in neutral) across a barely registering accretion of force relations."[12] The open notion of a felt in-between-ness that moves one to action can apply to the space between reader and text but also to spaces opened within texts that create moments of intuitive recognition and emotional response. In the case of *Murmur*, the emphasis falls upon an intersubjective in-between-ness, not the subjectivity of any particular actor in the text, nor the voice of the author, nor any invitation to an extended analysis of genre. Rather, the real action of this work is the mood and *movement toward* another that is experienced in the affective act of reading—characters who are moved to a sort of suspended insight by reading each other and reading texts, and we as readers inhabiting this affective field as ourselves socially embedded subjects. Indeed, Mullen's *Murmur* is, among other things, an extraordinarily dense network of such transmissions, a thoroughgoing investigation of the radical forms and implications of a felt in-between-ness in a culture that so relentlessly isolates people and reduces them to fixed categories of gendered, raced, and classed types.

Immediately following The Audience there is a major shift in perspective, tone, and form—a floating murmur, unaccounted for in the Table:

> Memory Marriage Murder Mother Mystery Muse Marker Men Mere Misplaced Memory Market Mulled Monument Mendacity Misprint Mr. Mrs. Meshes Machine Milk Marble Menstruation Mercenary Mound Model Mutter Mercury Monsoon Mistral Mond Mess Masterpieces Master Masturbate Movement Moments Mention Marry Murmur. (n.p.)

The Steinian sonic play here amid alliterative words charged with social meanings that will mean differently for different readers produces not a narrative or plot but rather a variable field of affect, one that resonates like discordant notes in a musical system (as in Stein's *Stanzas in Meditation*, the appearance of "May" later on in this section pointing to this allusion) but that also resonates outside the text in readers' memories and imaginations. It is a field of communication between text and reader in which the nouns themselves carry affective weight and content; the text thus uses the surfeit of affect produced in this semiotic "murmur" to wage a commentary on social convention, gender, and history. There are numerous references to women's bodies (Menstruation, Miscarriage, Menopause, Milk) and counterbalancing references to masculine authority (Master, Masterpiece, Men, Monument), interspersed with mention of Modernism, Memorialized, Mistake (another of Stein's favorite words, as Mullen herself points to[13]), and Movements. In its linguistic structure this portion of the text demands to be read as some of Stein's texts do, that is, as other than narrative or description of an object world beyond language; at the same time, the sensation of the language produces a somatic response in the reader akin to the experience of the "tactile erotics" governing *Tender Buttons,* a sensory phenomenon that works as a site of knowledge, and that Rebecca Scherr has brilliantly elucidated in relation to Stein's work.[14] Transferred between this portion of Mullen's text and her reader, then, is a pleasurably sonic yet discordant experience that produces rich feeling, feeling that then inaugurates the move toward intellection and analysis.

In *The Particulars of Rapture: An Aesthetics of the Affects,* Charles Altieri argues for a necessary attention to the affects as an antidote to the academically driven overemphasis on critical practices that reduce artworks and texts to a "meaning" that is often merely validation of predetermined heuristic models imposed from the outside. For Altieri, affect is that which exceeds the controlling impulses of academic discourse, eluding the drive toward closure that is inherent in literary analysis.[15] Writing about affect in relation to modernist lyric poetry, Altieri shows the ways in which a poem such as William Carlos Williams's "The Young Housewife" creates an affect-laden scene (the woman described as *possibly* vulnerable, the man described as *possibly* predatory, the uncertain but nevertheless pregnant link between the woman as a fallen leaf and the leaves over which the man drives) that solicits readers' attempts to make meaning even as the tableau's affective register of contingency renders attempts to fix the meaning of the poem both futile but also revelatory of reader desire. For Altieri, it is in readers' experience of such contingency, together with their own frustrated desire for fixed meaning, that meaning is felt, if not made.[16]

For Altieri, affect instigates a critical contingency that surrounds the text and renders it impermeable to closure. He writes, "Affects are immediate modes of sensual responsiveness to the world characterized by an accompanying imaginative dimension"—his use of "responsiveness" pointing to readers' creative and engaged reaction to text and world. In elaborating upon what he views as the four main categories of affects (feelings, moods, emotions, and passions) Altieri writes,

> Moods are modes of feeling where the sense of subjectivity becomes diffuse and sensation merges into something close to atmosphere, something that seems to pervade an entire scene or situation. Emotions are affects involving the construction of attitudes that typically establish a particular case and so situate the agent within a narrative and generate some kind of action or identification.[17]

Here, as elsewhere in a discussion of Eliot's "The Love Song of J. Alfred Prufrock," Altieri shifts his attention away from the presumed interiority of the lyric subject and toward a diffuse subjectivity that merges into atmosphere, a shift that resonates with Laura Mullen's model of the lyric as open to all and her subsequent placement of the lyric subject in *Murmur*. Such a model of understanding subjectivity as capable of a diffusion into atmosphere allows in Mullen's work for subjects that are not interior but are mediated by the atmosphere in which they are situated; moreover, the presence of affective feeling moves the reader toward an identification with the feeling. Thus, in *Murmur*, affect works in at least three ways: the feeling surrounding a subject renders that subject's affective experience both pervasive and elusive, yet this space is one in which readers form identifications; and yet again, this space of feeling is also one in which the subject is mediated by other atmospheres—in this case, the ready-made affective atmospheres of genre fiction. Such a complex of lyric, affect, and genre would seem to produce a textual roller-coaster ride; and indeed, as we will see, Mullen doesn't disappoint.

In "Reading for Affect in the Lyric: From Modern to Contemporary," Altieri names the Language-oriented work of Lyn Hejinian and Leslie Scalapino as examples of work that explores the potential for social action in affect. At the same time, Altieri cites the less expressivist work of Charles Bernstein and Bob Perelman as examples of some Language poets' distrust of anything close to subjectivity. The gendered divide here is not inconsequential.[18] Indeed, the lyric and its attendant emotions and expressions have long been considered suspect by prominent male members of the Language community, and the currently hotly contested slip from lyric to hybrid comes along with anxieties that the new poetry is going to sink back into that old lyric (content-laden, emotionally driven, messily female) mode. But about the Language poetry by women that he takes up, Altieri argues that "it might be possible to stage writing as an activity with exemplary social force because it can envision a version of affect capable of organizing shareable resistance to dominant cultural habits for orienting our capacities for feeling and for investing in feeling."[19] And it is this notion of affect as capable of organizing shared resistance that I want to bring to bear on Mullen's *Murmur*.

But first, it is important to highlight the difference between the Language writing of Hejinian and Scalapino and the hybrid poetics of a text such as *Murmur*. Clearly, the forms and corresponding intentions are very different. Whereas some Language poets write work that is linguistically self-aware of artifice and the intricate made-ness of subjective and affective response, in *Murmur* Mullen pushes the lyric mode up against the ready-made structure of genre fiction. Although her work is also always in some way self-consciously about the act of writing, as Language poetry is, Mullen's work also ventures into the realm of the mainstream, where character types are presented whole cloth and narrative convention exerts control over readers' expectations for plot. Her experiments in her hybrid novel/poems do not sustain a metalevel of linguistic inquiry to the same degree as the Language writers; rather, Mullen is more interested in what happens when a contemporary, displaced, disjointed, and distinctly gendered *I* wanders into the vast territory of a normative mass culture that is fundamentally hostile to difference and the marginal subject.

What Mullen calls the activated spaces or gaps between genres and tone in her text function as sites of uncertainty or instability, legible as surprising moments of critical intuition that cannot be immediately coopted by dominant cultural modes of discourse precisely because they are formally undefined and therefore resistant to grander theoretical models. How does one exert control over flashes of shared yet contingent insight? And, following Altieri, what do such "identifications" between text and reader make possible? Turning back to *Murmur*, we are introduced in "A Nouns Meant" to yet another reading woman, this one rendered in the image of the Virgin Mary who exists as "a passage then or hollow place," prepared to receive the annunciation of her purpose or destiny—in this case, her own murder. Opening with the image of the woman "fall[ing] back from the open book the interrupted reader," Mullen paints the image of a reluctant woman/mother who will be lured into marriage and childbearing against her will and who will turn again and again to reading to escape her unhappy existence (3). The voice in this portion of the text is that of an observer but also, in the italics portions and later in a stated *I*, an interested interlocutor. The interrogator mocks this reading woman by rendering her as a trivial version of the Virgin, representing her alongside the white bird, which is iconic in classical portraiture of the Annunciation as a sign of the soul.[20] In Mullen's twenty-first-century scene of the Annunciation, the fugitive reading woman—who is here both elevated and debased—receives along with the symbol of her conscience tidings of her own death foretold. Indeed, we are to understand that her pursuit of the illicit pleasures of pulp transforms the woman into a symbol of profound absence. She becomes a sort of living corpse who craves stories of analogously dead women, a reader who through her consumption of these novels propagates a vicious cycle of death in domestic pleasures.[21] The bird, a visual/emotional complex derived from classical art and thus a symbol that is meant to signify in the absence of language, resignifies as the announcement of the mother's figurative death-in-life, an eventuality presumably produced through a blind consumption of texts that fetishize one's own annihilation. Yet it is crucial to point out the linguistic and formal density of this transmission. Mullen employs lyric, narrative, symbolism, and a realist aesthetic to produce a charged space of exchange; that which in any formal sense is perhaps loose and undefined resonates deeply in terms of affective register. The reader is not charged with sympathizing; rather, we are invited to *feel* the oppressive inescapability of this situation and to genuinely wonder about causes. Does the trope of the annunciation suggest an inevitability to this chain events? If so, then for whom is such a fate inevitable? Is this a commentary on a selfish, neglectful woman (a reading perhaps analogous to those who want Williams's housewife to be a tramp)? Or is it a scene of gender oppression represented in the imposition of domestic labor, a more political reading that is undercut somewhat by Mullen's attention here and elsewhere to the woman's intense desire for and complicity with these novels? But again following Altieri, perhaps the "meaning" here is to be found in the choices offered up to the reader and in an awareness of what our indentifications make possible. Indeed and at the same time, the text challenges readers to read beyond mere plot analysis, in an awareness of the materiality of language and the elusiveness of fixed content.

In sharp contrast to the fragmentary, disjointed site of a mother who appears to be escaping into her own destruction, the following section, "Beginning Again & Again," locates the reader in the thick of noir detective convention, complete with messy files splayed out on a desk, the signature telephone (dusty and silent in this case), cigarette butts (one stamped with lipstick) clogging an ashtray, shot glasses, tilted blinds, rumpled overcoats, and a cluster of cops on the beach surrounding the murdered woman's body, which in this case is described as "the relic of a mood that's passed" (15). Thus steeped in mood and dressed/undressed as a mermaid-like figure with a green lace bra, a string of pearls, and silver satin pumps, the woman who reads trash in "A Nouns Meant" has become herself trash on the beach, her wound "the exact wound so vividly described as given to her ex-husband, metaphorically of course, by her request for money—specifically, for child support. 'She's sticking a knife in my gut . . . and twisting it,'" says the very alive man about his fraught relationship to his physically mangled wife (20). There is pleasure here for the reader habituated to pulp detective fiction, and the obvious clue: of course the man did it, for aren't men always (justified in) killing ex-wives who demand "a piece of them" in the form of money? But if there is the aura here of a police procedural, there is also the suggestion of Frank Bidart's Herbert White, a serial killer who, in Laura Mullen's own description, "jacks off on the corpse"; for in a strange imitation of locker-room behavior, the cops here engage in a display of homosociality as they take off their clothes and joke with each other, a tableau that is naturalized in the text as a perfectly logical response to the presence of any sexually displayed woman, living or dead (16–17). Also, as Mullen has explicitly stated, the callousness of the men in this sequence is reminiscent of Robert Coover's *Gerald's Party*, in which a female guest turns up dead in the center of a room full of men milling about bragging about themselves and hitting on one another's wives and daughters, no one present having witnessed the murder in their midst, and numerous of those present proceeding to treat the body in the most offensively casual terms.[22] In all three texts, Mullen's, Bidart's, and Coover's, the scene of the dead female body is filmed over (in the physical sense, but also in the visual "filmic" sense) in the same affective tone—one of complete neutrality or indifference, together with the vague suggestion that the perpetrator of the violence could easily be among them, a point of no concern. That which would be productive of shock in a social material context is in these texts treated in a language entirely lacking of feeling; indeed, in the case of *Murmur*, the stock genre of the detective story serves to gloss over human feeling and to aestheticize death such that it can become pleasurable for an embodied woman to disembody herself through reading. In beginning "again and again," and with echoes of Stein's exhortation in *Blood on the Dining-Room Floor*, the reading/desiring woman and the reader of the text return repeatedly to a doubly-coded scene, one in which the dead woman offers and consumes herself, but also one in which there is no feeling associated with the death. Instead, Mullen's text slides across the culturally inscribed habit of mind that demands that the woman probably deserved it. Again, the reader doesn't know what to feel, even as s/he feels sensory overload, or—confused—feels an excess, too much.

Murmur's radical shifts in perspective, scene, and mood work through a kind of cinematic jump cutting, each cut containing within itself disjunction and fragmentation that is nevertheless marked with objects carrying clearly identifiable symbolic weight (the white bird, the lace bra, the cigarette butts, the shot glasses, the cops themselves). Given both its fragmentary nature but also its gesture toward an overarching cohesiveness, *Murmur* relies upon readers' ability to supply the visceral feeling of pleasure/recognition associated with the objects in each of these flash moments; the text cannot mean at all if readers don't experience these forms and generic conventions as already associated with particular affects. In *Ordinary Affects*, Kathleen Stewart, an anthropologist studying the role of affect in ways of processing information, writes,

> From the perspective of ordinary affects, then, things like narrative and identity become tentative through forceful compositions of disparate and moving elements: the watching and waiting for an event to unfold, the details of scenes, the strange or predictable progression in which one thing leads to another, the still life that gives pause, the resonance that lingers, the lines along which signs rush and form relays, the layering of immanent experience, the dreams of rest or redemption or revenge.[23]

Stewart's understanding of the role of affect in rendering narrative and identity "tentative" in material society resonates with Mullen's staging of "forceful compositions of disparate and moving elements," compositions that produce uncertainty precisely through the surfeit of affect surrounding a woman who exists both outside in a textual space of the real and inside the fictions she consumes. She is not fixed to one level of the narrative, but we don't need her to be. Indeed, we no longer need unified plot and narrative to tell such stories at all, Mullen demonstrates, for we have the tenor of such narratives already embedded in our collective unconscious, thanks to the dependable ubiquity of American popular culture.

In Mullen's work, narrative conventions are playfully scrambled in ways that do speak more directly to the gender hierarchies deeply embedded in American cultural productions. "Chewed *Vague*" (this section's italics resonant with both *Vogue* and vagina) begins "Okay, spill," as a male character cycles through motive for the crime of murder, which is of course money, and meditates on claims to have a limited memory and a good deal of confusion surrounding his own guilt or innocence. There is another female body with "flabby thighs" and the suggestion of multiple crimes of murder across a span of time, the details of these crimes blurring in recursive narration. This section is thick with detail but frustrating for the dogged reader who still desires a coherent narrative:

> The phone rings, but there's nobody there: an echoing silence. We prettied it up some before the law got it. I was practically spending the cash.
>
> "Her . . .—oh, it's horrible!— "Another aspect of the *False Self* syndrome.

> No footprints, no weapon, no signs of violence—very neat. "This *is* business." The sea at last.
>
> I sat in my cell and asked myself what I would say to whoever committed this hideous crime. It is, he said slowly, a lot of money.... We spent years trying to figure out how the bodies were got rid of. (25–27)

The reader strains to make this text legible in narrative terms; after all, there is a male speaker, a body (referenced as "it") or several bodies, a crime or crimes, guilt, money changing hands, and desire for escape. But it is as if Mullen has layered and spliced multiple narrative fantasies to create a thick description of this endlessly repeating tableau; at the same time, in the play between "The sea at last" and "Free at last," uttered as a man's sense of escape from a woman, Mullen embeds a sinister sign of masculine freedom in a discourse weighted with positive cultural significance. The section playfully concludes, "Sometimes I wonder what happened to the rest of it," as if Mullen herself were penetrating the frame to point to the loose ends of her poem/novel. But in the logic of *Murmur*, the loose ends aren't characterized by disorder of detail, for control of details is irrelevant; the key to the text is to be found in the readers' full sensation of our collective cultural familiarity with the workings of such fictions.

In "Demonstrating Bodies," Mullen opens a new frame, that of the courtroom drama. Here a traditional and therefore necessarily sympathetic detective attempts to produce evidence at a trial, but he loses focus and can't sort the details: "He dozes off over the report he's reading again for the gaps, the lack of connections between events, wakes with a photograph of the body *in situ* stuck to his face" (emphasis in original; 38). The image suggests the detective's figurative "eating" of this corpse ("in situ" carrying an erotic connotation), another glancing reference to the woman as sexualized in death. Indeed, the gaps in the case are matched by the physical gaps in the corpse's body, which she obligingly "demonstrates" for her juridical audience: "She waits there, relaxed, holding apart the clean edges of the cut as far as possible and no blood impedes the gaze meant to penetrate though there might be a stain on the floor she stands on (impossible to be sure in the reproduction)" (37). Here is another image of the woman offering a view into her "cut," demurely bloodless as in the vagina of the available but properly nonmenstruating woman, as the men's gazes equate with another sort of penetration; Mullen's coy reference to reproduction completes this tripartite image of the woman as victim, mother, and whore all at once. And, of course, the court doesn't much care about the woman herself—it's all a game, and she is a forgettable and easily replaced provocation for the playing:

> "'Stabbed to death'? 'Tortured'? 'Mutilated'?" His laugh is perhaps a touch shrill. "'Found dismembered in . . .'—where was it? A shallow grave . . . ?" The medical examiner clutches his brow, "But we can't be talking about the same body, much less the same case! She took an overdose of barbiturates and then drank a bottle of vodka; she deliberately leapt to her death; she put her head in the oven to bake it like a cake, only she forgot to light the gas." He giggles. "The music she hoped somebody would get angry or concerned about (she wanted to be found!) just wasn't, finally, in *that* neighborhood, loud enough. It's suicide—no contest." . . . "Of course she was after a particular emotional result." (41)

One way of reading this schizophrenic testimony is for the obvious ways in which various modes of suicide are treated as themselves clichéd performances; the corpse could be that of any dead woman, and, anyway, her death is most likely her own fault and improperly executed (pun intended) at that. In such a reading, these men cannot help but treat the corpse disparagingly; it's already written into the genre and its long history of misogyny. But what emerges quite palpably from this section is also the reader's complicity in desiring these details. We've read these stories in which it doesn't matter who the victim is; it only matters that there be a victim: cause of death immaterial, corpse exchangeable, sordid details (note the reference to "*that* neighborhood") most definitely wanted. And of course the dead woman is always already guilty of something; even in death she fails. Giving the reader the option of reading this scene as testament to male depravity versus the option of reading the scene conscious of one's own habits of consumption, Mullen activates a space of choice; what do our identifications with the text say about us as readers?

In "Forensics," inaugurated with Stein's words "Forensics is so true," Mullen does the work of what the dictionary defines as "extracting the facts from skeletal remains" yet what Stein considers to be the science of argument through a writing of the tableau of the frustrated wife/mother banging pots and pans to show her resentment at her domestic imprisonment before she retreats into the bedroom to read pulp novels:

> She lay down. She went to bed early but it wasn't just that. She "took to her bed." She lay down more often in the middle of the

> day, not to sleep but to be left alone, to take up again the threads of an absorbing plot. She brought the books home by the armload, stacked them on her nighttable, on the floor by the side of the bed, in piles a foot or so deep: skulls and guns and daggers, spilled bottles of pills or poison, broken necklaces on the gleaming dustjackets, the broad-shouldered shadow of a man in a doorway, a woman fleeing in moonlight. She lay there, smoking, twisting a lock of hair, eyes on the page, anxious. (57–58)

There is a haunting, moody quality to this scene, the woman "taking to her bed" as though she is herself a literary construct, and in fact she is, as the product of the displaced speaker's imagination. This stand-in is herself an object or artifact rendered in high relief, as are the women in the pulp fiction she so hungrily consumes. The woman's pathetic desire in this cycle of traumatic repetition is palpable beyond the text; she who suffers is desperately seeking relief for her suffering that not only cannot be found in the novels but which this specific attachment to the novels perforce serves to foreclose. In what Lauren Berlant describes as the workings of cruel optimism, the reading woman is addicted to these pulp novels for the pleasure and promise of escape that they seem to offer, even as her life will be impoverished by her consumption.[24] Significantly, it is the heightened visual quality of this section that carries the weight of affect, as the reader takes in piles of details about the woman's posture, her tics, her bedroom full of trash novels. It is a suffocating tableaux, and one about which the reader is asked to make a judgment. Is she a victim, or trash, or both?

There is a shift in perspective and tone in "Forensics" as, for the first time, Mullen inserts footnotes into the text. A form customary in modernist long poems (*The Waste Land*, to take but one example), nonfiction, and critical theory is used here to detail the blending of the reading woman's two realities and the impact of her absence on a family, specifically her daughter. It is a creative move borrowed from Williams's *Paterson* (Mullen herself points to the influence of *Paterson* on her work) that elevates personal content to the status of authoritative critical information requiring responsible documentation. The footnote form gives clout to the speaker even as the intimacy of the content reveals the instability of the home environment. In its strange compilation of academic form and personal content, this section suggests that the speaker needs to prove that she is telling the truth about her own past. The first footnote:

1. She has to choose correctly between two men: one of the men wants her to be happy, the other wants her dead; it isn't clear which (until almost the last page we won't know which is which). Needless to add that each of them is, in their own way, compellingly attractive. She reluctantly marks her place in that more glamorous life before getting up to make dinner. I can hear the creak of the bedsprings as she gets up. In the book she's reading everything depends—oh, say it's all taking place on the Costa del Sol: the emerald water, that astonishing light...—on which man she chooses to turn to for help. She leaves the book lying face up on the bed: the lurid cover (*The Body on the Beach*) catches my eye as I follow her into the kitchen to ask what I can do, hearing a clatter of dishes meant, I thought, to tell me she wanted help or that it wasn't fair if I went on reading. (58–59)

There is a palpable visual/narrative quality to "Forensics"; indeed, the allusion to "Red Wheelbarrow" in "everything depends" intensifies the imagistic quality of this passage even as the reference to modernist poetry reflects a certain bathos in this scene. It is a scene thick with vivid detail of movements and behaviors, even as Mullen suggests the woman's complicity in her own fate (reading/becoming *The Body on the Beach*) and her dereliction of duty in nurturing her child. Speaking to the visual quality of her art, Mullen has said that she often storyboards her poems in order to determine their narrative coherence: "I think visually, and I am constantly transferring written images into their visual counterparts and concerned when they don't match . . . I think of the poem cinematically."[25] And indeed, these scenes have the look and feel of mid-1970s cinematic representations of broken homes and—for lack of a better word—slatternly women who are both victims of a classist and misogynistic society and, in the logic of conservative backlash, somehow responsible for their trashy lives.

The cinematic quality of Mullen's work invites us to read *Murmur* in relation to the visual arts, and a turn to theory of the abject in art turns up another layer to the text's hybrid structure. In "Obscene, Abject, Traumatic," Hal Foster examines the work of Cindy Sherman and artists in the shit movement of the 1990s whose work shifts viewer attention away from the image-screen (in which the viewer is outside the artwork) and toward what Foster identifies as the object-gaze, in which the subject of the image is self-policing and the viewer is implicated or complicit. He argues that Sherman evokes the subject under the gaze, the subject-as-picture.... Her subjects see, of course, but they are much more *seen*, captured by the gaze. Often, in the film stills and the centerfolds, this gaze seems to come from another subject, with whom the viewer may be implicated; sometimes, in the rear projections, it seems to come from the spectacle of the world; yet sometimes, too, it seems to come from within. Here Sherman shows her female subjects as self-surveyed, not in phenomenological reflexivity (*I see myself seeing myself*) but in psychological estrangement (*I am not what I imagined myself to be*).[26]

Echoed in Mullen's *Murmur*, Sherman's film stills exteriorize *and* interiorize the workings of the gaze, revealing the affective freight carried by the stock imagery of 1950s and 1960s films that, Sherman's choices of scene suggests, are interchangeable as dramas, films noir, or slasher films. At the same time, the subject of the self-objectifying image provides a heavily but also ambiguous affective tenor to the artwork, her abject consumption of her own debased image proliferating simultaneously with the viewer's uncertain, uncomfortable consumption of same. Indeed, the woman framed in states of self-estranged vulnerability throws the viewer back on his/her own desires in looking at such images, and the result is a kind of holographic triple-vision in which we see the subject who is simultaneously an object, this subject/object's desire made palpable but unknowable, and our own desire, which Sherman so brilliantly confuses. Sherman's critical images insist that we think about who is framing that which we are looking *at* and what we want from such images, much as *Murmur* asks a similar question of female consumers of mass culture who become strangers to themselves through self-destructive reading habits. That is, like Sherman, Mullen shows her subject/self-consumer to be complicit in her own estrangement from her life even as said consumer is thoroughly mediated by mainstream consumer values that carry a generalized hostility toward marginal subjects in particular.

Murmur actualizes the viewer's response to images of the abject female body using snatches of descriptive, pulpy narrative to create a sensation of pleasure/disgust that the reader of murder books seeks. In "Gravida Loca," Mullen compresses the provocative femme fatale with the dismembered corpse:

> "She trips into my office": for me it starts there ("beautiful, alive, desperate"), for her it began somewhere else, that mechanism which

delivers her violated remains later as symptom and excuse. I swear I could feel her impatience ripening into disgust. . . . Now around the body the furtive experts, their handkerchiefs pressed to their mouths. (72)

"The feminine form." Nothing for it. . . . Naked, of corpse—I mean *course*. . . . Arc of thigh, sharp angle of the lifted arm bent so as to protect the face. The graceful lines of. (Suddenly anxious to demarcate specific areas: This is where that [named section] of the body starts, and this . . . Cunt, for instance, ass.) "I'd like to assert that we're held, *if not by the formality of the composition*, then by the coldness of the values." (emphasis in original; 74)

But a severed head, he reminded us, weighs more than you think. (74)

Literally dismembering the female body in a revolting corruption of the blazon, Mullen charts the mundane progress of female-as-seductress to female body-as-abjection in a manner echoing both Sherman's and Acker's compressions of sexuality and disgust. At the same time, Mullen links the absurd grotesquerie of pulp to high art through a surprising insertion of a quote from Leonardo da Vinci: "*And as one single body did not suffice for so long a time, it was necessary to proceed with so many bodies as would render my knowledge complete*" (76).[27] The quotation—which could just as well be attributed to Jack the Ripper—trails off without end punctuation or closing quotation marks, signaling the openness and transhistoricity of painterly abstraction/mutilation/consumption of the female image/body. As an answer to da Vinci, a few pages later Mullen then inserts a well-known cultural marker of women's extreme self-destruction, Plath's "Lady Lazarus": "Dying / Is an art, like everything else" (78).[28] These contrasting yet strangely consonant markers compress language, genre, image, and time while also synthesizing the perverse actions of high art with those of the low, and murder with self-destruction; the use of "feminine form" and "composition" suggest the feminized status of pulp fiction as a low genre at the same time that feminine form in the text refers to the torn-apart body. The density of affective registers here is profound, as readers experience the commonplace as both satisfyingly familiar and horrifically grotesque; to be female is to be cut up, one way or another. What's more, Mullen suggests, we have come to crave and even stage our own dismemberment, or so the sales of murder mysteries would seem to indicate.

To speak of abjection is to rely on a psychoanalytic model of the discrete subject, which may seem contradictory to my own argument regarding affect as a diffuse and subtextual excess driving Mullen's work. But again, it is in the intersubjective, affective transmission of feeling that informs this argument, and a turn to Colin Davis's analysis of Julia Kristeva's detective fiction offers a particularly useful way of thinking about the relationship of telling a story in fiction to the practice making meaning in a therapeutic context. Davis shows how, in Kristeva's own novels, "the detective novel represents the immersion in desires that can no longer be identified with any particular subject. Like the psychoanalytic encounter, the novel does not offer innocence; instead, as it tracks the emergence of story out of the troubled material of the mind, it points toward the possibility of meaning."[29] It is this coupling of unlocatable desire with a search for the possibility of meaning that strikes me as the affective playing field on which Mullen's own detective fiction functions. In the assemblage of forms and diffusion of points of view, Mullen invites the reader to experience uncertain desire and to search for meanings that this text does not finally produce. For to say that the text is "about" a woman's self-consumption is to reduce the complicated workings of the text to a single straight narrative, which in its reductiveness runs counter to the demands of experimental art. Rather than be about such a mundane story, Mullen's text is also about what happens in the transmission of a story, as well as about how the story is told, or, in other words, how the story is mediated through affect and form. As Davis says of Kristeva and as we might also say of Mullen's *Murmur*, "[T]he relation of teller to listener inherently is part of the structure and the meaning of any narrative text, since such a text (like any text) exists only insofar as it is transmitted, insofar as it becomes part of a process of exchange."[30] That is, the relation is part of the meaning, and the meaning takes shape as part of the space between teller and listener, a space in which affect will necessarily come with any assemblage of details. Moreover, in any telling, desire determines the details provided, a fact that is foregrounded in psychoanalysis but sublimated to the belief in the possibility of empirical truth that attends readings of mass-market fiction. In *Murmur*, this combination of desire and details can be understood as a complex of affective transmission that does not aim for certain meanings so much as for a sense that there *is* meaning to be made from the disparate elements of contemporary culture.

In what can be read as a demonstration—however accidental—of Kristeva's model of detective fiction as an immersion in nonlocatable desires, *Murmur* makes manifest the processes by which diffuse desires and quests for meaning are mapped onto the plot of detection. Mullen begins the section titled "I Shadow (Private)" with a gesture toward the encounter between analyst and patient in the epigraph "My biggest concern is what all of this has done to me inside." The vague reference to "all of this" and the voice of the "me" work to pull the reader toward the promise of character depth even as the inability to locate the action and its apparent object keep the reader skating across a surface of potential meanings. What follows is a description of the form of the detective story as "a kind of intellectual game. It is more—it is a sporting event . . . there are very definite laws—unwritten perhaps, but ('if these walls could talk') nonetheless" (93–94). The voice here is presumably masculine, Mullen's linking of "sporting event" to detection calling up the homosocial bonding that takes place in, for instance, hunting, even as the "unwritten" laws necessarily privilege those in power who can determine which unwritten laws apply at any given time. The stage is thus set for the ensuing list of instructions for how to write a good tale, a set of rules in which pressure points are activated between rules for good (read: authoritative) writing and the resistance to such closure that comes from a language that wanders away from each directive and toward "evidence" in other forms:

> 4. The detective himself, or one of the official investigators, should never turn out to be the perpetrator who singeth all night with open eye in the third person while his appeals append. I will certainly be wary of men with good manners: they appear content and then walk out one afternoon after folding the laundry, citing a failure of desire. But she was perfectly harmless, the last person I'd have said to invite violence. One can't go on saying how shocking it is: words seem to lose their meaning with repetition. The parts were scattered. (95)

In Rule Number 4, Mullen jams the language of great literature up against the banality of everyday life, warning writers of detective fiction away from the pitfalls found in Act I of *Hamlet,* "who singeth all night," pitfalls of self-reflection and mediatation of guilt. With a jarring switch in diction, Mullen places the reader in the experience of an abandoned woman before shifting again to the voice of a witness who didn't see it (whatever "it" is) coming. Moreover, Mullen cannot help but invoke Gertrude Stein, who employs repetition to resounding effect throughout much of her work. But here the play is on how the meaning of shock has dissipated over time; echoing throughout this section is the ring of an exhausted postmodernism, wherein pastiche can only ever be the repetition of what has come before, and which has resulted in a loss of certain forms of meaning in commodity culture. Considered in this light, the scattering of the parts invites readers into the activity of gathering and arranging, a form of textual engagement that relies on reader participation and a sense of play.

But also in this section is a distinctly gendered argument, as the laying out of the rules is uttered in language of male authority and the interruptions and subversions take on the tone of a female accuser. For example, Rule Number 6: "The detective novel must have a detective in it; and a detective is not a detective unless he made a calculation, and went for it. I was the loser in that. With one hand she tries to hold the slick edges of her cut together" (96). Or Rule Number 12:

> There must be one culprit, no matter how many murders are committed . . . the entire indignation of the reader must be permitted to concentrate on A) a wonderful polisher of bronze or B) a single black nature. You are leaving me for a fantasy. Weak—and deadly. All of your relationships are ultimately about this ego of yours, your big needs and quests which you can't articulate but nonetheless are the point of your involvement with women. . . . Since the 1960s, every achievement in the space program has been covered so minutely by the news media that outer space has a familiar feel. But once you slip below the ocean's waves, you enter a dark, unpredictable and often claustrophobic. (97–98)

The jarring shifts in this rule, as in the others, force readers to locate references in a field with few markers, even as the rule trails off into a claustrophobic nothingness. The sentences don't cohere hypotactically, nor are they punctuated according to the rules of grammar; rather, the broken sentences function as paratactic musings on the many ways women are erased in American culture, from their invisibility in literature to their disposability in relationships to their status as thoroughly minor and marginal subjects during a time when the American space race dominated the collective imagination of those who would prefer not to think about the social changes precipitated by feminism and civil rights. The concluding reference to "claustrophobic" trails off into nothing, though the expected next word is "atmosphere"; this term, which comes up again in Rule Number 16, refers back to the structure of *Murmur*, wherein many of the tenets of this rule are flagrantly broken:

A detective novel should contain no long descriptive, no subtly worked-out, no "atmospheric"—such matters have no place in a record of. They hold up the action, and introduce issues irrelevant to the main purpose, which is to. There must be sufficient descriptiveness and character delineation to give. Lucky for me that there are people who care more about putting words together in a poignant way, who seek a more-than-aesthetic transformation. *That is not what I meant at all, that is not."* (emphasis in original; 99–100)

Here the text draws attention to Mullen's own breaking of the rules; indeed her book is *all* atmosphere, and the action is most decidedly "held up," while the "main purpose" remains as elusive as this sentence that can't finish itself. Prufrock's disembodied, emotive cry hovers as a reminder in the negative of "more-than-aesthetic" transformation, as if Mullen is seeking a readership that will participate in the political work of the text as opposed to looking for aesthetic evidence of beauty or gore. The reference in Rule 14 to John Keats's "Ode on a Grecian Urn" ("all ye know of truth") seems also to draw readers toward affective response to this—by comparison—decidedly low form (99).

The concluding Rule Number 20 is a symphonic complex of resistance to narrative closure, in which references to romance and sentimentality converge with detective fiction while the woman struggles to identify with other women in the lexicon of ethical feminism ("Not to speak *for* but *with*"):

I herewith list a few of the devices which no self-respecting. They have been employed too often, they are familiar to all true lovers. To use them is a confession of the author's. (A) ... the woman who writes, I don't want to be a commodity anymore. Hacked into a series of failed explanations because the problem of identification. Not to speak *for* but *with*. . . . (G) The hypodermic syringe and the knockout drops. So this is the last thing I have to say. Thanks for all the sentimentality. (H) The commission of the murder in a locked room after the police have actually broken in . . . I don't want to be a commodity anymore: you can be discarded. (emphasis in original; 100–101)

Embedded in this chopped-up amalgamation romance and noir, and of "the woman," "I," and "you," is she-who-writes but who also reads herself in mass-culture terms, who doesn't want to be a commodity anymore, and who in the end can be discarded. The many indicators of gender conflict, together with the overwhelming presence of signifiers of male superiority, reduce the woman/speaker of the text to a whimper, one who seeks rules and conventions in a genre within which she is already a nonentity. Rather than overcome her tormenters or undermine the genre of detective fiction, Mullen's narrator remains fixed in her own traumatic repetition, telling again and again a disjointed story in a genre that will kill her off every time. And indeed, as she avers later in "L'Aura," a self-referring section told in the same tones as the narrator of the Otto Preminger film, Mullen writes, "The struggle of the sexes is the motor of history" (133), a clear misquote of Marx's famous "All history has been a history of class struggle." And yet, lest the reader begin to feel too far into an old and boring rehashing of sexism, Mullen reminds us that although the struggle endures, the old rules no longer apply: "Confusion has made his masterpiece. At this point I like to ask the troubled reader to solve it for . . ." and the sentence ends there (111). And thus is the reader returned to her own desires and expectations for the text, forced to acknowledge her own exhaustion with an old story but also now implicated in the search for new terms.

Still, Mullen is not done with her reader. Shifting genre once again, in "The Killer Confesses to Unspeakable Acts" she takes us through a series of dramatic monologues ushered in by an epigraph from Gertrude Stein: "There is no such thing as being good to your wife." This section carries with it the pure if perverse pleasure of overheard confession as the articulate killer conjures his wife in various ugly or demeaning images, calling her only "my wife," and usually introducing the term in the first or second line of each poem. The speaker renders his deceased wife in physically gross or mangled terms as he repeats in whining, pleading tones his own petty frustrations (mostly having to do with unsatisfying sex) at living with her. Mullen inserts references to film, including the Jack Lemmon comedy of 1965 *How to Murder Your Wife*, as well as *Rear Window* (in which Jimmy Stewart watches Raymond Burr murder *his* wife), and she writes a fair corruption of Shakespeare's Sonnet 130 in "Errata," which begins "She stinks of gas, my wife" (125). Taken together, the poems represent the killer as cruel and pathetic alike, immature and demanding, and dangerous in his self-justifying simplicity. As in Browning's "My Last Duchess," the reader understands far more about circumstances than does the speaker, even as the reader gets caught up in, again, desiring details of these awful crimes—which include crimes of neglect and humiliation.

Mullen's use of dramatic monologue places the text in yet another critical context. In *Women's Poetry and Popular Culture*, Marsha Bryant examines dramatic monologues by Ai and Carol Ann Duffy, pointing to these poets' effectiveness at frustrating expectations for women's poetry. Coining the term "killer lyrics," Bryant details Ai's and Duffys' uses of images and events taken from mass culture to produce works that reenter culture as both criticism and indictment of desiring audiences.[31] For Mullen, Ai, and Duffy alike, the monologues make possible a transmission of affect to a reading public; it is through the feeling of each speaker's jealousy, rage, dissatisfaction, or petty self-interest that the reader is moved toward understanding and intellection. Indeed, it is the strength of these affective transmissions that forces a reader to respond imaginatively to representations of sociopathology, violence, and criminal indifference.

But how then are we to reconcile the apparently obvious condemnation of the killer in Mullen's monologues with the pathetic woman who consumes her own death in mystery novels, presumably inviting her own murder or annihilation in more literal terms? Indeed, at several points in the text the woman is obviously complicit in covering up the murderer, framed quite passively as a woman preparing for a date, though in this case she is linked to garbage as she primps for a more gruesome occasion: "[She] perched fussily on the living room couch (she'd opened a plastic garbage bag to sit on so as not to stain the upholstery), the corpse refuses to remove the bloody dress . . . she's afraid she might have caught a thread from his suit there, or some skin from his wrists. I've been trying to tell her she reads too many detective novels. She sighs. . . . She doesn't think I'm going deep enough. . . . *Honestly*, she says, *do I have to do everything*?" (emphasis in original; 64). If the male speaker in the dramatic monologues confesses to his crimes, then what do we do with a corpse who seems intimately—desirously—involved with her killer?

The concluding section of the book makes explicit that we are dealing on a couple of levels with a locked-room mystery in which the dead woman has murdered herself through reading. Images of a female body bloated, wrapped in seaweed, and so on proliferate in small narrative sections that go nowhere, as Mullen places this woman both within the fiction of her choice and external to that fiction in the outer layer of the book's narrative shell. Musing, "I cannot unravel the complexities of this case" (139), this section's narrator connects the body in the pulp novel to the woman of the domestic scene when she says, "To live with the recognition of one's complete betrayal of one's self: a suspicion growing more relentless in its rising estimate of exactly how much one gave up, for what?" (146). Here in the space between language and mixed-genre text is this plaintive voice seeking to know how and why a woman would throw her life away, an accusatory question that does not entirely obviate the guilt of the men in the book but that lays aside their roles as mere symptoms of a larger cultural sickness.

With the bent cry "Habitus corpus!" (147), Mullen twists the legal term for "you must produce the body" to resonate also with Pierre Bourdieu's theory of the "habitus," which Joan Retallack explains as "culturally congealed values and practices carried largely unconscious from one generation to the next."[32] Recalling Lauren Berlant's theory of cruel optimism, which names that affective mode of attachment to the very thing that will be one's undoing yet which appears to the contrary to be the very thing/object/practice that will be one's rescue, we see Mullen's poem/novel tracing the intricate workings of cruel optimism in the lives of women who retreat into mass-market fiction as a pleasurable escape from the demands of mundane domestic life. Showing their own complicity in their emotional/intellectual demise by placing their choices in the context of a traditionally misogynist genre, Mullen crafts images of contemporary femmes fatales who imagine themselves outside of oppressive social conditions even as they willingly enter the ideology embedded within detective fiction and desire for murdered women. In a layering of the experimental open lyric with pulp fiction and the material of daily living, Mullen creates activated spaces of intersubjective affective communication between reader and text, subtly underscoring these transmissions through attention to the affective communication between the woman in the text and the woman she reads about. In the end, this richly composite and multigenre text suspends readers in a state of both awareness and impotence, refusing in the end to move readers toward any final readings even as we are exposed to a system of cultural production and consumption as it repeats itself through those culturally congealed values theorized by Bourdieu. Reserving judgment while gesturing outward to future possibility, Mullen concludes *Murmur* with a description of the reading woman holding out her empty hands "as if she were reading her own palms... a text which changed at every instant" (151), suggesting the open-ness of the future and the possibility of another form of escape, leaving it to the reader to identify, to imagine, to be moved toward another mode of being.

3 / Alice Notley's *Disobedience*: The Postmodern Subject, Paranoia, and a New Poetics of Noir

> *"I find I need a plot to show us truth, the graph's coordinates quotidian life."*
>
> —ALICE NOTLEY, *DISOBEDIENCE*, 2001

Perhaps because of the many formal, generic, and thematic crossings within Alice Notley's large and ever-growing oeuvre, attempts to place her work within any single community of contemporary experimental writing necessarily fail at the same time that such failure precisely identifies her work as among the most distinctively hybrid poetics of our current moment. At times Notley has been identified through her husband, Ted Berrigan, with the so-called Second Generation New York School, a later twentieth-century movement both bohemian and urbane that generated a dynamic, spontaneous, and speakerly poetics. Notley and her contemporaries in the New York School were extending Frank O'Hara's adaptation of Baudelaire's flâneur, these later versions engaged in sensual absorption of both city and historical present through playfully textured languages of material and personal immediacy.[1] At other times, perhaps especially in relation to the poems of *At Night the States* and *Close to Me and Closer*, Notley has been associated loosely with the Language movement because of her work in the breaking down of normative syntax and her opening of language to reader engagement and construction of meaning. In her 1980 lecture "Dr. Williams' Heiresses," Notley traces her lineage back through ancestors Emily Dickinson, Gertrude Stein, Ezra Pound, and William Carlos Williams, among others, claiming to inherit directly from a collective of innovators in disjunctive and distinctly American language.[2] One rather broad avenue of approach to Notley's work, then, might be with close attention to her use of language-as-such, its texture, structure, and political force, its power to unsettle the status quo, its deeply American orientation toward speech and the utterance and experience of the common person, but also—importantly—its attention to questions of gender and authority in poetry. And yet despite the attention to the structure, politics, and radical potential of language that constituted the core of much late-century American avant-garde poetry criticism, Notley remains an awkward fit in this context, largely ignored by leading critics of not only the avant-garde but also the mainstream.

Notley's neglect among the mainstream is hardly surprising; her work is not straightforward lyric, and her poems take unusual forms, frequently ranging across the page in a provocatively connective dissonance and/or invoking the tradition of epic only to unsettle the gender identifications imbricated in the genre's history. These formal features appear to have been enough to make her work impenetrable to mainstream critics writing in the seventies and eighties, most of whom were writing about the work of Sylvia Plath, Anne Sexton, Adrienne Rich, and Audre Lorde when they were writing about poetry by women at all. With regard to what many poets have recognized as the opposing camp, the avant-garde community's neglect of Notley can be attributed to some degree to the abiding gender politics informing the innovative/experimental poetry scene of her moment, a moment that in aesthetic terms stretches from the seventies into the present. In *Leaving Lines of Gender: A Feminist Genealogy of Language Writing*, Ann Vickery documents this phenomenon, showing the multiple ways in which women's disjunctive poetics have been treated as marginal to men's in experimental/Language writing communities and rendered all but invisible amid male-dominant readings, public conversations, and publishing venues.[3] More recently, Juliana Spahr and Stephanie Young have rearticulated the degree to which the work of women poets has been elided in the criticism and anthologies of the various innovative poetry communities of the late twentieth/early twenty-first century, a practice that Spahr and Young argue continues into our current moment, appearances to the contrary notwithstanding.[4]

In histories and overviews of Language writing, a select few women, namely Lyn Hejinian and Susan Howe, have been consistently singled out by critics for their unique contributions to innovative poetry, and the reasons for this special status are clear. Reflecting the primary doctrine informing the Language movement's collective project of dismantling the lyric, Hejinian and Howe have either avoided or openly problematized the trope of the lyric *I* and have composed work that encourages reader engagement with the word as such, at a critical distance from any psychological or deeply personal content. There are of course many distinctions to be made between the poetics of Hejinian and Howe, yet nevertheless their work undermining the trope of the lyric subject and negotiating language as a world unto itself has made it possible for influential critics to analyze the work for its formal, linguistic, and ideological-political properties while entirely avoiding the question of gender and the politics of the poet's orientation to the world outside the poem. Numerous critics of avant-garde writing, including Bob Perelman, Marjorie Perloff, and Ron Silliman, have openly celebrated Hejinian and Howe as female adherents to the foundational—and inherently masculinist—Language aesthetics and poetics. Yet, in Romana Huk's trenchant critique of the Language movement's sweeping denunciation of the lyric *I* on neo-Marxian political grounds—the argument being that the *I* is a holdover of bourgeois ideology and as such is a form that serves to obscure rather than interrogate the workings of power—Huk shows how the entirely negated subject of Language theorizing is actually a mirror image of the universal subject, undifferentiated by race, class, gender, culture, historical place, and so on.[5] As such, this thoroughly unsituated nonsubject is, by the very fact of its unmarked status, white, male, and heterosexual, an assertion that is confirmed by Ron Silliman in a famous exchange with Leslie Scalapino.[6] Whereas male leaders in the Language movement were clearly opposed to the expressive lyric poetries of the various politicized identity groups who were their contemporaries, women Language poets who were included among that group were also writing work that did not invite analysis of the relationship of the embodied speaking subject to any content within the poem. And although Lyn Hejinian's and Susan Howe's work is of course not limited to assaults on the traditional model of the lyric or a noticeable absence of an embodied, emotive subject, nevertheless the terms of the discussions in which these poets were recognized and validated by their early supporters in the Language movement confirm the fact that theirs was decidedly language-based, antilyric work.

In contrast to the linguistically abstract and arguably disembodied poetics of Hejinian and Howe, Alice Notley's evolving poetics continually force the engagement of a nontraditional lyric subject with the immediate, extralinguistic present (as Notley has said, "I don't in the least feel that everything is language"[7]), while also sowing the seeds of future work in reinventing the epic as a hybrid genre uniquely suited to the interrogation of the immediate present. In what follows, I argue for a progression in Notley's oeuvre, from early work locating and describing the historically situated lyric subject to later work placing the embodied subject in a contemporary history conceived as simultaneously epic in scope and materialist in relation to a present mediated by totalizing systems of power, within a global mass culture. As I will show, beginning in the late 1990s, Notley deploys the culturally embedded and physically embodied subjects she develops in her earlier work in neoepic journeys of tremendous formal and thematic complexity, adapting the classical form to make it resonate with many coexistent cultural forces defining the material/historical moments of its creation. The evolution of Notley's hybrid work will be the focus of this chapter, as I examine her later fusions of lyric and narrative elements and place her uniquely innovative forms specifically in the context of American mass culture. Yet in order to fully appreciate the many dimensions of her later materialist epics, and given the relative scarcity of criticism on Notley's work, it is necessary to sketch as background the properties of the lyric voice she was producing at a time when the notion of voice was all but dead in avant-garde poetics.

In *Lyric Interventions: Feminism, Experimental Poetry, and Contemporary Discourse*, Linda Kinnahan argues against detractors of the lyric who claim that the form is simplistic and intrinsically closed, and she shows the ways in which the lyric form is inherently diverse and complex, a form that constitutes an "animat[ing] [of] the lyric subject in relation to the social rather than removed from it."[8] Moreover, Kinnahan analyzes the structure and cultural relevance of "a multiply located 'I' as product of social discourse and potential conductor of its change," making a powerful argument for the retention of the lyric as a viable mode of social critique. Although Kinnahan does not include discussion of Notley's work in *Lyric Interventions*, nevertheless she provides a model for understanding Notley's experimental/disjunctive lyric poetics as political engagements of and with the socially situated subject, one whose very situatedness makes it possible for her to critique the speeded-up contemporary culture in which her *I* lives. Indeed, flying in the face of the moderns' self-positioning at a remove from the gritty and increasingly debased society about which they wrote, Notley's work attempts to deliver in a language of immediacy the pressing chaos of daily experience and its impact on the fragile and ever-fragmenting female subject. Notley's speaking subjects often are modeled on Baudelaire's, the flâneur who emerges from the Romantic ideal of the radically insightful individual poet only to find herself embedded in a rapidly changing mechanized and relentlessly dehumanizing culture. To bring the immediacy of her subject's visceral experience to the reader, Notley's work is consequently often messy and apparently randomly irregular in form, reflective of the speaker's disorientation within a culture that produces and does violence to gendered and otherwise disempowered subjects. Most often, the speaker is declared to be herself, Alice Notley, a choice that points to Notley's seriousness in writing out of her personally experienced yet always linguistically mediated moment, and she acknowledges the particular difficulties faced by women poets whose voices are so frequently dismissed as what she calls "'too' something: flat, strident, emotional."[9] In her collection of essays *Coming After*, Notley critiques the trend in discussions of contemporary poetry to call into question the relevance of authorial voice. She says, "There is in Western poetry no decentered self, perhaps unfortunately; but I have read no work produced in Western society that doesn't reflect, among other things, the personality, experience, motivation, and ambition of the person who wrote it ... a poem ... is ... of a person, one person, not society."[10] Quite consciously, Notley situates her unapologetically voice-driven poetics at the fulcrum of debates surrounding the postmodern subject and the vexed status of the late twentieth-century lyric.

Yet, Notley's earlier work cannot be defined as only or "purely" lyric; throughout her poetry, Notley situates her subjects simultaneously in self-aware metalanguage *and* within specific and immediate cultural contexts, as in her poem "I'm Just Rigid Enough" from her 1998 collection *Mysteries of Small Houses*:

> How did I get to be born. And recognize the events
>   of my life
> Some of them were always going to be
> But I don't want any events—I have, even early, revulsion
>   for their names:
> Graduation, marriage, childbirth
> The meteor's named by science
> We name us and then we are lost, tamed
> I choose words, more words, to cure the tameness, not the wildness.[11]

This sociocultural specificity of a subject both embodied and self-consciously textual defines Notley's poetics, resulting over time in the creation of a voice distinguished in equal parts by assertiveness and a cosmic confusion. Indeed, from her earliest published work into the present, Notley has pursued various means of expression for that subject through play with idiomatic speech, adapting the playful speakerly poetics of William Carlos Williams and Frank O'Hara to her own female and feminist perspective, as in her poem "January":

>   Mommy what's this fork doing?
>   What?
>   It's being Donald Duck.
>
>   What could I eat this?
>   Eat what?
>   This cookie.
>   What do you mean?
>   What could I eat it?
>   . . . .
>
>   I didn't lose any weight today
>   I had clean hair but I drove
>   Ted nuts and spanked Anselm on
>   the arm and wouldn't converse
>   with him about the letter C. And
>   didn't take Edmund out or change
>   the way the house smells or not
>   drink and take a pill and had to watch
>   John Adams on TV
>   and fantasized
>   about powers of ESP when on LSD—[12]

In this speeded-up lyric poem, Notley displays the fast-talking style of O'Hara and the quick-change pop culture scenery of John Ashbery to a specifically feminist representation of women's place—and labor—in the home of the 1970s. The material of her moment—the felt texture of her body, the pungent smell of the home she is charged with keeping, her children's needs, television, and drugs as the only escape—comprise an atmosphere of despair reminiscent of the scene of T. S. Eliot's "Preludes," yet here the woman clasping "the yellow soles of feet / In the palms of both soiled hands" is Notley herself, active agent in a debased world that too frequently has been described from the position of critical male speakers for whom the embodied woman is the ultimate sign of filth.[13] Here is an example of Notley's career-long investigation of gender and power as conducted in a rapid-fire, highly compressed deployment of the lyric *I*; her litany of associations with body and filth, as well as her perhaps mock guilt over her perceived female inadequacy, add thick texture to a trope that is literally disappearing in other circles. In a related vein, in "How Spring Comes," the title of which calls up Williams's "Spring and All," Notley's speaker critiques her culture's control over women even as her title calls up ambivalent feelings related to the powerful influence male naysayers have on her work:

> ... She addressed in uneloquent hatred
> SMUG LIFE
>   the one who soothes one's foolishness the
> Great Face Construct who loves you for your kinks child
> anyway, the Guru God:
>
> Oh I will come back a knockout tomorrow
>   Useless to you!
>   You're not it you smug face
> I'm not doing your yoga not wearing
> Your moondrops using your cream
> Rinse letting you fuck me Exquisite
> Like I was one of the Ones With Brains Too!
>   Intelligence in panties with peekaboo
>   holes—
> No I'm coming back raw[14]

In interviews Notley has spoken of her anger at the various sites of male domination in her own personal/public life (the two are always interwoven in Notley's poetics), telling Judith Goldman that "the whole idea of a literary movement, the academy, the avant-garde, are all male forms."[15] Taking note of the influence of Williams and O'Hara in particular, we can nevertheless read these poems as emblematic of Notley's consistently feminist stance against male authority, as well as her chafing against poetic movements and social structures controlled by men. Indeed, her threat to "come back a knockout tomorrow" recalls Plath's similar promise in "Lady Lazarus" to return to "eat men like air."[16] Grounding her poetics in the central preoccupation of feminist Confessionalism while pushing into new territory, in her 1998 talk "The Poetics of Disobedience" Notley rearticulates what for her are "the problems ... of subjects that hadn't been broached much in poetry and of how it seemed one had to disobey the past and the practices of literary males in order to talk about what was going on most literarily around one, the pregnant body, and babies for example. There were no babies in poetry then. How could there have been? What are we leaving out now?"[17] As becomes evident in her melding of a radical feminist voice with alternative syntax and open form, Notley's has been from the outset an implicitly hybrid consciousness—one that uses established canonical tropes to her own contracanonical ends, and one that reflects that female double consciousness that her contemporary Eileen Myles argues is forged out of the cultural necessity of understanding one's own subject position as well as the privileged and authorized one.[18]

In a good deal of her work leading up to and including her *Mysteries of Small Houses*, the personal/public collection published in 1998, Notley's development of alternative aesthetics for the interrogation of economics, gender, and power take place in the context of domestic life and her complicated marriage to Ted Berrigan. Yet, unlike her precursors in the Confessional mode, Notley consistently renders home as a public space mediated by the marketplace rather than as a private family drama rooted in generations of dysfunction and individual psychodramas. To this end, she forces emotional content into highly compressed lines that suggest idiomatically the dual pressures of economic hardship and a corresponding gender imbalance within a heterosexual couple. In "But He Says I Misunderstood," Notley's speaker says, "He & I had a fight in the pub / 5 scotch on the rocks 1 beer I remember / only that he said 'No women poets are any / good, if you want it / Straight, because they don't handle money.'"[19] Withholding any internal emotional response to these highly charged remarks that, in that emphasis on "straight," carry the hint of critique of the power dynamics inherent in heterosexual relations, the speaker wittily concludes, "This poem is in the Mainstream American Tradition." Here Notley defines the mainstream tradition not as psychologically interior workshop poetry derived from Confessionalism but rather as poetry rooted in a populist American bar scene and engaged in a pointed critique of the culturally produced instability of relationships, a context far distant from Robert Lowell's rooms "longitudinal as Versailles" in Boston's "hardly passionate Marlborough Street."[20] For although the postmodern subjective lyric pioneered in Lowell's *Life Studies* is perhaps unfairly considered popular and mainstream by the 1980s, still the middle- and upper-class context of Notley's precursors in Confessionalism render that earlier lyric tradition distant from the economic realities of the lower strata of the American populous. Indeed, in her densely packed and rushing speech-based poetics, Notley plays with what it means to be mainstream but also poor; her idiom's texture and rhythm chafes against the controlled cadences within the mainstream journals at the same time that her materialist class representations render bourgeois notions of the family romance irrelevant to her own life. Personality and any notion of the Freudian unconscious aside, this family's dysfunction is defined by class conflict and entrenched gender codes even as the players struggle presumably as equals to be artists.

By mixing innovative poetic form with low/prosaic content, Notley effectively raises questions about the status of the lyric both in mainstream poetry circles and in the avant-garde, playfully asserting that her version of the lyric does not reflect mainstream/workshop aesthetics even as she writes of everyday social concerns. Here we can read Notley's work in the lyric as playing in that space of American culture that Jed Rasula defines as an oscillation "between high and low . . . exaggerated respect for the unique combined with routine embrace of the mundane."[21] That is, rather than gesturing toward the rarified avant-garde aesthetics associated—some would say erroneously—with an utter rejection of populist ideals, Notley constructs a radical aesthetic out of a populist sensibility. In these ways her work both engages and works against the avant-garde that wants to consider itself a part of the world in neo-Marxian political terms but also apart from it in aesthetic ones.

Published in 1998, Notley's disjunctively lyric and deeply autobiographical *Mysteries of Small Houses* emerged at a time when debate over the lyric *I* had reached a fever pitch. In response to this interdiction against a form of vital importance to women poets in particular, numerous women experimentalists interrogated the masculinist politics of Language writing through critique of its values surrounding the lyric; this position was articulated perhaps most famously by Kathleen Fraser, founder of *HOW(ever)*, who argued that innovative writers who are women could not well afford the abandonment of a textual subject position that they were at the time only just then establishing.[22] In accord with this oppositional stance against the law of the moment, yet also characteristically open to reconsideration of her own thinking, Notley has said,

> I decided to go against my own sense that certain styles and forms I'd participated in formerly might be used up, that autobiography was, that the personal-sounding I (as opposed to the fictional I) might be, against the rumor that there's no self, though I've never understood that word very well and how people use it now in any of the camps that use it pro or con—I guess I partly wrote *Mysteries* to understand it better.[23]

As a linguistically exploratory text, *Mysteries of Small Houses* is important for the ways in which Notley traces her speaker's growth as a gendered subject through a constructivist orientation to syntax and form, from early childhood and learning the mechanics of how to write to adulthood and recognition of the politics of gender and war. Notley's poems of early childhood are marked by hesitancy and indeterminacy of language poetics, but these elements are associated with subject development rather than with a neo-Marxian rejection of the so-called bourgeois subject. *Mysteries of Small Houses* thus constitutes a pointedly feminist intervention in the male-dominant experimental poetry scene at the end of the last century, an intervention that reframes the relationship of disjunctive language to the speaking woman subject.[24] Significantly, not too long after the publication of *Mysteries*, critics of Language writing, including Marjorie Perloff, began to acknowledge the relevance of author signature—if not subject presence—in works associated with the avant-garde, a critical shift that in its moment appeared to herald the arrival of a new orientation to experimental writing at the beginning of the twenty-first century. Yet, and not surprisingly, the shift was entirely one-directional; the avant-garde could now be seen to display signs or signatures of the subject, but the subject of the lyric remains well outside the realm of the avant-garde, reflecting a fear of the mainstream that continues to inform the avant-garde's skepticism surrounding hybrid poetics.[25]

Further exploring gender inequity, poverty, and the public/private economics of the poetry world, Notley's "The Trouble with You Girls" situates the poet/speaker in her small apartment, peacefully drinking coffee and writing or trying to write, as her bombastic (and quite funny) husband declares, "'You have no philosophy' [. . . / . . .] 'That's the one thing you need to be great,'" and

> "The trouble with you girls . . . you think it's all
> Sunshine and coffee. It's money, lots of it
> Everything's money. My ass is money, yours too
> Even if your asses aren't as ugly as mine. . . . Got any
> Money for cigarettes, Marion?" Marion and I
> Cleaned this apartment, when I first took it and
> It was so small, before everyone came in.
> "How about a little extra, for a pepsi, and the paper?
> How about some doughnuts for us all?"[26]

Notley sketches a home life characterized by a theatricalized gender imbalance through the voice of a marginalized female speaker living simultaneously in a private context and a "mainstream American" one. That is, this marriage and the aesthetic work composed within it are immediately affected by American economic values and gender norms, even as the tenor of the life here reproduced is showily public. With recourse to Berrigan's outsized personality, Notley manages to connect bald economics to her physical body quite neatly in this poem, suggesting that a woman's creative output (diminished in the male speaker's caustic reference to "sunshine and coffee") is measurably less valuable than her body, at the same time that in her poverty she is expected to financially support this obviously unemployed man who comprises part of the "everyone" invading the apartment that was originally entirely her own space. Yet these are not bland first-person laments; rather, Notley runs over normative syntax and compresses speech in the production of a post-O'Hara fast-talking feminist subject whose experience of the dominant culture is both interior/emotional and exterior/economic—both, in equal parts, at once.

Running throughout Notley's work is her firm insistence on the necessity and viability of the lyric speaking subject, be that the sometime-flâneuse of the contemporary material world or the developing psyche of the inward-looking, isolate individual. The allure of such subjects flagrantly transgresses the poetic values of many of Notley's contemporaries who write so skeptically of the bourgeois implications of the *I*, and it is perhaps because of the firmness of that community's rejection of the trope that Notley's play with it functions so seductively. In a climate marked by a binarized separation of the abstract/material/structural from the sensuous/affective/emotive, it is very tempting to follow a woman of words down an alternative path, particularly because Notley herself is cognizant of the danger and fallibility of the trope. For in much of her work, her speaking subject functions illusorily as a beguiling gesture toward order in the text, an order that a reader expects against her better judgment to coalesce around this construct, even as that subject most often self-divides and crosses into the selves of others. In this sense, Notley's *I* flags danger in at least two registers—danger that the *I* will fall apart, or not suffice in these post-Language times as a viable guide, and the danger that the reader thus immediately attaches to the circumstances of that *I* in the text. Indeed, Notley's speaking subjects are always doubly vulnerable as they negotiate worlds layered with hostile spaces of the fictive and the everyday in the only language afforded them, a language they must continually fracture in order to make it suit meanings heretofore unarticulated.

Yet at the same time that the linguistically unstable gendered and embodied subject can be seen to emerge in *Mysteries* through these various sites of cultural mediation, these mediating factors fuse and come into view as a composite field of cultural domination that the embodied and gendered subject—feminine and at times masculine—must negotiate in order to survive. She names such forces in plainly material yet also deeply personal terms, as in the poem revealing Notley's overwhelming sadness surrounding the Vietnam War and its immediate impact on the brother she lost to its aftereffects. Notley writes in "Sept 17 / Aug 29, '88":

> Al thinks that at a certain point he was supposed
> to die because he knew too much, about the killing of
> civilians, Operation Phoenix, and so on.
> Members of his sniper unit stopped ever coming back
> from missions . . .
>
> . . . .
>
> "When I got back they were getting ready to send out
> an MIA to Mom and Dad. They sent me *instantly*
> into North Vietnam. Then I *knew* they wanted to
> be rid of me." . . .
>
> . . . .
>
> I love my brother so much this visiting day, but wonder
> if he doesn't know too much to live. He's been
> remembering and remembering—the therapists want him
> to remember even more, but he doesn't want to, he wants
> to go home and see his kids. . . .
>
> . . . .
>
> . . . He emanates too much knowledge, power;
> his self is huge, bigger than any I've ever witnessed.
> His boundaries are too painful and too small:
> they keep him where he remembers, they keep his
> knowledge concentrated, personal.[27]

Here we see the beginnings of Notley's vision of the subject in history on a grander scale, even as her emotional, affective responses to the Vietnam War contrast sharply with the poststructuralist/Marxian linguistic response the war movement activated among her male contemporaries in the Language movement.[28] In the face of such grief, it is difficult to dismiss the lyric as insufficiently political; the weight carried by the witness to the personal as Notley records it here resists any easy dismissal of the power of the lyric. At the same time, as we see in her later narrative works, to be a self for Notley is necessarily to be a site of oppositional knowledge; to exist as a thinking subject is to be in constant engagement with and resistance to a shadowy sociopolitical system of control.

In an interview with Claudia Keelan that took place over several months from 2002 to 2003, Notley says that it was her family's experience of the Vietnam War and the losses they suffered that precipitated her turn to the epic long poem: "I wouldn't have chosen epic if I hadn't had to deal in some part of myself with the fact of that war."[29] Her comment points to the power of epic to narrate history at the same time that she transfers to her idea of the epic an immediate experience with the shadowy systems of power governing war. Looking back to "Sept 17 / Aug 29, '88," we see how Notley frames her brother as a reluctant witness to the inner workings of a totalizing system governed by hidden, sinister motives in a historical moment steeped in confusion and political uncertainty. Read in this way, Notley's brother in this poem is simultaneously a beloved family member and a marked marker within a grand narrative of control—an individual person in material historical terms, yet also in significant ways the embodiment of the alienated subject within the American Cold War culture of containment. And indeed it is with an acute awareness of the vulnerable subject situated in material chaos and battered by forces beyond his/her control that Notley finally turns to the form of the epic, saying that she needed a narrative form to trace the trajectory of her oftentimes invisible experiences of war and loss. Notley writes,

> I began to grapple with the idea of a female or feminist epic—but not calling it that in my mind, rather, an epic by a woman or from a woman's vantage. Suddenly I, and more than myself, my sister-in-law and my mother, were being used, mangled, by the forces which produce epic, and we had no say in the matter, never had, and worse had no story ourselves. We hadn't acted. We hadn't gone to war. We certainly hadn't been "at court" (in the regal sense), weren't involved in governmental power structures, didn't have voices which participated in public discussion. We got to suffer, but without a trajectory.[30]

Notley's first epic, *The Descent of Alette*, is a shadowy quest story, a detective fiction of sorts, in which the heroine searches through underground tunnels—the New York subway system—to destroy the male Tyrant who threatens all of civilization. In her own words, she "deliberately reversed the Dantean, Christian, and other religious direction of 'enlightenment,' making it a descent into darkness. That is explicit in the poem as a defiance of male tradition. Enlightenment is seen as a male luxury. One of the major story elements . . . is the search for the First Woman."[31] Susan Stanford Friedman associates the move on the part of some women poets to occupy ancient forms with "a belief that sacred texts have degraded or repressed the feminine [and] an insistence on the need for women to experience and narrate the sacred," and indeed in this long work rife with fiery imagery it is possible to read Alette's quest to destroy the Tyrant in terms of a sacred mission to save the earth from masculine domination.[32] Yet Friedman also points to the tendency in women's long poems of mixing the material present with the ancient past, creating worlds that are immediately contemporary and familiar as well as strange; in *The Descent of Alette*, we see this merging reflected in the underground shadowy atmosphere that is just as descriptive of a contemporary urban underbelly as it is of Dante's circles of hell. Linking Notley's innovative speakerly meter—comprising discrete phrasal units offset by quotation marks—to ancient oral tradition, Page duBois summarizes *The Descent of Alette* as "a stunning intervention in a brutal present, connecting its details with a long history of poetry, insisting on particularity within generality and on the historical intensities of Vietnam and the New York City subway even as it locates itself scandalously in the genealogy of Homer and Dante."[33] Dubois reads Notley's return to the epic as an immediately materialist orientation to history, unfolding the ways in which Notley's poetics expand and spread into territory—literary, material, and linguistic—historically held by men.[34] *The Descent of Alette* remains the most frequently studied and commented-upon work Notley has produced, drawing critical attention perhaps in part because it can be interpreted in clearly gendered terms, her feminist innovations in language and hero-type intervening in a great Western tradition and thus opening new spaces of being for women poets. And yet, at the same time that this text and its interpretations offer exciting ways of thinking about new feminist forms that are alternative to the lyric, *Descent* also exemplifies more broadly the many ways in which Notley continually forces the engagement of radically disparate elements, in this case the engagement of the sweeping literary-historical with the particularity of the concrete material, through an alternative/oppositional speech rhythm conceived of as at once feminist, material/contemporary, and ancient in origins.

Explicitly linking lyric to narrative in long poems by women, Lynn Keller defines the long poem as a generic hybrid, arguing that "in individual poems with multiple generic valences, the conventions of one genre or another may well be particularly evident, and awareness of those primary conventions can assist interpretation."³⁵ For Keller, contemporary long poems necessarily borrow from multiple forms and traditions, and it is this mixing that gives the genre its exciting and open diversity. In light of Keller's argument, the academic avant-garde's devaluing of both lyric and narrative poetry in favor of poetry that performs, in the words of Marjorie Perloff, "the linguistic turn," signals again this group's deep distrust of generic mixing, at the same time that their positioning of lyric and narrative as opposed to a linguistically oriented poetics underscores how Alice Notley's forays into linguistically disjunctive lyric/narrative hybrids fall well outside of any easy categories. Indeed, her exclusion from conversations surrounding experimental writing can be attributed not only to her attention to gender and female voice but also to her development over time of forms that elude easy categorization. And if her composite poetics were not enough to keep her outside the circle of the avant-garde, certainly the fact that her newly imagined spaces are not hospitable to a masculinist presence further casts a shadow over the possibility of her inclusion among a milieu that is more than dismissive of a certain feminist tone in radical art.

Sketching the foundation for Notley's more recent, boldly expansive hybrid work, we see in the poetry leading up to and including *The Descent of Alette* work that over time variously enacts blendings of form, tradition, sensibility, and idiom; furthermore, moving forward, we can read the lyric subject developed in *Mysteries of Small Houses* as carrying forward the epic project begun in *The Descent of Alette*. Together, these very different works form a joint precursor to Notley's later and surprisingly understudied work *Disobedience* (2001), a post-lyric/epic/narrative long poem that functions on a grand historical materialist scale while framing the isolate, alienated subject in multiple spaces simultaneously: in the historical present, in dream worlds and forays into earlier epics, and in the shadowy world of detective fiction and film noir. Notley has said that when she began *Disobedience*, she "wanted to see if [she] could combine all of the elements of [her] previous work into one work, that is, autobiography as daily commentary and daily involvement with politics (by virtue of being oneself), fictional narrative, with characters, fantasy and dream."³⁶ Her earlier development of a self-consciously speech-based lyric makes the world of *Disobedience* navigable for readers who become immersed in worlds both familiar and strange; having gotten to know Notley's "voice" and "self," her readers are invited to follow that self into a confusing and alienating universe productive of anxiety, paranoia, and desire for/uncertainty about the unknown. Yet crucially, that alienating universe is legible as simultaneously fictive and material, a self-consciously constructed cultural production that is also a recorded experience of life in the immediate present of the text.

Disobedience was released on October 1, 2001, composed in the late 1990s and in press at the time of 9/11. Situated in a layered facsimile of real time, a thirteen-month span during which Notley lived in Paris and followed the politics of the United States and Europe in the media, the book traces an extended displacement of the subject within lived history and, self-consciously, within the cultural productions that inform the subject's construction of herself. The tensions among her use of the lyric subject in real time, narrative, and pop culture idioms are flagged in her early references to temporality in the text. On line eleven of the first poem, Notley references the moment of writing as the eleventh day of her project, "Aug of late, early on the 9th ninety-five."[37] Taking pains to name the moments precisely, Notley draws attention to both the slow and deliberate act of writing and to the material content of history as it occurs. By foregrounding her placement as a material body in a specific time and place and setting out to write those moments as they are experienced, Notley is self-consciously locating herself as both witness to and agent of history. Yet, complicating the notion of historical accuracy are the playful section titles that are strongly reminiscent of Frank O'Hara's irreverent and quotidian sense of humor, titles that point to both a latter-day Personism and a sense of the absurdity of daily life: "Sun Is Very Near Hot and Buttockslike," "Lana Turner at Versailles," "There Isn't Much to Do If You Aren't Geology," "Do You Want to Be Excellent an A Actress No Not That Either," "Don't Think That Thought It Will Poison This Moment," and "A New Hairdo." Calling up on O'Hara while issuing a sly critique of her own, Notley writes at one point, "Lana Turner don't speak now" (37), as if she ever did in O'Hara's poem. (She didn't.) In moments such as these, the multiplanar walking around sensibility of O'Hara becomes a mantle under which Notley frames her own wittily subversive visions of society.

The tone of the book is casual and talky, at times written in the narrator's private musings, at other times in dialogue with a hard-boiled detective (more on him to follow), but mostly semipublic and conversational, as if the reader is walking next to Notley's *I* in some seedy Paris neighborhood, or descending with her into shadowy dream caves, listening to her account of the scene at hand in the voice of a contemporary feminist flâneuse. If that were the extent of the text, it could be effectively summarized as a postmodern neoepic in the New York School vein, or, in the words of Maggie Nelson, "a baggy monster offering unprecedented pleasures and exasperations,"[38] baggy apparently referring to *Disobedience*'s size, duration, and loose amalgamation of incident, episode, and witty observation. Contextualized as Nelson's analysis is within her compelling recent study of women in the New York School, it is not surprising that her attention turns to voice and mood, reading Notley's poetics as "a poetics of pure grouchiness."[39] And yet, Nelson's summary doesn't capture the many ways in which this baggy monster functions on multiple levels to situate the feminine/feminist subject in a hostile new realism, at the same time that Notley laments the wide reach of global multinational capitalism through concerted critique of the narratives informing mass culture productions that are disseminated at home and abroad. For the turn-of-the-century world that Notley's subject inhabits in *Disobedience* is an affect-laden combination of the material real, the epic/historical, and the pulp fictive, with the heightened paranoia of popular genre fiction suffusing Notley's experience of material history. Indeed, those cliché worlds of midcentury B film that nowadays seem to exude a nostalgia for a presumably simpler and more manageable past are reanimated in this long work such that those discursive fields of social control palpable in pulp fiction become operative again, and the collectivized anxiety and paranoia fostered by Cold War culture return as affective states descriptive of our own moment.

Notley begins *Disobedience* in medias res, blurring affect with material geography and the passage of time in interrelated points of location: "moved here for no reason. / don't seem to be anywhere" (3). As the text gets under way, diverging along multiple narrative planes, Notley foregrounds references to her detective and stock plot devices, cloaking the text in the familiar pop culture aura of noir fiction and film. Notley's *I* declares, "I find I need a plot to show us truth, / the graph's coordinates quotidian life" (4), and names her choice of plot: "a cheap Chandleresque detective device / a man with a coat and a gun / a room with mirrors because / I can't leave your company, your approval" (5). With her second-person address she summons the reader as witness to the poem while compressing "quotidian life" together with suggestion of the hardboiled plot; from the outset, Notley forces a merging of the real and the fictive while implicating her reader in the journey, even as she maps the present along that positivistic mathematical "graph." At the same time, the mirrors suggest Notley's speaker's desire to see herself reflected as the male half of the noir landscape, switching places with him in a dream: "I dream I'm a detective a man / trying to catch a woman / I'm in a barroom with small reflector mirrors" (5). The speaker's desire to be read as both male and female and in multiple frames indicates a polyvalent relationship to the visual image: here she situates herself as both subject/agent of the image and its object, even as the proliferation of mirrors here suggests noir conventions such as the Rita Hayworth mirror scene in Orson Welles's *The Lady from Shanghai*. At this moment, the text enters the realm of visual production and noir aesthetics, the affective tenor of the low genre suddenly pervading the space of the poem, even as this gender-switching subject is suspended in a liminal, unstable position. For what is seen in the small reflector mirrors? Is it the image of the male detective in pursuit, or of the pursued woman? Or both at once, holographically? That we cannot definitively fix the mirror image points to one of the central problematics in this text: how can the female *I* escape reification as a powerless, passive object in an aesthetic and material climate marked by the relentless disintegration of the textual and the material self? And if she can escape, what new form must she necessarily take?

Adding to the uncertainty surrounding agency in this text, Notley's morphing detective, modeled on Robert Mitchum and alternately named Hardwood, Hardwill, Hardone, and Mitch-ham, operates as a figure for the poet's "will" and engages in continual pursuit of and argument with his/her alter ego, the female "soul" of the piece, as both are witness to terrorist bombings, racial oppression, homelessness and economic injustice, the proliferation of images of American consumerism (Bill Gates and Windows make numerous appearances), the rise to power of the French arch-conservative Jean-Marie Le Pen, growing antiimmigration sentiment and legislation, and other large-scale incidences of human struggle that continue to resonate a decade later. These recorded details comprise the realistic context for the considerably murkier plot of detection, the tension between material history and the suggestion of plot revealing the inevitable move toward closure and silence that any tightly plotted narrative entails. For while on one level the detective device is comic and clearly tongue in cheek, a nod to noir conventions of the morally ambiguous detective and the elusive, mysterious woman he typically pursues, the heavily layered presence of sites of real struggle belie any comic reading of the work and also stand as critique of such seductively efficient, inherently perverse devices of information control and containment as such stock tropes necessarily represent. Notley's poem thus effectively deploys the tropes of the hard-boiled detective story such that they work against their own grain in a critique of those grittily realist fictional spaces that appear to reflect things as they are in the material world even as material history unravels in one disaster after another. In *Disobedience*'s temporally defined yet aesthetically changeable realism, the simulacral noir landscape of the text functions as both campy illusion and, in its ultimate inability to contain its present together with its efforts to distract audiences from the truth, as legitimate indicator of the tenor of a contemporary history that is always mediated by mass cultural production.

In its adaptations of popular culture as well as its self-consciousness about the subject/*I* in the text, *Disobedience* could be said in some ways resemble to Ed Dorn's revolutionary Pop Art long poem of the late sixties, *Gunslinger*, published in 1968. Hailed by Marjorie Perloff as "an epic of contemporary celluloid America, with its cartoon versions of Capitalist Entrepreneurs and Outlaw Heroes, its simulated folksiness, its Sci-Fi allusions and reductive academic clichés,"[40] Dorn's long poem is a quest through American cultural fantasy and capitalist ideology marked by witty engagement with the theoretical discourse popular in its time. In this long poem, the Slinger's horse is alternately called "Hi Digger" and "Claude Levi-Strauss," such nomenclature being but one example of Dorn's play with poststructuralist theory in a poem concerned in Perloff's view with "the archaeology of mass-produced myths." At the same time, Dorn's is a poem concerned with continually undermining the *I*-as-construct through rigorous play with the language in which the lyric subject is shown to be no longer viable.[41] Indicative of its contemporaneity with the rise of poststructuralist theory, Perloff argues that *Gunslinger* marked "a turn away from the monologic lyric of mid-century to the dialogic 'parapoem' of *fin de siècle*, with its amalgam of 'theory' and lyric, of prose narrative and sound-text, and especially of citation embedded in or superimposed upon the speech of a particular self."[42] As Perloff's assessment suggests, Dorn wrote theoretically investigative poetry and rent the traditional lyric subject asunder just ahead of those practitioners of Language poetry who would continue the project of dismantling normative conventions of language and narrative. Yet here is an important—and arguably quite gendered—difference between Dorn's poem and Notley's, for in *Gunslinger* the dismantling of the lyric *I* is precisely the point in a triumphant turn to poststructuralist theoretical discourse *as* the new poetry, whereas for Notley, writing at the historical fin de siècle and not an anticipated or imagined one, the *I* retains (or returns to) its viability at the very core of the long poem's proliferating narratives, narratives that are derived from the news of the material world as much as they are from pulp fiction.

Whereas *Gunslinger* stages a rollicking epic acid trip across the historically male-defined, simulacral, and what Perloff terms the highly gestural Wild West, Notley suggests a link between the paranoiac affect pervading noir and the real space of our contemporary present, such that the affect associated with the popular genre bleeds into her vision of the now. The difference here is crucial and signals competing attitudes toward postmodern aesthetics of pastiche. Dorn's aesthetic is reflective of what Patricia Waugh has shown to be the ahistorical turn in postmodernism that undercuts master narratives and literary genres without critiquing the ideology within them.[43] Contrastingly, in *Disobedience* Notley invokes the terms of noir to critique the old politics within the aesthetic at the same time that her work suggests that the politics and attitudes of pulp have penetrated the collective consciousness; her text is thus a critical examination of those cultural productions that have influenced culture and lived history in America and abroad. Indeed, Notley's creeping detective in all his forms remains a constant and amorphously threatening phantom presence that she/we can't quite shake, an elusive embodiment of abiding attitudes toward power and cultural domination that exceeds the boundaries of the text.

Theorizing what she terms the "return of story" in postmodern poetry, Perloff writes that

> [t]o tell a story is to find a way—sometimes the only way—of *knowing* one's world. But since, in the view of many of our poets, as in the view of comparable fiction writers, the world just doesn't—indeed shouldn't—make sense, the *gnosis* which is narration remains fragmentary. By frustrating our desire for closure . . . such stories foreground the narrative codes themselves and call them into question.[44]

As in *Gunslinger*, and fitting Perloff's theory of narrative in postmodern poetry, *Disobedience* extends the project of postmodern aesthetics by calling attention to the devices through which readers construct their own theoretical fictions. In so doing, *Disobedience* displays what Brian McHale has termed "weak narrativity," a trend in postmodern long poems motivated by a deconstructionist mistrust of master narratives and reflective of contemporary poets' and readers' understanding that every story is in some sense a fiction.[45] But in a different emphasis from Dorn's, Notley renders ostentatiously theoretical discourse as itself a hackneyed and distinctively masculinist narrative, a move that runs counter to the poststructuralist turn in late-century experimental poetry:

> I could say that the detective
> becomes even more interesting older
> wittier drunk a veritable piece
> of characterization for you
> isn't it marvelous he reads a lot
> an amateur critic/philosopher
> belongs to a Derridean study group (*siècle* drags on.) (6–7)

Notley's skepticism surrounding the cult of high theory is illuminated in this description of the male intellectual as a tired cliché; this attitude, together with her insistence on the sincere *I* as an agent and witness to history, stands as a refusal of the Language movement's celebration of its own power to subvert narrative and abolish the *I*. *Disobedience* thus directly contests those avant-garde aesthetics that Patricia Waugh and other theorists of postmodernism have linked to a male nostalgia for the universal, autonomous subject of the Enlightenment; against the celebration of the death of the *I* in postmodern poetics, Notley uses narrative and voice to show the struggle for the gendered *I* to exist. As she writes in "The 'Feminine' Epic,"

> I want to write that large public poem. I want to discover a woman's voice that can encompass our true story existing on conscious and unconscious levels, in the literal present, witnessing more than one culture. There will certainly be a Voice. I think it is essential that people like myself, and my brother, be heard: I can only do this by speaking out clearly. . . . A woman's voice.[46]

Yet, Notley's framing of the unstable, morphing agent in *Disobedience* speaks to the postmodern subject's uncertain position at multiple sites—in poststructuralist discourse and in poetry debates, as well as in a chaotic material present mediated by what seem in Notley's work to be competing totalizing forces. Connecting the unstable agent of *Disobedience* to Notley's comments about her brother and Vietnam as motivating her turn to epic, we can infer that this instability is rooted in Notley's knowledge and distrust of large-scale systems of power. At the same time, she retains the notion of the isolate individual as an integral entity, in open and confident rejection of the fashion in criticism and theory. Yet this is not to say that her integral subjects are not aesthetic productions, for in situating her record of daily life in Paris within the frame of noir fiction, she associates the subject of the poem with a fictional hero, a trope whose very existence is occasion for the playing out of a drama surrounding society and its assault on the individual. One productive way of reading the primary speaking subject of *Disobedience*, then, is as the suspended agent within a totalizing social order that is effectively metaphorized here as a generalized conspiracy plot against the individual, but the plot functions on two levels—at the level of the text (assault on the *I*) and at the level of material history (assault on the gendered self). Notley's agent thus takes shape as a singular and vulnerable individual who is "the result or flower of suppression" (6) and must negotiate a shifting textual and material landscape in order to survive intact. Yet, "intact" is not quite accurate either, for at the same time that Notley's textual *I* demands to be read as the central agent of this epic, the set of collisions among other texts and genres that *Disobedience* performs work to continually destabilize her speaker/self at every turn. As Notley writes in "Circorpse," "there's really only one, but there's hardly any interest / if there aren't two or more: / That's why I keep on letting Hardwood detect me" (17). The speaker acknowledges her fundamental sense of her own oneness in these lines at the same time that she insouciantly complicates that convention in mock deference to poststructuralist skepticism. In a multilayered framing, then, Notley's self both takes shape and fragments, hovering as a psychologically knowable and sociologically situated subject within a textual and material realm in which the subject and her voice are ever under threat of erasure.

Coupling Notley's chosen plot device with her statements about war and systems of social control, we are invited to read *Disobedience* as a narrative rooted in paranoia, an affective state associated with postmodern fiction but as yet not considered in relation to postmodern poetry. Writing about ambitiously postmodern fiction by writers such as Thomas Pynchon, Don DeLillo, and William Burroughs, Timothy Melley has shown the paranoid male protagonists within these novels to function as signs of agency panic, an affective state that Melley defines as the fear that the isolate and integral individual is under threat of destruction and/or feminization within large-scale conspiracy plots.[47] Critiquing yet also adapting Freud's analysis of Daniel Schreber, Melley argues that this fear of feminization in specifically postmodern fiction can be read as a fundamentally paranoid response to the late twentieth-century upheaval in normative systems of meaning and the lone individual's loss of control with the simultaneous proliferation of technologies and social systems that appear all-powerful. According to Melley, against the late-century deconstructionist view of the subject as always culturally and linguistically mediated such that there never was any core self in the first place, the paranoid narrative of agency panic reflects an abiding belief in the humanist model of the individual, a core being whose absorption into the larger culture necessarily means loss of self. Yet writing about female paranoia, Melley argues that paranoia functions in stalker novels by Atwood and Johnson as a marker of the instability of the female subject who cannot finally determine whether the threat she feels comes from the outside (a sociological reading) or her own consciousness (a psychological reading). In Melley's view, it is this lack of clarity, manifested as uncertainty about inside versus outside, that distinguishes the agency panic of women in these novels.[48] Considered in relation to *Disobedience*, Melley's masculine paradigm of agency panic is relevant to Notley's self-consciously unstable character construction, whereas his reading of female paranoia is altogether not; her cagey narrative of pursuit relies upon a masculinist pulp sensibility to call up the cultural climate Melley describes, yet her flagrant mocking of the tropes reveals a degree of control over that climate that the self-destructing heroines of stalker novels do not possess. In *Disobedience*, paranoia functions as a form of knowledge and critical inquiry as opposed to a fulcrum for self-destruction.

If paranoia stands as a comic indicator of postmodern anxiety about the integral male subject in the "big" novels of the late twentieth century, paranoia in *Disobedience* takes a feminist turn, functioning not to indicate insanity or a breaking apart of the integral subject, as Melley argues, but rather to indicate a specifically feminist epistemology capable of eluding attacks on the subject as such. In *Ugly Feelings*, Sianne Ngai's study of affect in the minor genres of American literature and film, Ngai argues for the value of reading paranoia in texts written by women as a site of Marcusian negative thinking; she shows the ways in which paranoia in certain texts—including Juliana Spahr's experimentalist *Response*—functions as a form of critical insight at a time when the integral subject has come under erasure and the critical community has lost the vocabulary for talking openly about patriarchy-capitalism.[49] Leaving aside the question of the subject and studying the affect surrounding a text as a legible indicator of oppositional thinking, Ngai shows how certain feelings suggest states of obstructed agency within larger systems of social and/or economic control. She argues that in a transmission of radical thinking, it is in readers' recognition of obstructed agency through experience of affective paranoia that political discourse returns to art in covert forms.

In this view, paranoia suffusing a text can function as a specifically feminist response to a set of conditions that the textual subject can neither represent nor change,[50] at the same time that interrogation of the integral subject is deferred as the affective tenor of the text takes precedence.

Notley's use of noir within her materialist epic suggests a view of American film more broadly as closely linked to her experience of the dailiness of living, a notion supported in Notley's unpublished autobiography, *Tell Me Again*, in which she lists a long string of movie titles as being central to her formation as a subject:

> If I had to choose between knowing my family and friends and going to the movies and reading books, I would have chosen movies and books.... Movies were the best alternative to that blank blue sky, which as I got older seemed to deny that there was such a thing as real life and I was part of it.... Robert Mitchum, Howard Duff, the young Paul Newman of *The Silver Chalice* and *The Long Hot Summer*... FROM HERE TO ETERNITY, CAROUSEL, IMITATION OF LIFE, GIANT, HUD, THE AFRICAN QUEEN, THE MOUNTAIN, VERTIGO, BELL, BOOK, AND CANDLE, FUNNY FACE, THE BAND WAGON, ONE EYED JACKS, GUNFIGHT AT THE OK CORRAL, I SHOT JESSE JAMES, THE UNFORGIVEN.[51]

And yet, even as noir, westerns, and film in general were the escape of choice for many growing up in the post–World War II era, for women, film—and noir in particular—poses special problems. Routinely about everyman's alienation within a corrupt society, noir is also just as routinely about woman's complicity in man's downfall. In Raymond Chandler's *The Big Sleep*, to take Notley's own example, multiple female characters are essentially interchangeable: grasping, perverse, psychologically unnatural, and in ruthless pursuit of power over men. In this and other novels of the genre, it is precisely the Feminine that must be vanquished and returned to her rightful place within the law and the patriarchal family, a schema that resonates somewhat comically in *Disobedience* but quite seriously throughout Notley's body of work. But in *Disobedience* Notley interrupts the now-commonplace circulation of such tropes by taking the role of producer of the images; no longer forced to watch herself represented in B films, she takes her place behind the lens and remakes the genre from a feminist perspective. Connecting style to politics as they work together in *Disobedience*, Notley writes, "It's very feminist but men do seem to enjoy it a lot, it possibly contains a rather virile approach to things riding roughshod and shooting at every little duck that seems to pop up."[52]

Notley's use of noir aesthetics constitutes Notley's return to the serious yet unfinished business with a dangerously underexamined American consumer culture. In fact, the text comprises a sophisticated critique of economics, gender, and power at the turn of this last century, layered in with Notley's historically situated political consciousness surrounding mass entertainment and its global impact. At first glance, and on its most commonly understood level, noir is the cinematic incarnation of the modern American hard-boiled crime story, both genres arising out of artists' dissatisfaction with the saccharine narratives of American society common to popular fiction and film in the 1930s and 1940s. Noir stages an anxious poetic realism of a hostile universe that the reluctant male protagonist must navigate in order to survive, and paranoia is central to the workings of the genre. Originally the stuff of B films, noir in the 1940s and 1950s both reflected and invited engagement with the American working class; as such, early examples of the style and storylines seem at times to suggest a proto-Marxian understanding of the man against a dehumanizing mechanized culture, even as big budget studio films churned out bourgeois notions of the powerful, autonomous individual and the promise of class mobility. Citing Raymond Borde and Étienne Chaumerton, whose 1955 *Paranoia du film noir américain* is considered a benchmark for later critical work on noir, James Naremore writes that

> *noir* is not merely a descriptive term, but a name for a critical tendency within the popular cinema—an antigenre that reveals the dark side of savage capitalism. Fot Borde and Chaumerton, the essence of noirness lies in a feeling of discontinuity, an intermingling of social realism and oneiricism, an anarcho-leftist critique of bourgeois ideology, and an eroticized treatment of violence. Above all, noir produces a psychological and moral disorientation, an inversion of capitalist and puritan values.[53]

Locating *Disobedience* within noir's international history produces eerie echoes of present with past, a linkage between America as an exporter of capitalist/democratic ideology through film in the 1940s to America as ultimate producer of global unrest via the success of this very project at the turn of the last century. Jennifer Fay and Justus Nieland have shown how 1940s-era French and Italian directors adapted the American crime story and noir aesthetic as a tool for critiquing fascist regimes and their impact on common people; for these directors, the new gritty realism of the alienated everyman navigating a new urban jungle served very well as a means of resistance against totalitarianism and fascism in Europe. Referencing the poetic realism that a few French and Italian directors adapted from American noir, Fay and Justus write that "American culture offered Italian and anti-fascists both a symbolic *elsewhere*—the lure of an other to fascist cultural life—and a way of reseeing the very *here-and-nowness* of Italian locality and Italian national character that had been suppressed by the fascist version of national life."[54] In one very important sense, then, the aesthetic itself made possible new forms of populist representation and political critique through presentation of another narrative to combat the chaos of the present. But lest noir seem antidote to oppression, following World War II, Hollywood began exporting big-budget films to Germany, France, and Japan in a move to associate democracy with capitalism. Writing about "Hollywood, Americanization, and Market Empire," Fay and Justus show how "American films could advertise American goods to foreign consumers . . . [and] . . . in the postwar era, Hollywood could help spread the English language, American culture, capitalism, and democracy as the basis for a new, much more homogenized, internationalism."[55] And indeed, throughout Notley's *Disobedience* the global reach of American capitalist values are palpable.

But at the same time that the studio pictures were indoctrinating European populations with consumerist values, the affect pervading noir was subversively paranoiac and anxious. According to Fay and Justus, "In this genre associated with subterranean economies and stolen goods, luxury was a sign of corruption and it was clear that American capitalism—if not also its presumed democratic culture—had run amock."[56] That is, even as American consumer culture was visually advertised across Europe and Asia as the way to the free world, noir retained its power at home and abroad to suggest unrest beneath the surface of polite society and the moral ambiguities—as opposed to the comfortable certitudes—pervading modern life. It is this tension between the allure of power and the sense of dis-ease that Notley's flâneuse must negotiate, continually threading the needle between the chaos of daily living in an increasingly fascist global environment and the desire to shape the chaos into a story legible for a critical audience.

Affective tone—paranoia in particular—is the only consistency in this work that veers from site to site and narrative to narrative in search of some ultimately unnameable goal; while the many narratives spin, paranoia suffuses the text such that the tone itself becomes its most consistent character. I want to suggest here that it is precisely Notley's creation of a paranoiac field that holds this "baggy monster" together. Ngai has shown how we can read a specifically *feminist* paranoia as a site of knowledge in the critically minor genres, an affective tone signaling a diffused understanding of cultural forces that otherwise remain unnamed in a time when we have lost our vocabulary for discussing patriarchal capitalism. For Ngai, who articulates her argument through discussion of Spahr's *Response*, feminist paranoia takes the place of the expressive yet fallible lyric subject; affect is harder to locate and at least for now impervious to methods of silencing, and it can act as character in texts that are predominantly metalinguistic in form.[57] As a critical lens through which we view the present moment of *Disobedience*, then, paranoia bridges the gap between lyric speaking subject and narrative genre, a rhetorical presence that serves to legitimize the text for readers trained to experience paranoia as a special form of insight in a world gone mad. The imbrication of her *I* into an affective field is signaled in Notley's naming of herself at times as a "dark woman," at others, "soul," and still others, "will," as she searches for the critical vantage point from which to understand and interpret the murky world she inhabits. Notley makes visible the complex of cultural productions through which this specific gendered self and writer has been defined, even as we trace her progress as she continues to search for some other narrative:

> Hypnotize self into a fantasy world
> A world of caves. (Yes, I *do* this, I can.)
> . . . .
>
> A shadowy man in a gun-coat has come to find me.
> Why do I like these caves so much?
> He seems to be asking the question.
> Because evidence left in them
> is our subject of detection. Is what's lost
> to the presumably awakened world.
>
> . . . .
>
> I'm, we're, the result or flower of suppression.
> Much of one is suppressed
> towards being another kind of one
> other colors, petal arrangements, scents
> you can only have one scent
> I want to know what I've forgotten

> for 50,000 years. Think of those ridiculous *déesses*
> so-called Venuses, in French museums.
> What do I know. It's so fatiguing to hate you men. (6)

Here again, Notley relies upon the idea of an authentic self as the primary locus of meaning, even as her plot line of the self is pocked with real or imagined traps and the bad memories of ancient history in which her explicitly and transhistorically gendered self is embedded. Here that history is more deeply layered than now versus then, for, simultaneous with a generalized gloom, the reference to caves also calls up Plato's allegory, in which the validity of human knowledge is assessed based on whether the subject can in fact see clearly. One way of reading the "evidence" left in the caves as "the subject of our detection" is as a floating signifier marking lies and distortions, the paradoxically ubiquitous and elusive rhetorical content of an official culture that works to keep women and marginalized subjects quite literally "in the dark" about the secret workings of power. Through breaks in metanarrative and self-conscious references to narrative device as controlling fictions, Notley opens a vacant space through which a displaced, decontextualized, and distinctly gendered subject slips this discursive trap, emerging—if only momentarily—as an agent and engaged witness of material history. Writes Notley, "the eye is slipping out in order / not to die, slipping out to see" (110).

Blending first-person narrative with the convention of a noir hero and plot, Notley emphasizes the determinism of noir narrative for women at the same time that she articulates an anxiety surrounding her inability to escape from "this thought" that "leads further and further in." At the same time that her *I* appears to collude with Hardwill/Mitch-ham, she also expresses her own alterity and pessimism. She exists inside the plot and outside at the same time, looking back at the scene half-humorously, knowing its artifice, but also acceding to the inevitability of this narrative. Indeed, at times she seems almost to claim the role of Walter Benjamin's angel of history, flying through time and possessing special knowledge about the pileup of human catastrophe, as in "I float alive, larger than history. / Better than history" (7), and "The Choros of the future howls quietly" (23). Blurring fictional plot and images of a witness to history, Notley suggests that the realism of noir becomes the realism of daily living, the plot of the one rather uncannily anticipating the terms of the other.

Through serious play with popular culture, Notley brings into high relief the obvious workings of power in mass culture forms at the same time that she indicates the ways in which mass culture values inform our material historical moment. Throughout her ambitious long poem *Disobedience*, Notley layers into the epic form a critical dance with what O'Hara termed "the despised daily" and the stuff of mainstream pulp, sketching the political unconscious of turn-of-the-century American culture as one that is steeped in regressive and deeply subliminal values surrounding the march of capitalism, entrenched gender ideology, and the same old distribution of power, but an unconscious that is also fleetingly visible in the gaps opened in Notley's generic and thematic collisions. In her development of hybrid forms that subvert expectations and critical demand for single genres, Notley bypasses the insidious rumors that there is no self and resists the move toward closure underpinning stock narrative genres. Hers constitutes a new poetics of the excluded middle—a poetics forged out of disaffection with binary thinking and situated in the gap Jed Rasula has identified between the high and the low in contemporary art. As such, Notley's turn-of-the-century work does not so much bridge a gap between the high and the low, the linguistic and the narrative, the poetic and the pulp, as it exposes the uselessness of these binary terms, even as she builds through new hybrid forms a populist poetics rooted in a strong and resistant "mainstream American" sensibility.

4 / Harryette Mullen's Poetics in Prose: A Return to the Modernist Hybrid

"I am curious about the 'unconscious' of language..."
—HARRYETTE MULLEN, "IMAGINING THE UNIMAGINED READER"

In this chapter I examine the ways in which Harryette Mullen's prose poetry in two of her collections—*S*PeRM**K*T* (1992) and *Sleeping with the Dictionary* (2002)—foregrounds and frustrates white desire for consumption of the black body, a desire that runs deep in American literature and history and that has played out in a multitude of ways—aesthetic and material—since well before the dawn of modern poetry. Taking recourse to Aldon Lynn Nielsen's critical work on African American poetry and his insightful analysis of the trope of cannibalism as it has long functioned in public and literary discourse to incite fear in whites as well as African Americans,[1] I build my argument surrounding Mullen's resistant prose poetics of the body upon a deeper argument for the ways in which this desire to consume can be found in the modern prose poetry of Charles Baudelaire. Considered by many to be the pioneer of the intrinsically hybrid genre of the prose poem, Baudelaire published his better known verse work, *Les Fleurs du mal*, in 1857, the same year as Flaubert's controversial *Madame Bovary*. Like Flaubert's novel, *Les Fleurs* constituted an avant-garde breakthrough in form as well as in the way it presented scenes of debased urban life. Yet as Jonathan Monroe has shown in *A Poverty of Objects: The Prose Poem and the Politics of Genre*, it is Baudelaire's prose poetry that more closely aligns with Flaubert's work given that the poet turned to prose as a means of reaching a broader audience, in this case one made up of bourgeois consumers of novels and mass media.[2] Moreover, just as Flaubert's formal transgressions and innovations in the language are accompanied by the writer's deeply regressive representation of the embodied woman,[3] so, too, are Baudelaire's prose and verse poems, which are written to produce a shock of recognition in the reader, reliant upon established cultural biases surrounding gender and race. In what follows I examine the ways in which Mullen's work replicates and resists such representations, making visible the literary, cultural, and linguistic ways in which black women in particular have been objectified and contained in modern poetry and visual art. At the same time, I chart the ways in which Mullen's language games revolutionize the prose poem genre.

To begin, some history of the prose poem as a genre and its current place in American poetry will serve as a context for my argument surrounding Mullen's work in the wake of Baudelaire's and will further locate Mullen's poetics in the current conversation surrounding hybrid aesthetics. Defined by Margueritte Murphy as "a genre formed in violation of genre, a seeming hybrid, in name a contradiction in terms,"[4] the prose poem has taken many forms in modern and postmodern poetry and has retained an aura of subversion or transgression in all of them. Made famous if not entirely invented by Baudelaire,[5] the prose poem genre turns up in the modernist Anglo-American poetry of Gertrude Stein, William Carlos Williams, and T. S. Eliot (whose prose poem, "Hysteria," is a study in misogyny), later appearing in the midcentury experimentalist poetry of John Ashbery and taking another form in the work of the Language poets who used its confines as a locus for subversions of normative syntax and literary convention; Lyn Hejinian's prose poems in *My Life* are one important example of this. The prose poem is somewhat in vogue in our current moment, appearing in the work of poets who are modifying and compressing the lyric and also in the work of those designated as avant-garde or experimental poets. Surveying this field, one might conclude that the prose poem takes so many different forms in so many different contexts that it is in fact somewhat meaningless as a designation, yet a growing body of scholarship on the genre would seem to suggest otherwise. As Michael Delville argues in *The American Prose Poem: Poetic Form and the Boundaries of Genre* and as Stephen Monte details in *Invisible Fences: Prose Poetry as a Genre in French and American Literature*, the prose poem when read in historical context can perhaps best be described as a form that intrinsically challenges the boundaries of form, and as such one that exists always in relation to other forms, though never firmly fixed in its own.[6] At the same time, with the exception of Gertrude Stein, the overwhelming majority of prose poets currently anthologized and studied are men.

In his introduction to the 2003 Scribner anthology *Great American Prose Poems: From Poe to the Present*, an anthology that publishes the work of male to female prose poets at a ratio of roughly 3:2 and that contains the work of few poets of color, David Lehman consolidates this genre under the sign of the hybrid. Writes Lehman, "The prose poem is, you might say, poetry that disguises its true nature. In the prose poem the poet can appropriate such unlikely models as the newspaper article, the memo, the list, the parable, the speech, the dialogue. . . . It is an insistently modern form. Some would argue further that it is, or was, an inherently subversive one. . . . The prose poem is a *hybrid* form, an *anomaly* if not a *paradox* or *oxymoron*."[7] In Lehman's definition of the prose poem as a genre that mixes genres, we hear echoes of Cole Swensen's and Stephen Burt's descriptions of the hybrid that appear in their introductions to their own anthologies of hybrid poetics, and that I take up in the introduction to this book. Indeed, the similarities among Swensen's, Burt's, and Lehman's accounts of their respective outlaw genres' place in American literary culture are striking; it also bears noting that the arrival of the prose poem in Scribner's commercially appealing anthology (John Ashbery's color-rich and kitchily provocative collage *L'Heure Exquise* is reproduced on the cover) coincides roughly with the emergence of the hybrid in Norton's own market-savvy presentation. Linking the subgenres of hybrid and prose poem even more closely together is Lehman's explicit claim that the prose poem is by definition a hybrid, at the same time that the target audience for *Great American Prose Poems: From Poe to the Present* seems fairly clearly to be white male readers.

In *Boxing Inside the Box: Women's Prose Poetry*, poet and scholar Holly Iglesias examines the inherently experimental nature of the prose poem form when written by women even as she addresses the absence of women prose poets from discussions of the genre. She argues that contemporary women writing in this genre are in various ways writing from within a container—a box—that stands as metaphor for both women's experience of containment in the broader culture and their confinement within the limits placed upon them in the field of contemporary poetry. In delimiting this container out of which women prose poets are seen to write, Iglesias traces the development of the American prose poem since the midtwentieth century by noting the omnipresence of a "new" or "hybrid" form, but one that is associated with male writers. Iglesias points to Robert Pinsky's definition of the prose poem as the site of "one-of-the-guys surrealism," a characterization echoed by Peter Johnson, editor of *The Prose Poem: An International Journal*, who terms the genre "The Wise-Guy School of Poetry." Iglesias names this work "template poetry," a subgenre of the prose poem in which the speaker is presumed to be male and "the focus is inward, cerebral, singular, ephemeral, anxious, insubstantial—a talking head, disembodied, laughing skittishly in isolation."[8] Iglesias links the privileged position of famed prose poets such as Pinsky, Charles Simic, and Russell Edson to their style of writing, a style that is palatable to mainstream bourgeois audiences even as it appears to be exciting, quixotic, and new. In Iglesias's view, the revolutionary potential of prose poetry in these cases is submerged under new articulations of mastery and self-importance, written by poets from the dominant group whose work already enjoys considerable visibility in major magazines and journals. And it is in fact the case that many venues for prose poetry emergent since the 1990s have published the work of male poets in greater numbers, while the work of women poets writing in the genre lingers at the margins of both the anthologies and the criticism.[9]

Against this clubby trend in which a select few poets from the dominant group write presumably revolutionary new work with what in Iglesias's view amounts to a template of stylistic and thematic consistency, Iglesias foregrounds the possibilities for restraint and rupture in other, minoritarian subjects' uses of the form, turning to the work of poets including Susan Howe, Kimiko Hahn, Carolyn Forchè, María Rosa Menocal, C. D. Wright, and Maxine Chernoff to show that "[i]t doesn't take a visionary to see the box, just the experience inside one. And it doesn't take a theorist to explain captivity, or conversion, or a life sentence in narrative. As Gertrude already told us a box is a box is a box. Dainty containment, the domestic box. Male fantasy and fear. Her tight box."[10] At the same time that Iglesias points to the experimental origins and the potential for rupture in the prose poem as written by women, she makes a direct link between prose itself and the idea of containment when she summons Gertrude Stein's revolutionary *Tender Buttons* and directs our attention to Howe's innovative *Articulation of Sound Forms in Time*, in which Howe returns to the captivity narrative of Mary Rowlandson in order to "sing the holes in history," in the words of Howe critic Paul Naylor.[11] Both Stein's and Howe's prose poetry in fact foreground structures of containment and control that hold women in place, even as each develops poetics of social rupture. Maxine Chernoff's "I linger in the shadows. I learned how to do that by writing prose poems" succinctly underscores Iglesias's argument about the form and its metonymic relationship to the containment of women and their histories, and Chernoff's suggestive linking of gendered subjectivity to lingering in shadows functions as a keynote to Iglesias's work and is a point I will examine in more depth shortly.[12]

From its inception the prose poem has entailed a subversion of the very idea of what is considered poetic, in terms of both language and subject matter, as Baudelaire's groundbreaking verse in *Les Fleurs du mal* anticipates. In Baudelaire's case, that revolutionary work, together with the prose poems eventually collected in *Petits poèmes en prose* (*Le Spleen de Paris*), subverts not only traditional verse form but also, in its attempts to represent life in the streets, bourgeois French cultural standards for decency and propriety. Crucial to Baudelaire's poetics of close observation, and a trope very much alive today in the "Wise-Guy School," is the trope of the flâneur, a shadowy witness (always male) to the degradations of modern life whose observations about debased humanity are given in realist/surrealist terms. And yet, central to Baudelaire's *Les Fleurs du mal*, and at the near center of my own argument surrounding Harryette Mullen's work, is a cycle of poems addressed to the poet's black female lover and muse, the Haitian-born Jeanne Duval. In these poems, commonly referred to as the "Venus noire" cycle, the black female body is on view in peculiar ways as the object of the speaker's illicit desire but also as an opportunity for the speaker's narcissistic reflection upon himself. Consider Keith Waldrop's recent translation of poem 28, "Dancing Serpent," one of the so-called Black Venus poems:

> How I love, dear lazybones, to see how the skin of your beautiful body sparkles like cloth billowing.
> Over the depths of your hair with its acrid perfume, sweet-smelling vagrant sea of blue and brown,
> my dreamy soul, like a ship waking to morning wind, weighs anchor for a distant sky.[13]

Here and elsewhere, Baudelaire's speaker, adrift in melancholy reverie, pays homage in exoticizing terms to his mistress as she (or rather, the serpent) moves across the screen of Baudelaire's desire. In a close and repetitive exchange between male speaker/viewer and black female/object, the objectification of the female body in fact creates the terms for the speaker's "dreamy soul" to exist and flourish. That this representation of Baudelaire's Venus should resonate with the tenor of Laura Mullen's treatment of the female victim of noir fiction is worth noting. In other words, the woman's capture under the male gaze functions as the site of the flâneur's musings upon his alienation from bourgeois society, a dreamy alienation produced through his suspended attention upon the body of the woman whose status in society is far more precarious than his own.

Baudelaire's representations of the black female body foretell the modernist fascination with primitivism, a trope visible in the writings of Gertrude Stein, Carl Van Vechten, Ezra Pound, and others, and one that Michael North explores at length in *The Dialect of Modernism*.[14] Keeping in mind the black female body's imbrication in modernist poetry, the prose poem in particular, Harryette Mullen's own contributions to the genre can be read productively as revisionary constructions in which the African American body is simultaneously on view and concealed, a now-you-see-it-now-you-don't figure that appears and disappears in Mullen's innovative language and forms. For against the trend toward representation and fetishization of the black female body, Mullen's prose poetry can be seen to invoke and conceal the African American body in ways that resist her/his enclosure within the dominant culture's commodity fetishism, literally reinscribing this body as the site of active intellection even as s/he remains unavailable for readers' consumption.

Nathaniel Mackey has called for scholarship and criticism of African American cultural productions that attends to the unique aesthetics of these works and that does not ascribe "only the most obvious orders of statement to the work of black writers, the confinement of the work to racial readings that tell us only what we already know." For Mackey, criticism of African American literature that traffics in sociology rather than aesthetics "is a symptom of the social othering such readings presumably oppose."[15] At the same time that Mullen's work is embedded in African American culture, history, and experience, her poetry demands committed readers and complex readings that far exceed simplistic sociological observations. Like her 1991 *Trimmings* and her 1995 *Muse & Drudge*, *S*PeRM**K*T* and *Sleeping with the Dictionary* play with the very idea of representations of the black body by foregrounding multiple sites of mediation and object formation, at the same time that in these latter two collections she lifts the body out of such fixed positions. It is frankly impossible to reduce Mullen's presentations of African Americans and black women in particular to sociological readings, for the body in her work always eludes us, morphing, moving, shifting, and receding in a playful language of innuendo and evasion. At the same time, in breaking down normative syntax and foregrounding the materiality of language, Mullen's work can be read in the context of Language writing. The significance of Mullen's work to the genres of modern and postmodern poetry therefore is manifold, for as we will see, the aesthetics of the

European avant-garde that continues to influence Language writing and prose poetry alike contain certain critical aporias that call the current understanding of avant-gardism into question, even as Mullen's work opens new ways of thinking about the slippery slope of race in language as a foundation for radical art.

Locating her poetics in the space of "language per se" but also in the complex workings of the global and imperialistic American economy, Mullen has said that she "happen[s] to be working in what is currently the global language of international capitalism, or what some call 'Imperial English,' the quirks, contradictions, even the inanities, in the language of the declining Anglo-American empire."[16] In her oft-cited and forward-looking essay "Imagining the Unimagined Reader," she names some of the many linguistic idiosyncrasies that attract her, including "puns, double entendres, taboo words, Freudian slips, jokes, riddles, proverbs, folk poetry, found poetry, idiomatic expressions, slang and jargon, coinages, neologisms, nonce words, portmanteaus, pidgins and creoles, nicknames, diminutives, baby talk, tongue twisters," adding that she is interested in what is "minor, marginal, idiosyncratic, trivial, debased, or aberrant."[17] Notable here are the several references to language associated with the body and its desires (conscious or unconscious) as well as the body's location in society (marginality referring at once to the status of the child and of who or what is aberrant). Yet furthermore, it bears noting that Mullen locates a great many of these games circulating around the desiring body and the socially categorized within the generic frame of the prose poem, a minor and marginal literary form unto itself and yet one capacious enough to assemble—if not contain—these many forays and explorations into the languages of the minor and the debased. In fact, the blues quatrains of *Muse & Drudge* being the major exception, Mullen has written within the prose poem form more often than any other, meaning that the many innovations she achieves at the micro level or "unconscious" of language are embedded within a larger generic frame possessing a long history in modern poetry and a complicated ideological structure all its own.

Mullen's work has been the subject of numerous studies addressing its formally innovative poetics and its challenges to static representations and stereotypes of African American women. Evie Shockley's recent book *Renegade Poetics: Black Aesthetics and Formal Innovation in African American Poetry*, is one example of a study giving attention to Mullen's experimental poetics that is also grounded in questions of African American identity and history. Quoting from Arlene Keizer, scholar of

African American literature, Shockley writes that "[e]schewing racial essentialism, but maintaining a healthy respect for 'the integrity ... of black cultures,' I suggest that the term 'black aesthetics,' from which many contemporary critics have distanced themselves, need not be inevitably linked to static understandings of how blackness is inscribed in literary texts."[18] Shockley interprets Mullen's work for the ways in which it invites new ways of thinking about racial identity as inherently open and ever in flux, and she argues that *Muse & Drudge* "insist[s] upon the manifold and diasporic nature of black women's experiences. The result is a new form—an African American blues epic—that takes its language, structural cues, and expansive, nonautobiographical first person subjects primarily from the blues and African American literary traditions, even as it foregrounds the extent to which American poetic traditions, and other aspects of American culture, have always themselves comprised complex, polymorphous mixtures."[19] Identifying the ways in which Mullen's work complicates received notions surrounding the makeup of American culture, Shockley grounds her inquiry into Mullen's work in the distinct tradition of African American aesthetics. Anchoring her own analysis within the context of African American expressive tradition, Meta DuEwa Jones reads *Muse & Drudge* for its links to both the blues and jazz.[20] Also starting from a position of racial identification and African American history, Robin Tremblay-McGaw draws upon the legacy of slavery to articulate a theory of enclosure and escape in what she creatively terms Mullen's "fugitive poetics," a poetics characterized by "a productive tension between 'enclosure' and 'run,' between an archive of cultural, linguistic and historical references, images, and information and the fugitivity that is both a thematics and a formal strategy."[21]

Tremblay-McGaw's argument surrounding fugitivity as a thematic in Mullen's writing raises interesting questions about captivity and about those enclosures from which Mullen's writing might be escaping. Whereas this notion immediately calls up the history of slavery and the literal capture and containment of African and African American women, and whereas Tremblay-McGaw deepens and complicates this initial association by looking at Mullen's many "recyclings" of terms and historical references as a medium of escape from the enclosure of stock identity positions, I propose that we read fugitivity and captivity in Mullen in relation to innovative forms within modern poetry, the field in which Mullen writes and in which she produces culturally critical work. Elsewhere I have analyzed Mullen's innovations in avant-garde Language writing and her development of poetic forms of high artifice within which she layers race as a constitutive presence; indeed, some of her poems intervene quite provocatively in the Language movement's preference for the elision of the embodied subject within the text.[22] In a continuation of that earlier investigation into Mullen's politically interested rewritings of form, here I want to look more closely at Mullen's return to the prose poem, a genre in which the presence and position of the body has been absolutely central, as the foundational prose poetry of Baudelaire initiates. Indeed, moving from the gendered body to the status of the subject, and thinking about the particulars of subject position in relation to the prose poem in particular, Holly Iglesias's argument that the very form of the prose poem can be read as an enclosure and a space out of which women poets attempt to escape can be applied quite usefully to Mullen's work.

Considering Mullen's aesthetics of subject position, captivity, and escape in relation to modernist poetry, we ought to first recall Mullen's return to and revisions of Gertrude Stein's *Tender Buttons*, in which Stein inscribes a lesbian domestic space through the form of the prose poem. In *Trimmings*, Mullen adopts and adapts Stein's paratactic style and her disjunctive, metonymic description to write race into Stein's linguistic encounters with the female body and her playfully erotic suggestions of sexuality. Intriguingly, in *Trimmings* Mullen also takes up another item from the early days of modernism, Édouard Manet's *Olympia* (1863), the painting in which the transgressive representation of white female sexuality is undermined for contemporary viewers by the predictable and problematic representation of the black woman as a nearly invisible servant within the frame, an embodied black woman linked to Olympia's housecat through use of color. As is the case in Stein's novella *Melanctha*, Manet shocked his audience with a new style of representation even as within that representation old ideas about race, subjectivity, and subjection are reinforced. In Mullen's return to Stein's "A PETTICOAT," which reads, "A light white, a disgrace, an ink spot, a rosy charm,"[23] the poet answers Stein's as well as Manet's fetishistic modernist primitivism thus: "A light white disgraceful sugar looks pink, wears an air, pale compared to shadow standing by.... Behind her shadow wears her color."[24] In what Elisabeth A. Frost notes is a Black Arts–inspired "critique of white dominance in American life,"[25] Mullen's poem brings the modernist aesthetics of Stein and Manet into the present moment, to foreground black women's enclosure in art forms that are presented as radical breaks with an oppressive bourgeois culture.

Mullen articulates the status of the black woman as the object "ink" within her ekphrastic re-creation of Manet's painting, a metaphor that can be interpreted to indicate a position of either powerlessness—as the one who is inscribed—or power—as in the case of the one doing the inscribing, as Deborah Mix has shown.[26] For Mix, the black female body in Manet's painting, when read through Mullen's playful rewriting of Stein, is returned to us as a figure of resistance to the dominant culture. Related to white art's use of the black body, Michael North argues in *The Dialect of Modernism* that the languages of African America, and black bodies, objectified, are central tropes of modernist art, standing in for the otherness felt by avant-garde artists wishing to represent their exile from bourgeois culture through associations with the unfamiliar and what they viewed as the strange. North writes that "primitivism seems necessary to accompany a condition of exile,"[27] and in discussing the racializing writing of Sherwood Anderson, North argues that the author "implicitly aligns the free language of the modern artist with the despised dialect of African America. . . . Artistic language is, by virtue of its deviation from [standard 'white' English] black."[28] That is, for modernist artists including Anderson, Stein, Eliot, Pound, Van Vechten, and others, to be avant-garde meant to be aligned with the marginality experienced by African Americans, and the language of African Americans was available for deformation in the form of white dialect constructions, even as these subjects *as subjects* disappear within accounts of history and poetry. Indeed, as Aldon Lynn Nielsen notes and as the history bears out, "Among the many benefits of white privilege in American culture is the power to make race appear and disappear at will."[29]

There is a curious correspondence here with Gustav Flaubert's claiming of the feminine as the trope for his own marginality, expressed in his "Madame Bovary, c'est moi," which was coexistent with a thoroughgoing elision of the subjecthood of actual women, a point made by Andreas Huyssen and one that I take up in chapter 1. Huyssen argues that white male modernist writers such as Flaubert claimed the feminine as a privileged site of alterity even as these writers considered actual women to be little more than consumers of mass culture. According to Huyssen, the very structure of modernist art is a dialectical one in which the producers of the art mine mass culture for material that they convert into avant-garde art that ignores or elides the actual lives of the marginal.[30] Here I want to suggest that in some ways analogous to Flaubert's simultaneous cooptation of the abstract feminine and erasure of the woman as subject, white modernist artists have appropriated the black body and objects from African and African American cultures as signs of a profound otherness, even as Africans and African Americans themselves are relegated to the shadows.

Such is the case in the revolutionary verse and prose poetry of Charles Baudelaire, whose flâneur passes through the streets of Paris witnessing poverty and illness as these are presumably produced by the conditions of modernity, even as these very conditions are reproduced and reenforced in a poetry that celebrates the materiality of the degraded black female body. Borrowing from the Romantic trope of the lone individual whose poetry spouts whole cloth from the imagination that is sublime unto itself, Baudelaire modernizes the Romantic poet by placing him in constant contact with the urban materiality of his cultural and historical present, yet the flâneur remains above or outside of the world he witnesses and recounts. Baudelaire's poems are thus presented as the reflections of a lone bohemian outcast, a trope necessary for the effusive recounting of a tactility and sensuality that is often represented doubly as the flâneur's experience of both desire and revulsion for his muse, a muse who is often indistinguishable from the figure of a prostitute. In the words of Rebecca Munford, who quotes from Nicole Ward Jouve's *Baudelaire: A Fire to Conquer Darkness*, "[T]he muse is no longer identified with the purity of the Madonna but, rather, her dark shadow, the vampish whore. The prostitute thus becomes the site over which Baudelaire negotiates his 'declared aesthetic intention of extracting beauty from evil.'"[31] Consider poem 25:

> You would take the whole universe to your couch, lewd woman! Ennui makes your soul cruel. To exercise your jaws in this singular game, you need each day another heart off the heap. . . .
>
> Blind dumb machine, fertile in cruelties, salutary instrument, world bloodsucker, have you no shame? And can you not see in every mirror how your charms grow pale? . . .
>
> Filthy grandeur! Sublime disgrace![32]

At the same time, the Black Venus, embodied, is figured as an entire geography unto herself, as in poem 23, "Hair":

> O fleece, billowing down even to breastline! O ringlets! O apathy-filled perfume! Ecstasy! This evening, to populate our hideaway with the memories that sleep in your hair, I want to wave it in the air like a hanky!

Langourous Asia, burning Africa, a whole world distant, absent, almost dead, lives within your depths, aromatic forest! As other spirits sail on music, mine, my love, swims in your perfume![33]

Thus imprisoned within the flâneur's gaze, the Black Venus takes various forms as foreign lands to be explored, exotic experiences to be consumed, African cannibal to be feared, machine, insect, betrayer, and beast; Carol Clark and Robert Sykes have pointed to these poems' "sharp eroticism and sadistic themes."[34] Elsewhere, on the subject of a black woman appearing in Baudelaire's "La Cygne," Gayatri Chravorty Spivak has written of "the immense vagueness of the negress' geography" that Baudelaire succeeds in representing through only three words, "la superbe Afrique."[35] Central to an understanding of Baudelaire's Black Venus, then, is his lust for the African muse who in turn devours him, a racialized figure of "beauty extracted from evil" and—in Keith Waldrop's eloquent translation—a sublime disgrace, all contained within the firmly locked box of Baudelaire's revolutionary poetic idiom. For indeed, "Hair" in *Les Fleurs* has its complement in Baudelaire's prose poem, "Un hémisphère dans une chevelure" ("A Hemisphere in a Head of Hair"), which in Michael Hamburger's translation begins "Long let me inhale, deeply, the odour of your hair, into it plunge the whole of my face," and progresses as a celebration of the speaker's imaginative ocean travel to foreign ports "where eternal heat languidly quivers" and where he takes in the lushly described exotic through his five senses. The prose poem concludes with the speaker literally eating the woman's hair, gnawing at her "heavy, black tresses" and thereby "eating memories."[36] Here the devouring muse is devoured, the speaker intoxicated by the mistress whom he voraciously consumes even as she is reduced to the physical attribute that for centuries has functioned as the quintessential marker of racial difference. Moreover, the consistency among Baudelaire's various portrayals of his muse throughout his poetry—even as she exists in the twinned roles of food and cannibal—allows us to read her as always doubly encoded in verse and prose, consumer and consumable.

Baudelaire's construction of the black female body as both dark continent and cannibal has its roots in a long history of white Western mythologizing of Africa as a site of profound and threatening otherness. In his introduction to *Reading Race in American Poetry: "An Area of Act,"* Aldon Lynn Nielsen traces whites' fear of being eaten by Africans to Columbus's arrival in Cuba, pointing out that although there has never been direct evidence of Africans eating whites, the fear or perception of the practice has appeared for hundreds of years not only in public and political discourse of Europeans but also, more recently, in white modernist poets' constructions of African Americans and black writers.[37] Arguing that "the critical currency of cannibalism as a trope for primitivism, exoticism, Africanness, and poetry" has circulated for centuries, Nielsen points to T. S. Eliot's verse play *The Cocktail Party* as but one instance of a modernist's representation of Africans as cannibals. Focusing on the moderns precisely because that is where primitivism as a white construction held such heightened fascination, Nielsen goes on to argue that

> [f]rom the beginning of the Atlantic slave trade, through its eventual abolition, and well into the present century, Anglo-American literature recorded and transmitted a discursive formation that posited the "Basic Savagery," as Vachel Lindsay terms it in "The Congo" (47), of African persons and that codes Africanist savagery in self-authenticating narratives of pervasive cannibalism. Africanist discourse so thoroughly formed the terms of American thinking about Africans, was so deeply embedded in the ideologies of poets and critics alike, that it has continued to operate within the critical reception of American poetry into the recent past.[38]

Nielsen's argument centers on Anglo-American literature, yet his observations about the trope of the African cannibal in European discourse can also apply to Baudelaire's mid-nineteenth-century construction of the black female body as voracious and profoundly other, even as the relevance of this trope to American poetry will become clearer in my discussion of Mullen's poetics. But it is crucial to note, as Nielsen does, that at the same time whites believed in the trope of the African cannibal, blacks held their own fear of being consumed by whites, a fear founded in Africans' experience of being kidnapped into forced labor and treated as animals to be used. Certainly, this fear is far more logical than whites' fear of the very people they were consuming as laborers, sexual objects, and reproducers of slaves. Nielsen writes, "While millions of whites read and repeated narratives of African cannibalism, weaving them into their fiction, their poems, their politics, and their humor, Africans, from the end of the fifteenth century on, witnessed the mass disappearance of their brethren into the seemingly insatiable appetites of the whites. Whites were, as [Patricia] Turner puts it, 'large-scale consumers of African peoples.'"[39] In other words, from well before the time of Baudelaire, and on into the work of T. S. Eliot, Vachel Lindsay, and Kenneth Rexroth (whose rather more recent naming of Black Arts poetry as being "like Ornette

Coleman ... cooking missionaries" is worth noting),[40] the figure of the African cannibal has circulated widely in literature and poetry and has functioned to fix the black body in threatening and hideous terms.

Tropes of cannibalism and eating can be read in relation to Mullen's S*PeRM**K*T and Sleeping with the Dictionary in several ways, beginning with Mullen's refusal to construct a visible African American body for readers' consumption, but circulating also in many metaphors of eating and being eaten that are embedded in a linguistic playfulness that never settles into realism. In other words, Mullen's representations of the body are incomplete, vaguely sketched, but also surreal; her bodies are made up of metaphors and metonyms that point to but that do not place the body on view, constituting a provocative absence that refuses American cultural containment and consumption of the female body in particular. Hortense Spillers has argued that the black female body in American culture historically has been so relentlessly misnamed in terms such as "Sapphire," "Peaches," and "Brown Sugar" that her presence in the flesh remains ever overdetermined. According to Spillers, in order to fully recognize the person so (mis)named, one must "strip down through layers of attenuated meaning," searching for the "history of naming in the history of slavery."[41] For both Spillers and Mullen, then, the mark of race on the body is both highly visible and utterly misleading in its superficiality; only by digging deeper into the history behind such language can one find the human truth.

This being the case, we can also read Mullen's poetics in light of Patricia Hill Collins's argument surrounding the "new politics of containment" through which black women's bodies are highly visible, scrutinize-able, and consumable in public roles—think of women such as Oprah Winfrey, Condoleezza Rice, and Michelle Obama—even as the realities of many or most black women's lives are elided in mainstream culture such that long working hours, efforts to get a good education, exploitation by employers, low pay, and institutional poverty are not on view, meaning that black women labor bodily in the marketplace even as they remain invisible in the larger culture.[42] Considered thus, the black female, embodied, is available for either consumption, in the case of the public figure or the one who comes to voice about black experience, or, in the case of many others, containment within the racializing ideology of the dominant culture that will not recognize the realities of black women's lives. Speaking to the problem of claiming personal experience as a site of authority from which to speak, Collins argues that the notion of "coming to voice," a strategy foundational to black women's fiction and much of the lyric poetry coming out of Black Arts and multicultural poetries, is no longer effective as political discourse. She notes, "In the new politics of containment in which visibility can bring increased surveillance, breaking silence by claiming the authority of experience has less oppositional impact than in the past."[43] It could be said, then, that one way of eluding these processes of consumption and containment in literature could be to refuse to place the black female body on view, instead representing black women metalinguistically or metonymically, as Mullen has done in *Muse & Drudge* and elsewhere. Indeed, as a physical presence that is paradoxically disembodied, in some of Mullen's work the figure of the black woman enters the text even as her voice and her experience cannot be consumed and contained by the reader. Accordingly, I suggest that we read Mullen's linguistically experimental, disembodied poetics through a triangulated theory that takes into account the pervasive trope of cannibalism (the black woman figured as both consumer and consumed), the buried history of slavery, and the new politics of containment, examining the ways in which Mullen uses the ideologically freighted form of the prose poem—itself a container—as a means of escape.

Returning to Baudelaire for the moment, Griselda Pollock writes that Baudelaire's flâneur "symbolizes the privilege or freedom to move about the public arenas of the city observing but never interacting, consuming the sights through a controlling but rarely acknowledged gaze, directed as much at other people as at goods for sale."[44] One notes in Pollock's description both the total freedom enjoyed by the flâneur and the proximity of people to goods, simultaneously linked and commodified in the gaze of the privileged one. Looking far into a literary future Baudelaire presages though could never have imagined, Harryette Mullen's prose poems in *S*PeRM**K*T* revive and revise the figure of the commodity-making flâneur into a uniquely disembodied witness who cruises not the streets of the city but rather the aisles of the supermarket, observing the many ways in which (post)modern mass culture delimits, controls, and contains the identity formations of subjects who are marked by race but also defined by their relationship to consumer goods—defined, that is, by marketers' versions of themselves. Linking the formation of the physical body to commodity fetishism, Mullen's prose poems indicate the ways packaged goods convey or construct subtle meanings that are insidiously involved in our self-fashioning as social subjects. As Mullen avers in a recent interview, "We have to critique and resist rampant consumerism, if only because it's an unsustainable way of life.... We have to think critically when we're bombarded every hour with messages that are designed to affect us on an emotional level."[45] Suggesting that American consumers are in danger of becoming no longer individuals but rather saleable products, Mullen's S*PeRM**K*T reveals the ways in which we as consumers are taking in images and projections of ourselves in a new, postmodern version of the urban environment, even as her disembodied flâneur resists any attempts to fix a body in these aisles.

Consider the opening poem in S*PeRM**K*T, beginning "Kills bugs dead. Redundancy is syntactical overkill,"[46] in which Mullen summons the advertising idiom used for the sale of pesticides in order to foreground Americans' desire—conditioned by the culture industry but also and more deeply endemic to a history of imperialism, genocide, and slavery—to eradicate the black, the aberrant, and the disruptive. Note the proximity of black people to cockroaches: "In black kitchens they foul the food, walk on our bodies as we sleep over oceans of pirate flags. Skull and crossbones, they crunch like candy. When we die they will eat us, unless we kill them first. Invest in better mousetraps. Take no prisoners on board ship, to rock the boat . . . " The layers of meaning here are dizzying, as we are meant to acknowledge and slide away from the fact that it is the black kitchen that is perceived to be dirty, while several references to the ocean and ships point separately to a position over the ocean (masters) and below deck (prisoners or slaves). The poem's reference to "steriliz[ing] the vermin" alludes to those whom the dominant culture wishes to stamp out and the means by which it has done so in the past, even as the poem summons quite clearly white fear of black cannibalism with "When we die they will eat us, unless we kill them first." This reference to fear of cockroaches presented as an anxiety justified by fear of cannibalism is at the center of this prose poem, where the language flattens out and the linguistic play stops momentarily over a cultural (dys)logic that will be familiar to any reader of Herman Melville or Joseph Conrad, or any consumer of popular American films such as *Apocalypse Now*. Here we recall Aldon Lynn Nielsen's point about "the critical currency of cannibalism,"[47] and yet in Mullen's poem, beyond an unmarked statement of "they" and "us," there is no clearly defined racialized body on view; rather, Mullen makes visible the unconscious of the English language that comes already inflected with centuries of barbaric acts and fear-based justifications for those acts.

If "Kills bugs dead" can be said to reflect white fear of a blackness that is metaphorized into a cannibalistic insect, the poem beginning "Off the pig, ya dig?" can be read as reflecting black fear of white cannibalism as it plays out in lynching.⁴⁸ The poem continues, "He squeals, grease the sucker. Hack the fatback, pour the pork. Pig out, rib the fellas. . . . Pork belly futures, larded accounts, hog heaven." In one reading, and such readings are always highly contingent in Mullen, the language of this poem calls up the voices—not quite the image—of southern whites at a barbecue, but the true nature of the meat on the spit is somewhat in question. With "He squeals, grease the sucker," we hear one man telling another how to exert control over a recalcitrant beast, and with "Hack the fatback" one can read the whip and the lash. "[R]ib the fellas" reads as a disturbing reminder of the revelry that often surrounded a lynching as well as a reference to the clubbiness ("the fellas") of those enjoying ease and privilege. With "Pork belly futures" and "larded accounts," we hear tones of greed and self-satisfaction coming from people who have made fortunes off the backs of others. Even further, the very wealth that has been accumulated remains in the form of the flesh, a gruesome notion that disappears as quickly as it appears. In language that slips and slides from the idiomatic to the sinister to the breezily casual, the body of the African American man is invoked but also elided as the threat to such a person is made manifest in language carrying its own historical unconscious. We hear the complicated language of oppression even as the tableaux of slavery or lynching never materializes. In this way, the reader encounters her/his language anew as an ideologically freighted site of pervasive violence and historical/cultural domination.

As Deborah Mix has shown, the prose poems of *S*PeRM**K*T* continue the theme of the domestic first introduced in *Trimmings*, with an important shift away from *Trimmings*'s concentration on the linguistically decorated body and onto the body as it is constituted by the marketplace. In an important topical and formal shift, Mullen's more recent collection, *Sleeping with the Dictionary*, both summons and displaces the body in a series of prose poems that invoke and slide off of historical and cultural references that inform the location of African Americans in the immediate present, even as themes of cannibalism, consumption, and containment carry forward in subtle ways. The poems are organized in an abecedarian list, the formal constraint reflecting the aesthetics of Language writing in which high artifice takes the place of lyric sincerity, yet the title invokes the presence of the sexualized black woman whose erotic connection to the language marks a shift away from her sexualization in history and visual culture. That is, this body that sleeps with the dictionary is not the body that sleeps with men, but is rather immediately marked by intellection and refusal of the dominant culture's attempt to contain her.

In "Bleeding Hearts," a raw poem invoking stereotypes of blackness, black fear of whites that is based on a long history of oppression, and the cycle of violence in urban areas produced by this history and portrayed in the media, Mullen's linking of the black body to food reveals its perishability in American culture.[49] Invoking the name of a predominately black neighborhood in South Central Los Angeles where the 1992 Rodney King incident took place, Mullen's poem begins, "Crenshaw is a juicy melon. Don't spit, and when you're finished, wash your neck. Tonight we lead with bleeding hearts, sliced raw or scooped with a spoon."[50] Remarkable here is the paratactic juxtaposition of African Americans' anxiety about being perceived by whites as dirty (don't spit, wash your neck) with the idea that the very core of African Americans' bodies have been eaten out—cannibalized—by white culture. The people limned but not physically described in the text live at a site marked by racism (black people necessarily like melon, though in this case Crenshaw is a place) and mark themselves as "monkey" and "beady-eyed bug," one speaker claiming that he/they can be "re-hash[ed]" for breakfast just as they must continually rehash a racist history. The layers of meaning that proliferate here are complex, as Mullen's making of multiple anagrams from the term "Crenshaw" produces a surprising array of legible signifiers associated with African American culture and history.[51] Functioning at the level of language, then, this prose poem is able to invoke and also refuse the embodiment of African American individuals.

In a poem meditating on the metaphorization of the female body into a cocktail to be drunk, "Daisy Pearl" calls up the body of the woman and/as the shape of the margarita glass, "[r]apidly spread and rubbed with a wedge" (18). Mullen has said her own idea of the body in question is that of a Mexican woman in a border town during the time of the maquiladora murders,[52] her "[r]im rubbed" equated with a "great show of suffering in order to arouse" (18). Fixed at the site of metaphor, raced, gendered, and murdered but never fully on view, the body of this woman exists in a permanent state of danger, yet precisely because she moves chimerically from glass to body she eludes another kind of danger. That is, Mullen's linguistic play creates and maintains a distance between the desiring reader/viewer who might encounter elsewhere lurid news accounts of mutilated female bodies offered up for audience consumption. Indeed, the poem's linking of body and thirst can be read against the exoticization of the racially marked body in Baudelaire's "Sed Non Satiata" ("Insatiable Thirst"), that other body being one that the speaker longs in eroticized terms to consume. In both cases the body is objectified and eminently vulnerable, yet in Mullen's version she eludes consumption because her construction in language renders her unavailable and effectively disembodied.

In fact, the playful language of eating as a form of capture pervades *Sleeping with the Dictionary*, the subject of "Dim Lady"—which plays on Shakespeare's Sonnet 130—metaphorized into a "scrumptious Twinkie" (20); one of Mullen's fleeting characters in "Free Radicals" having "her history preserved in a jar of pickled pig feet" (29); and the "you" of "Resistance is Fertile" being "indigestible, and it's undeniably true it's tough to swallow you" (60). In these particular cases, the signs of food and consumption register as attempts to contain, control, or rebuke the recalcitrant body, attempts to fix in place one who continually slips away through language that refuses to resolve at any site of permanent visual tableaux. In many of the poems in *Sleeping with the Dictionary*, the site of the body is ever in tension with the unconscious of Mullen's own particular English language that often can be seen to function dually as space of confinement and medium of escape.

But the poem in *Sleeping with the Dictionary* that entangles Mullen's work perhaps most closely in the enclosures of Baudelaire's early prose poems is "The Gene for Music," a long and relatively straightforward narrative prose piece in which the female speaker/subject responds to the pressing needs of a "he" who wishes to contain her. Consider: "He wants to know if I am happy here and if I have eaten any apples yet. I tell him no, I like to let them fall off the trees and rot.... They are eaten. They are never wasted. They have their use, when they fall, never far from the proverbial tree. Yellow apples with brown leaves move slowly onto grass that's greener than ever. Green in winter, tawny in summer. Don't burn. Consume yourself more slowly" (30). The speaker, a modern Eve, is both obedient and enraged, the tightness of "[t]hey are never wasted" suggesting servility but also a buried hostility, even as "Don't burn. Consume yourself more slowly" suggests an attempt at self-control that leads only to self-destruction. Captive, Eve speaks in simple sentences as she describes an enclosed natural environment, yet the point of view changes in the second paragraph such that the two characters are represented in the third person and the walls quite literally close in upon the female:

> Try not to burn. Try not to alarm. Later he will ask her where she went and she will say, "To the laundromat or the library, I forget which." He might seem hurt but his honesty will prevail.... At times like these he's most endearing and yet she'll have no place to hide because the house has no walls.

> He can see her from another room. He likes to whisper at her while a record is playing. That's how cool he can be. He'll ask which books she has been reading. She could give him a list and we could discuss them later.... He didn't want to forbid her singing in the bathtub, but she would notice that he flinched a little, so she tried not to do it when he was around. She had not inherited the gene for music.(31)

Presented as the object of male desire, the woman in this poem in surveilled and controlled, primarily through her awareness of the needs of the man who watches her. She exists in his image (a phrase doubly resonant in the case of Eve), attempting to mold herself to his desires, even as subtle allusions to her not living up to the promise of her ancestry suggest that he chose her under the assumption that her body would equate with certain talents—that she would necessarily be musical. As the poem continues, the man's desires are figured in ever more constricting terms:

> he noted that each time he touched her, her body was there, which had not always been the case with her predecessors.
>
> She listened to his lists and made her own in secret. A grocery list was necessary because he avoided buying food, preferring to spend cash on inessentials because they brought more satisfaction. "But you," he told her, "are impossible to satisfy because you never seem to want, except to sleep and eat." She lives in his house like a sleepy cat though once he joked he might pay to keep her here....
>
> Nothing touches him now except her hands, her mouth. He touches her hair. Her wet hair. He makes her a gift of his solitude. Solitude is something she misses. He takes hers with him when he leaves. She goes out for short walks, looking at sidewalks. He takes her to mountains and deserts. He seeks out old trees. They walk until she's out of breath. "Chill," he says, and she feels cold, suddenly noticing the air.

The enclosure of the man's house functions much as the enclosure of the poem does, capturing a woman who remains invisible to the reader yet physically available—hyperembodied and stalked by her captor. Comparing her body to the bodies of her predecessors, the poem suggests that she is interchangeable with other women of her type, women whose hair also would attract and delight the sense of the man. And with "She lives in his house like a sleepy cat though once he joked he might pay" the woman is cast as both beast and prostitute, an object to be enjoyed, petted, and contained. Given Mullen's poem that reenvisages Manet's *Olympia*, readers might here see evidence of Manet's black servant at Olympia's bedside, the small black cat nearly invisible at the foot of the bed.

Moreover, and particularly intriguing when compared to Baudelaire's "Dancing Serpent," the man in "The Gene for Music" controls and defines the woman's relationship to nature, which she is both associated with and forcibly distant from as she walks with head bent only feeling the air when his words allow her to. In this last, she is imprisoned not merely in his gaze and his desire, but also in his language. As a point of comparison, consider now the remainder of Baudelaire's "Dancing Serpent":

> Your eyes, that reveal neither sweet nor bitter, are two cold ornaments blended of gold and iron.
> To see you walk in cadence, fair unconstrained, brings to mind a serpent dancing at the prodding of a stick.
> Under its lazy weight your childish head rocks softly as that of a young elephant
> and your body leans and reclines, like a first-class ship that rolls from side to side, plunging her yard in the water.
> When, like a torrent fed by the thaw of roaring glaciers, your mouth, watering, wets your teeth,
> then I think I drink a wine of Bohemia, sour and overpowering, a liquid sky that spreads stars across my heart![53]

We note that Baudelaire's muse never speaks but is thoroughly spoken as an object of desire, imprisoned and silent within his self-conscious metaphors for all that she might mean to him. In contrast, Mullen's "The Gene for Music" begs to be read as the limning of the consciousness of just such a woman who is trapped by male desire, a desire as old as poetry itself—as old, it would seem, as the original garden. Indeed, in Mullen's description of one of the only women embodied and given a full narrative in her work, she writes an imprisoned Eve eerily mirrored in the serpent who dances among Baudelaire's flowers of evil.

I want to return to Mullen's Steinian response in *Trimmings* to Manet's *Olympia*, in which Mullen writes a prose-poem critique of the politics of race as evident or concealed in both Stein's *Tender Buttons* and Manet's painting—two major works of modern art. It bears noting that there is a near companion piece to *Olympia*, this being Manet's 1862 *Baudelaire's Mistress, Reclining*, a portrait of Jeanne Duval toward the end of her life when she was wasted by illness and approaching death. According to Therese Dolan, it has become standard in Manet scholarship to assume that both *Olympia* and *Baudelaire's Mistress, Reclining* were inspired by Baudelaire's poetry,[54] a discovery that renders Mullen's poetry of the body—specifically, the black female body imprisoned within the confines of the prose poem and yet simultaneously escaping the frame—more deeply resonant with modern visual art than scholars have perhaps realized. This is not to say that Mullen is engaging *Baudelaire's Mistress, Reclining* directly in her poetry, but rather that the trope of the black subject-as-object captured in the "box" built by the white male artist can be seen to inform Mullen's innovative prose poetics in which it is crucial that the body almost never appears, and when it does, as in "The Gene for Music," it appears only to reveal the terms of its imprisonment.

Edgar Allan Poe—himself an early prose poet, and one whose work was translated by Baudelaire—famously averred that "[t]he death then of a beautiful woman is unquestionably the most poetical topic in the world, and equally it is beyond doubt that the lips best suited for such a topic are those of a bereaved lover."[55] Such a claim when read in relation to Iglesias's notion of the prose poem as box suggests that the prose poem in its original form can be in fact a coffin in which the woman is permanently contained; as an intriguing side point, Therese Dolan points out that in Manet's portrait of Duval, the divan on which she rests at an odd angle does resemble a coffin. Moreover, Dolan points out that Baudelaire "opened his *Salon* of 1846 with the observation that the best criticism of a picture may well be a sonnet or an elegy . . . Manet's portrait of the poet's mistress could have been offered as a response in kind, a demonstration that the best response to poetry about love gained and lost in this instance may well be a painting."[56] In each of these cases, the black woman (Dolan refers to her as "mulatto") is trapped by the white male artist, imprisoned by the poet's waning desire and delivered to another man for permanent encasement in visual art, her body transacted. This being the case, Mullen's prose poetics of linguistic rupture and bodily escape takes on a new urgency, suggesting as her work does a long history of containment and consumption in art, at the same time that she refuses to offer a static image or a sociologically realist representation of the African American body to the reader. For consider the fate of such a body when thoroughly used up and no longer an object of desire, here in Baudelaire's "Une Charogne," or "Carrion":

Recall, my soul, the thing we saw that fine mild summer morning:

> there at a bend in the path, loathsome carrion on a bed sown with cobbles,
> Legs in the air, like a lewd woman, scorching and sweating poisons, reeking belly split open nonchalantly, cynically.
> ....
> —And to think, you will be like that filth, like that horrible stench: you, my eyes' guiding star, sun of my life, you my angel, my passion! Yes! such you will become, O queen of graces, after the last sacrament when, under the grass and gross flowering, you mold with the other bones.
> Then, O my beauty! tell the worms that feed on you with kisses, that I have kept both the form and the divine essence of my loves-in-decay.[57]

As the object of the flâneur's gaze and devotion, the black woman is available to serve the function of both lover and reviled corpse, to be so rendered at the whim of the artist. This poem's tone of frank abjection—the black woman is the one desired and the one discarded, even as she cannot be entirely eradicated from the speaker's memory—ensnares the woman permanently in the trap of the speaker's psyche and encases her for all time in the frame (coffin) of his poem.

Moving toward conclusion if not closure, in "Wino Rhino," one of the last poems of *Sleeping with the Dictionary*, we can read one sort of response to a long history of such representations—literary and visual—of the black body as object of fascination and the gaze, as beast to be controlled and contained, and as a site of filth and decay. For in Mullen's rewriting of the hunted "other" whom the camera aims to capture, the tables are turned and what comes into view is a culture that continues to figure the black body as animal, even as the voice of the elusive unicorn registers a deep knowledge of such cultural logic, a knowledge that constitutes resistance and revolt:

> For no specific reason I have become one of the city's unicorns. No rare species, but one in range of danger. No mythical animal, but a common creature of urban legend. No potent stallion woven into poetry and song. Just the tough horny beast you may observe, roaming at large in our habitat. I'm known to adventurers whose drive-by safari is this circumscribed wilderness. Denatured photographers like to shoot me tipping the bottle, capture me snorting dust, mount on the wall my horn of empties that spilled the grape's blood. My flesh crawls with itchy insects. My heart quivers

as arrows on street maps target me for urban removal. You can see that my hair's stiffened and my skin's thick, but the bravest camera can't document what my armor hides. *How I know you so well.* (79; my emphasis)

In this poem of many boxes—the prose poem form itself, yet also the camera lens and the gaze of the onlooker/hunter—the movement is outward as the speaker breaks free of his enclosure precisely through his intimate knowledge of his oppressor; his ability to look back equates with his escape from objectification and capture. The Wino Rhino as "a common creature of urban legend" lives in the space very similar to that described by Baudelaire, the degraded urban landscape where the flâneur enjoys a walk among the poor and the abject. Yet unlike the Dancing Serpent or the woman who is carrion, trapped in the gaze and the language of the onlooker, this character speaks back to the flâneur/photographer/desiring gaze of the dominant culture, asserting a countervailing knowledge position through recourse to the language of poetry. As in the case of the titular woman who sleeps with the dictionary, Mullen summons the vulnerable African American body only to foreground its refusal to comply, substituting intellection and powers of observation—s/he who looks back at the viewer—for one who would be on view in coming to voice or in testifying to experience of oppression. In a posttestimonial poetics of race and refusal, then, Mullen's prose poetry thus constructs and dismantles those enclosures that historically have rendered black people, and black women in particular, invisible in the dominant culture. Hers is a poetics of creative release, a release that can be fully appreciated only when the many traps (literary, material, cultural, historical) laid along the way are on view, and it is through the intrinsically hybrid form of the prose poem-as-box that Mullen accomplishes this daunting task.

5 / Claudia Rankine's *Don't Let Me Be Lonely*: A Lyrical Long Poem in a Post-Language Age

> *Hence the poem is that—*
> *Here. I am here.*
> —CLAUDIA RANKINE, *DON'T LET ME BE LONELY*, 2004

Claudia Rankine's *Don't Let Me Be Lonely: An American Lyric* is a thoroughly revolutionary twenty-first-century hybrid work that expands the limits of the long poem form in order to investigate the status of the politically situated, socially mediated human subject in contemporary American culture. Rankine's poem merges the epiphanic lyric, visual media, journalistic/academic writing in the form of prolific endnotes, and the cultural-critical essay in a formally complex critique of subject production and regulation at various sites in our current historical moment, including sites of official culture, media culture, and literary culture. Thematically, *Don't Let Me Be Lonely* is at once an internal meditation on the private and public meanings of death and loneliness (death-in-life); an interrogation of the politics of racial violence as they play out in public spectacle; a critique of the American media's function as a means of subject interpellation and social control; a condemnation of war; and a single-voiced song of hope for the American body politic that takes inspiration from precursor poets as well as sustenance from the field of ethical philosophy. For even as *Don't Let Me Be Lonely* enacts an immediately contemporary critique of American culture as it is produced in visual-media spaces beyond the reach of language, the poem also draws upon the work of Emmanuel Levinas, Paul Celan, Cornel West, Wallace Stevens, Czesław Miłosz, Aimé Césaire, Myung Mi Kim, and Gertrude Stein in producing a network of, to borrow Joan Retallack's useful phrase, "poethical thinking,"[1] an investigative countercultural poetics, assembled in this case collectively, which is designed to intervene in and foment resistance to the deadening effects of our mass-produced, quotidian American life. Working at multiple sites formally and thematically, *Don't Let Me Be Lonely* functions as a searching and far-reaching poetic response to our material, historical, American moment, a formally complex calling-out that is itself an occasion of hope in a globally violent and politically chaotic time. Simultaneously, as part of Rankine's commitment to social change through the development of innovative art forms, *Don't Let Me Be Lonely* constitutes a grand experiment with the long poem genre, an experiment that draws upon the form's varied history in modernism while arguing for its new uses as political discourse, achievable through expansion, hybridization, and—at times—return to the spirit of a usable past.

Given Rankine's earlier, more disjunctive work, and especially given the thirty years of aesthetically radical political poetry preceding it, it is indeed quite striking that *Don't Let Me Be Lonely* is—for all its many parts—immediately legible as a lyric long poem, and one resonant variously with modernist, midcentury, and postmodernist iterations of the form. As such, this work marks a pronounced turn away from the various forms of Language-y writing that have dominated the experimental poetry scene since the late 1970s. Although *Don't Let Me Be Lonely* does layer photographs, drawings, lists, and footnotes into the prose poem/essay form, and although the work quotes at times ironically and at others sincerely from other sources, there is no linguistic interpretive guesswork here for the contemporary reader, no need to swim in new syntaxes or interpret broken words, no gestures toward indeterminacy of language or subject, no winking commentary on the word as such. Instead, the book makes clear its assumption that the trope of the speaking subject of poetry is a viable means of engaging larger sociopolitical issues, demonstrated not only by Rankine's use of the lyric *I* but also in the several references to the speaker's actual body riddled with physical suffering as a result of what she witnesses in a debased society. For in addition to the mere presence of this witness, the notion of pain as a communicable affective response to information is central to this text, pain being that feeling that marks the body's permeability but that also, in its very expression, commands the attention of another, as Elaine Scarry argues in *The Body in Pain*. Writes Scarry, "[A]t particular moments when there is within a society a crisis of belief—that is, when some central idea or ideology or cultural construct has ceased to elicit a population's belief either because it is manifestly fictitious or because it has for some reason been divested of ordinary forms of substantiation—the sheer material factualness of the human body will be borrowed to lend that cultural construct the aura of 'realness' and 'certainty.'"[2] Following Scarry, I want to suggest that Rankine uses the body to register the effects of a fundamentally asocial, antihumanist American culture.

Given Rankine's chosen form of the lyric/long poem, it is not at all surprising that *Don't Let Me Be Lonely* should carry echoes of a litany of forebears in modern and postmodern poetry, and brief attention to a few of these is useful in showing the ways in which such a deceptively simple lyric/hybrid long poem conducts its sweepingly subversive cultural work. In originating from the locus of pain and alienation as the space from which to speak, the poem inherits from "The Love Song of J. Alfred Prufrock," T. S. Eliot's modernist lyric poem that tells of one man's uncertainty and despair and that relies heavily—as Jennifer Ashton has argued—upon the affective response of the reader.[3] Much like Prufrock, though in a more layered and complicated aesthetic field, Rankine's *Don't Let Me Be Lonely* compels the reader, the implied "you," to respond to this embodied social subject as she struggles to make sense of the alienation produced by our collective American everyday. In Rankine's own words, *Don't Let Me Be Lonely* "focuses on one's inability to affect change, which is deeply crippling."[4]

But this hybrid long poem can also be said also to inherit from Walt Whitman's *Song of Myself*, a protomodernist long poem that uses the trope of the embodied speaker as a catalyst for a call to unity among the American body politic. As in the case of Whitman, Rankine's speaker leads her interlocutor through the vagaries of her vision and perspective, establishing an intimacy that carries the potential for surprising insight through a shared affective response. Unlike Whitman, however, Rankine's speaker is abraded by all she sees, negatively impressed with the pileup of historical events and fundamentally disturbed in a way that Whitman's speaker rarely is. In just this way, *Don't Let Me Be Lonely* carries echoes of Baudelaire's *Les Fleurs du mal*, with its oscillation between the speaker's internal musings and his material experiences as he proceeds through the streets of a familiar yet aesthetically defamiliarized city. Closer to the present, in its paratactic arrangement of lyric sections interspersed with photos and language taken from the media, *Don't Let Me Be Lonely* resonates with Mark Nowak's *Shut Up Shut Down*, a collection of discordant long poems that explore the impact of federal policies on unions and the increasingly marginalized labor class.[5] As in the case of Nowak, *Don't Let Me Be Lonely* also inherits from Charles Olson's theory of projective verse, in which "form is never more than an extension of content."⁶ Still further, Rankine's poem can be compared to Theresa Cha's lyric hybrid/epic *Dictée*, a work concerned with the many forces—linguistic, religious, and sociocultural—at work in colonizing a people and subjugating a person. In one interview, Rankine explicitly cites Cha's work as a model "because of its freedoms, its willingness to go wherever it needs to go in order to document the kind of strife present in the creation of her Korean identity."⁷ Yet if it seems counterintuitive to name Cha alongside Baudelaire and Eliot alongside Nowak, the fact that we can do so in this case is quite telling. Throughout this chapter, I will be showing the various ways in which *Don't Let Me Be Lonely* is in conversation with a broad expanse of poetic tradition, finding its own form amid the remnants of the past and the poetics theory of our present, and speaking back to the current critical conversation that is just now trying—once again—to establish clear taxonomies of modernist and postmodernist literature.⁸ Indeed, among the poem's many other contributions to contemporary poetry, *Don't Let Me Be Lonely* offers an entirely new, post-Language way of conceiving of the work—aesthetic, political, and cultural—that innovative hybrid poetry can perform.

Don't Let Me Be Lonely is distinguished by its threading through of multiple discourses and influences at once, a layered structure in which the echo of other writers can be heard amid the cacophony of contemporary material events. It is a text in which images taken from mass culture are effectively reframed in the language of the lyric speaker such that they are defamiliarized and rendered strange, where elemental drawings of human anatomy serve as counterpoint to American rhetoric of nationalism, and where a long section of endnotes—not referenced in the body of the text but encountered by the reader at the end—constitute both a prose commentary and re-vision of all that has come before. If we were to attempt to paraphrase the poem, a move that always necessarily falls short of accuracy, we might say that *Don't Let Me Be Lonely* stands as a new hybrid long poem lyric for the twenty-first century, one that reaches back to the sweeping vision of the moderns and later politically activist poetry while pushing past the abstract intellectualism associated with some contemporary experimental aesthetics. In Rankine's own words, the poem is the result of her search for "a form that accommodates an investigative poetics," one which "attempt[s] to acknowledge a total experience of being—to involve as many of our senses as possible."⁹ As such, this poem can be usefully characterized as a work that enacts the search for its own form while questioning that form from within, a work that finally—in its humanistic groping for connection and meaning in a fractured society—returns us to the modernist long poem's reach for what Ezra Pound once termed "the tale of the tribe."[10]

In borrowing from and extending the admittedly various tradition of the long poem, Rankine necessarily must deal with the gendered history of this particular form, a history that stretches from the Homeric epic to Whitman's *Song of Myself* to the work of high modernist poets such as Pound, Eliot, Wallace Stevens, and William Carlos Williams, and still further into Charles Olson's midcentury poetics of expansive voice. For it remains the case that in the shadow of the most famous of these works, long poems by women—including works by Gertrude Stein, H. D., Muriel Rukeyser, Marilyn Hacker, Bernadette Mayer, and Alice Notley—have been relegated to the margins of the canon, discussed far less often than their male contemporaries and to this day nearly invisible in criticism of American poetry. Addressing this very dynamic in her influential essay "When a 'Long' Poem Is a 'Big' Poem," Susan Stanford Friedman has argued that the absence of women's long poems from the canon can be attributed to the fact that the very form of the long poem is predicated on a gender hierarchy in which "long" equals "big" on a gender-coded scale.[11] Arguing that the long poem form is rooted in the masculinist epic that presumes to "ask very big questions in a very long way—historical, metaphysical, religious, and aesthetic questions," Friedman writes,

> As poems on the greatest historical-metaphysical-religious-aesthetic questions, big-long-important poems have assumed the authority of the dominant cultural discourses—even when they speak from the position of alienation, like Ezra Pound in *The Cantos* or William Carlos Williams in *Paterson*. The generic grid within which these and other big long poems are read has been established pre-eminently by the epic, which has a very big-long history of importance in western culture. . . . It reflects a comprehensive sweep of history, a cosmic universality of theme. . . . In Pound's words, the epic is "the speech of the nation through the mouth of one man" . . . it is "a poem containing history."[12]

The terms of Pound's definitions are obviously coded masculine, just as *The Cantos* and *Paterson*—and more recent works such as Melvin Tolson's *Harlem Gallery* and Ed Dorn's *Gunslinger*—undoubtedly are; witness the sexualized female bodies in the latter two texts. In response to this history of the big-long poem as the purview and output of the male writer, and in what is essentially a recovery project, Friedman introduces the work of women poets writing from the time of modernism and up until the late 1990s that has achieved the scope and scale of the long poem; in Friedman's estimation these poems are simultaneously in debt to and subversive of the male tradition.[13] Creating a new set of categories for what she has positioned as subgenre, Friedman offers four strategies of women's subversion of the male tradition, showing how such strategies constitute a "feminization of form" in which women "dismantle the boundaries so as to position themselves *as women* writing inside a tradition in which women have been outsiders."[14] Temporarily laying aside this way of framing aesthetic innovation in gendered terms, a problem I will return to shortly, Friedman also shows how the long poem as written by women is intrinsically hybrid in form, stating that "a generic hybrid gains its status as anomaly through the tension created by a 'mixing' of preexisting 'unmixed' genres."[15] She cites the foundational work of Sandra Gilbert and Susan Gubar, as well as Jacques Derrida and Julia Kristeva, all of whom have addressed the politics of genre in showing "how the most prestigious genres (like poetry, drama, and epic) erected threatening boundaries against women; how marginal new genres (like letters, the novel, the gothic) invited women's participation."[16] According to Friedman, then, long poems written by women are self-consciously feminine in their hybridization of form, the terms of their innovations representing a feminine and inherently feminist subversion of masculinist values surrounding the high and the low. For Friedman, these mixings of feminine low forms with the stuff of high culture must be understood primarily as aesthetic innovations rooted in the realm of gender difference.

More recently and similarly concerned with the gender of the long poem genre, Lynn Keller's *Forms of Expansion: Recent Long Poems by Women* is a helpful book-length study of recent iterations of the long poem that includes a history of the criticism surrounding the genre together with a critique of the masculinist bias undergirding lack of critical discussion of works by women.[17] Citing the work of Smaro Kamboureli, who has written a study on Canadian women's long poems, Keller argues that "[t]he long poem is, by most accounts, a generic hybrid; one can well argue...that generic interplay or dialogue is the long poem's most distinguished characteristic."[18] At the same time, Keller shares Friedman's interest in showing the ways in which women poets have responded to the male tradition of the genre. Keller writes, "[P]artly because the recovery of earlier long poems by women is so recent a development—women attempting to write long poems have been conscious of entering a territory previously mapped by male poets and traditions. Consequently, these women have tended...to work with, struggle against, and re-vise the approaches of their fathers."[19] Keller's study is more expansive in scope than Friedman's in that she does not attempt to contain long poems by women within new taxonomies, and she studies the work of black poets and lesbian poets alongside the work of women from the dominant group.[20] Keller's strategy is to make visible the broad diversity of women's contributions to the genre, and she provides capacious models through which to consider women's innovations while arguing against imposing limiting new categories upon these works.

Helpful as these studies most certainly are, particularly in their attention to the implicitly hybrid structure of the long poem, problems arise when we attempt to fit Rankine's *Don't Let Me Be Lonely* into Friedman's or Keller's models of feminine subversion of a masculine genre. For, in the very first place, and as Joan Retallack has argued in *The Poethical Wager*, to write of feminine "subversion" is to render the work of a woman writer always in an inferior position to a dominant "version";[21] and indeed, although it goes without saying that gender binaries are still operative in our culture, to agree to think uncritically in these terms is to risk granting credence and authority to a deeply problematic way of categorizing the work of women in relation to that of men. Responding to the version/subversion problem and advancing a theory for poetics that will take us outside of what she calls "business as usual," Retallack has shown how some writers—women as well as men—have developed a variety of new forms and languages that, in their absolute otherness, constitute politically radical aesthetics and/as newly creative intellection. Naming such poetics the "experimental feminine," Retallack points to the work of James Joyce, Samuel Beckett, and John Cage, as well as to the work of Gertrude Stein, as exemplars of this poetic principle, highlighting the uses of disjunctive language, antinarrative, sound, and silence as these artists' means of undermining the totalizing operations of the status quo.[22] And yet, still other problems arise when we attempt to place Rankine's poetics in the realm of the experimental feminine, for *Don't Let Me Be Lonely* is not so much a text of linguistic otherness as it is a text predicated upon a deep cultural familiarity, a poem that literally, in its material/visual form, contains history. As such, it is a poem written by a woman that traffics in and expands upon poetics traditionally coded masculine, effectively hybridizing the very gender of the long poem form while, in the words of Muriel Rukeyser, "extend[ing] the document."[23] Indeed, even as Rankine expands the possibilities of the genre, pushing the form into new shapes through a mixing of what has heretofore been unmixed, she is also regendering the genre as neither male nor female, but generously inclusive of both; hers is a twenty-first-century lyric that is not so much an ecstatic calling out to Everyman but that is rather the establishing of a culturally adrift lost soul, that being whom Alicia Suskind Ostriker once termed "the confused actual person," alone—lonely—in our shared present.[24]

As a central part of my argument against locating Rankine's work within a discourse of feminine adaptation of a historically masculine form, I want to take up the issue of subject position as it is made manifest in the speaking subject of *Don't Let Me Be Lonely*, precisely because feminist scholars have long argued for the centrality of the lyric as a marker of subject position in poetry by women and people of color. When asked by an interviewer to comment on the relevance to her work of her own subject position as a black woman, Rankine affirms the relevance of these factors while emphasizing the importance of integrity and social responsibility of the self, whoever that self might be.[25] Rankine has directly addressed the problematic (and in her view, disappointing) results of allowing her subject position to determine the direction of her poetry, looking back with regret upon her debut collection, *Nothing in Nature Is Private*, a book that attempted to work through the complexities of subject position. In a 1999 interview with Katy Lederer, Rankine says,

> Very soon after receiving the published version of *Nothing in Nature Is Private* I felt it did not represent my understanding of the world closely enough.... In the end it was disappointing to me because the characters, race, and gender acted throughout rather than embodying the text. My intent had been to write poetry that explored the conflicting ambiguities and complexities comprising our notions of race and gender. Beginning with such a specific field allowed me to think my way through the poems to the extent that, in the end, the point of view began to typecast itself in a performance of blackness and immigration. The poems began to enact a preconceived condition.[26]

Reflecting upon the problem of writing about identity in socially prescribed terms, Rankine echoes the sentiments of her contemporary, Harryette Mullen, who has also spoken to the complexities of writing as a black woman. Separately, both Rankine and Mullen have pointed out that, although they inevitably are writing from this specific subject position, to allow this fact to determine meaning in the work, or to imagine that readers occupying other social spaces cannot participate in the text, is to mistake an open text for a closed set of identity markers.[27] In response to this very real danger, Rankine and Mullen in their own ways suggest that subject position in their work is simultaneously visible and elusive and ever in flux.

Looking more closely at Rankine's use of the lyric *I*, it is important to note that she is quite conscious of the exacting theoretical principles of Language writing, and her use of the trope is not to be taken as a nostalgic return to some presumably simpler lyric past. Rather, Rankine's speaker muses on the constructedness of *I* while at key moments taking the question of subject formation out of the realm of the linguistic, locating the subject in terms of the mass-mediated American social sphere. To take one example, in which Rankine's speaker moves from consideration of television advertising and investment culture into articulation of her own conditioned responses to signs of the heightened fear and paranoia since the events of September 2001, she then segues from this fear of attack immediately into anxiety about material goods. In a quick-change movement that mirrors patterns of distracted thinking endemic to this media age, Rankine's speaker says,

> To roll over or not to roll over that IRA? To have a new iMac or not to have it? To eTrade or not to eTrade? Again and again these were Kodak moments, full of individuation. . . .
>
> It strikes me that what the attack on the World Trade Center stole from us is our willingness to be complex. Or what the attack on the World Trade Center revealed to us is that we were never complex. . . .
>
> As the days pass I begin to watch myself closely. The America that I am is washing her hands. She is checking for a return address. She is noticing the postage amount. . . . Do I like who I am becoming? Is this me? . . .
>
> My flushing toilet, my hot water, my air conditioner, my health insurance, my, my, my—all my my's were American-made. This is how I was alive. Or I wasn't alive. I was a product, or I was like a product, a product of and like Walt Disney's cell animation—stylishly animated, somewhat comic. I used to think of myself as a fearless person. (91–93)

Reducing the self to a product of a paranoid culture and consumer values, a concern shared by Harryette Mullen in *S*PeRM**K*T*, Rankine's speaker wonders where the *I* resides amid such fear and materialism, and fear *as* materialism. Even more, she connects the stuff of a "developed" nation—conveniences such as running water and health care—to the turning of the subject into an alienated American product herself. Echoing the tone and spirit of Joan Didion's anomie-laden critical essays on the banal paradoxes of American culture, the speaker in the poem suggests that in fact, the very technologies that make us American are those that are also killing us.[28]

Layered into her exploration of what constitutes a distinctly American identity, elsewhere Rankine addresses the linguistic complexity of the trope of the *I*, pointing to and artfully sliding away from the notion that *I* is a trick of language rather than a social being. At one point in the text, and amid meditations on death and what constitutes life, Rankine's speaker performs a series of sleights of hand/eye/I in which her speaker points to the mechanical workings of the first-person pronoun while slyly shifting the locus of meaning off the trope of the lyric subject as it is contested in the space of relatively recent poetry criticism and onto the philosophical tradition concerned with defining the social subject in ethical relation to another. Echoing the sentiment of a quote from Emanuel Levinas that appears later in the text—"[t]he subject who speaks is situated in relation to the other"[29]—Rankine's speaker says, "If I am present in the subject position what responsibility do I have to the content, to the truth value, of the words themselves? Is 'I' even me or am 'I' a gearshift to get from one sentence to the next? Should I say we? Is the voice various if I take responsibility for it? What does my subject mean to me?" (54). Separating terms that would seem to be bound to each other while leveraging the skepticism *I* never fails to invite, Rankine sets up a series of conundrums in which it becomes difficult to determine where that skepticism should lie. She then playfully leads her reader to make a series of choices that turn out not to be choices at all but that instead draw upon readers' beliefs about our own agency as a means of reaffirming the value of the lyric as stand-in for the ethical subject. To begin, "If I am present in the subject position" is a curious statement in that if there is one "present" in the subject position in a text, then *I* must be that person. But although we as readers have been taught to doubt "I," no one has seemed all that invested in doubting subject *position* (indeed, how would we go about doubting this, as it would seem to lead to doubting our own position?), so it would seem that both *I* and subject position must exist and indeed might just be one and the same. This satisfactory conclusion to a temporary discomfort then nicely shores up the idea of the speaking subject as one "present" who takes "responsibility"—another cozy conclusion—at the same time that "content," "truth value," and "words themselves" are rendered synonymous through syntactic rhythm, an aural equivalence that discourages us from stopping to make any distinction among the definitions of these terms. Content, truth, and words themselves have come together in a textual convergence suggestive of the modernist search for meaning through form. In the next sentence about pronouns and gearshifts, the most interesting word is undoubtedly "even," for used here this term implies intensity and implicit validation of the *reality* of "me," forestalling our impulse to think about whether "me" is equivalent ("even with") linguistic construct. That is, through that emphatic "even," the reader is persuaded to believe that the "me" in this text really does exist, whether or not "I" is the proper name for it and regardless of any gear-shifting going on among sentences, the latter part of that syntactic equation perhaps aimed at those holdouts still inclined to prefer looking at language as a system of pure abstractions. For if there is an "even me" in the text, then whether it is *I* and/or whether it functions as a gearshift on occasion, is all beside the point. Indeed, the presence of "me" is tantamount to saying there is a *person* in the text, a conclusion we've arrived at—or that has arrived in us—in spite of our keen lookout for any sign of that "shifty" *I*. From there, "I" gives way to "we," which we readers can be happy about since now we get to play, too, and "voice," another beleaguered notion in poetry today, thus indeed becomes multiple. The concluding "What does my subject mean to me?" playfully harks back to elementary school essay prompts ("What does my mother/brother/puppy/name mean to me?"), even as buried within the play is a call to define "subject," which—as we will see—is somewhat holographic throughout this text while remaining in essence profoundly, woundedly, the same.

Thus, and throughout the poem, Rankine's speaker is self-consciously poised—often in the form of *I* but also in the reflected image coming from the reader—always at the very point where the subject coheres as a social being in some relation to another, forming in and being formed by exchange, and existing beyond the reach of—as well as in spite of—old prohibitions against the lyric voice. Coming at the end of the text, the speaker's citation of Celan's view of the poem as handshake serves to underscore Rankine's belief in the lyric and the social subject as intricately interwoven; but also, the invocation of Celan suggests the poem's rootedness in historical and political urgency, the terms of our own historical moment having changed from—yet also having grown out of—those informing Celan's time (130). Moreover, Rankine's emphasis on the integral subject as formed in exchange with another marks an ethically driven turn away from late twentieth century trends in experimental poetry, a turn underscored in a recent interview in which Rankine says, "[W]hat does it mean to be the speaker of the piece you are working on—that is crucial to the integrity of the piece."[30] Such explicit statements regarding the poet/speaker's responsibility to society at once suggests the centrality of lyric to political poetry but also goes against the old claim that the lyric subject cannot do political work. For counter to this bias, Rankine insists upon a subject that is coherent as a respondent who has an immediate obligation to society, even as her *I* investigates the sorts of social mediation that work variously and insidiously to control outcomes, including but not limited to the outcome of her own subject construction. Moreover, the affective dimension of the speaker's experience remains of particular importance in *Don't Let Me Be Lonely*, in the sense that Rankine often relies upon readers' affective relationships to pieces resurrected from our shared media past to structure meaning in the text; but affect works two ways, making meaning from "what is" but also making what will be out of feeling that is shared with the reader. Rankine has said that her aim is to write "a feeling of feelings (a core sense of basic humility) that is capable of taking into account a knowledge (including its chaos) of thought" and that "the moment when we are able to intersect into another's consciousness happens when we are allowed into the process, the flux of feeling and thought."[31] Borrowing the words of Clair Wills, who has written about experimentalism and expressivity, we could usefully say that Rankine's social subject "reveals the ways in which that private or intimate realm of experience is constructed 'through' the public,"[32] yet Rankine also insists upon that intimate realm of subjective experience as potentially, radically constitutive of the public and the social.

To return to the question of the poem's undergirding structure while keeping in mind Rankine's reliance upon lyric address, it is important to note that although *Don't Let Me Be Lonely* borrows in significant ways—formal as well as thematic—from the modernist lyric long poem, Rankine is careful to establish her poem's situatedness in a postmodern age. In a recent interview she avers, "I'm not interested in creating anything that contributes to the fiction of wholeness; instead, I continue to try to find a mode that can accommodate without pretending to transcend, that manages to stay in the mess and continue an exploration of thought in the imagination."[33] Rankine's description of her project resonates with

Brian McHale's characterization of the postmodernist long poem as "a difficult whole," and indeed *Don't Let Me Be Lonely* exhibits at least some of McHale's primary distinguishing features. For example, Rankine's foregrounding of various media as the very presence of material culture corresponds to what McHale calls—borrowing from Fredric Jameson— "the spatial turn," in which a postmodern long poem might "foreground ... the spaces of the worlds it projects."[34] Too, in its self-consciousness of the use of the *I, Don't Let Me Be Lonely* nods to postmodernism's/ poststructuralism's/Language poetry's critique of the lyric subject as a device. Indeed, Rankine's description, above, of her own project is consonant with the primary tenet of experimental poetics more generally, this being a commitment to the open text. She has cited Charles Olson, John Ashbery, Juliana Spahr, and Theresa Cha—all "open form" poets— as important pioneers in expanding the formal and political range of what poetry can do while refusing to close off final meanings.

Yet, more subtly, Rankine's choice of phrasing—"the fiction of wholeness" versus "a mode that can accommodate"—echoes a central concern of high modernist Wallace Stevens, whose "Of Modern Poetry" both performs and calls out for "The poem of the mind in the act of finding / what will suffice,"[35] and, moreover, whose "Notes toward a Supreme Fiction" can be heard in that reference to a "fiction of wholeness." In Rankine's choice of phrasing, and "mess" notwithstanding, the terms of an old struggle—the modernists' search for good forms—can be heard. Such a connection between Rankine's hybrid long poem and a giant of the high modernist lyric would perhaps seem somewhat dubious, were it not for the quotation from Stevens's "The Noble Rider and the Sound of Words" that shows up in *Don't Let Me Be Lonely*. Even so, something is lost in translation, as Rankine draws upon the loveliness of Stevens's articulation of the imagination while pointing to contemporary mass culture's degradation of same. Following a prose section in which the speaker muses on the scene of New York mayor Rudy Giuliani's knighting by Queen Elizabeth, a scene of the making of American "nobility" that American television viewers were not allowed to see, the speaker turns to Stevens for the tools to interpret what the postmodern subject yearns for and thus imagines:

> Wallace Stevens wrote, "the peculiarity of the imagination is nobility ... nobility which is our spiritual height and depth; and while I know how difficult it is to express it, nevertheless I am bound to give a sense of it. Nothing could be more evasive and inaccessible.

Nothing distorts itself and seeks disguise more quickly. There is a shame of disclosing it and in its definite presentation a horror of it. But there it is." (81)

Here, and in a bathetic twist, the elevated nobility of imagination in Stevens's definition of lyric poetry gives way to New York mayor Rudy Giuliani's ersatz nobility, which must be desirously "imagined" by mainstream audiences because there wasn't a TV camera present to record it. Thus, the "shame" and "horror" marking the imagination in our own time are mere indicators of petty emotions, rather far removed from Stevens's intimations of the sublime. The endnote to the page on which this quotation appears states that "The Noble Rider and the Sound of Words" "addresses [Stevens's] and other poets' removal from political concerns in their work. He suggests that such poets play a greater social role than those contemporary poets who create politically didactic verse" (146). In playing Stevens just this way, Rankine redraws the boundary between a lyric poetry of the imagination that is ostensibly removed from politics and its apparent opposite, didactic verse; in doing so, she underscores the blended lyric didacticism of her own meditations on American cultural and political life. Indeed, *Don't Let Me Be Lonely* shows precisely how political discourse can again take lyric form, though the lyric must be reimagined if it is to extend beyond the reach of "the political" into the impoverished imagining lives of a numbed populous. In moments such as these, Rankine announces *Don't Let Me Be Lonely*'s debt to, derivation from, and expansion upon lyric poetry as we have come to understand it in both political and aesthetic terms.

In another example of the interplay between epiphanic or meditative lyric and the stuff of contemporary material life, Rankine includes a vignette that offers lyric poetry as hedge against the repressive function of the state. In this vignette, a young woman on a hot day goes up to the roof of her thirty-story apartment building to lie in the sun, dangling her legs over the side of the building and thus attracting the attention of onlookers who think she is about to jump. The police are called, and the rules and social protocols this young woman is breaking are apparent in reference to the sign that says TENANTS NOT ALLOWED ON ROOF as well as in the would-be rescuer's practiced, hushed tones as she tries to talk the woman out of a suicide she has no intention of committing. Here one can detect a certain resonance with Didion's heavily affective voice of cultural critique in the flat tones of the speaker as she describes a situation that is essentially absurd—a bald misapprehension of simple human activity that causes the machinery of the state to intervene with rhetoric designed to bring the wayward individual back into the fold. In contrast to the actions of the rescuers is this sudden turn to Czeslaw Milosz's "The Gift":

> The sky is drowning in blue with clouds that billow like sails, a blue sea of sails. After a while of just lying there, the girl decides to shout a Milosz poem to the sky.
>
> > A day so happy
> > Fog lifted early, I worked in the garden.
> > Hummingbirds were stopping over honeysuckle flowers.
> > There was no thing on earth I wanted to possess.
> > I knew no one worth my envying him.
> > Whatever evil I had suffered, I forgot.
> > To think that once I was the same man did not embarrass me.
> > In my body I felt no pain.
> > When straightening up, I saw the blue sea and sails. (35)

Located between two of the text's floating television sets with George W. Bush hidden in the snow (and thus subliminally present as surveillance), this section stands out for its intensely lyric quality, its unironic use of metaphoric language to describe the day, and its summoning of Lithuanian/Polish political and lyric poet Miłosz, whose last line is foreshadowed in Rankine's own prose. Laid in amid the many surrounding sections on death and the heavy presence of the media, this small scene foregrounds the way in which the beauty to be found in the epiphanic lyric might yet be a route to freedom. Even further, here in a brief instant the state is revealed as repressive at the most private level of personhood yet also impotent in its attempt to regulate the activity of the girl, as her recitation of the poem amounts to a fleeting yet total freedom for the girl and reader alike. And even as the girl's choice of poem connects her experience on a rooftop in late-capitalist urban America to the experience of a political exile, her recitation into the sky reminds one of all that we have ceded to the state in this ostensibly free country even as her choice is testament to the abiding revolutionary potential in lyric poetry.

Yet, lest *Don't Let Me Be Lonely* seem naïve in its summoning of the epiphanic lyric, Rankine modulates her uses of the form with commentary designed to draw attention to its unique functionality *as* lyric. In the endnote to the foregoing section, encountered on page 138 of the text and thus long after the reader has moved through the scene of the girl and her Miłosz poem, Rankine writes, "There is a good chance that Czeslaw Milosz spent some time on the roofs of New York buildings in the late 1940s when he lived there as a diplomat for the Polish government" (138). There are several ways to take this ambiguous note, some of them comic. In the first place, and given how far the reader has traveled through other moments in the text, the reader might have forgotten the section entirely and will here simply note that the famous poet was once in New York. This is an easily digestible factoid for the literalist who would mine a prose-y poem for information, but it is also a "and so what?" for the reader who recalls the poem's striking appearance many pages previous. In one reading, the image of the poet himself on a rooftop is banal and says next to nothing about the poem's function in this new moment, uttered by a girl yearning to exist outside of the bounds of normative culture. For if the endnote's naming of the poet and his diplomatic function in the United States seems a gesture to the political, the text would seem to argue that the revolutionary potential embodied in the idea of Miłosz is not to be found in his later-life role within official culture, but is instead evident in the verse that he has released to the world and that might well bubble up elsewhere, shaking things up in another context. With this literal treatment of Miłosz as distinct from the appearance of his words, Rankine underscores the limited way in which Americans have come to understand politics, as though monitoring diplomatic relations or voting for candidates or staying up on the news could wrest freedom from necessity. To the contrary, and in a witty yet also quite moving turn, Rankine posits lyric poetry as the surer route to that freedom as we are witness to the image of Miłosz himself shouting to the sky.

Consider another dimension to the work's political engagement, and the dimension taken up most often in criticism surrounding *Don't Let Me Be Lonely*: amid such lyric passages and internal musings, the exchange between speaker and reader is at times triangulated with still images taken from visual mass culture. At various moments, and with recourse to photos and cartoons taken from the national news or other public sources, Rankine's speaker invites readers into shared visual spaces that are immediately recognizable by virtue of their ubiquity in the popular media or—in the case of the floating television set with the screen covered by snow, the shadow of Bush barely visible in outline—by their ubiquity in our very homes. Our primary relation to the text at these moments is a residual affective response to a familiar and quite loaded image, as well as a felt connection to the self-aware speaker who also stands apart from these images in the position of critical witness. It is just this invitation to stand side by side with the speaker in front of a visual display that brings readers into sudden and involuntary engagement with the text as we are hailed into a relationship with the speaker as well as into the field of a mass mediated American body politic.

Through deployment of the image, the text moves fluidly between the psychosocial space of individual *I* into the shared public space of a collectively constituted social body, a move noted by Alan Gilbert in his insightful review of the text.[36] Rankine's reliance on readers' affective engagement with voice and image as a means of forming a critical community stands in stark contrast to the work produced by some of her more visible contemporaries in the experimental poetry community. For against the more abstract concepts undergirding readers' play with and deciphering of new linguistic constructs—which often mark the elision of the social subject of poetry—the shared witnessing enacted by *Don't Let Me Be Lonely* testifies to the responsibility incumbent upon embodied subjects in a social space. At the same time, however, the text implicates the reader in the process of constructing society through the choice to respond either passively or actively to American media and/as politics. As in the premise of Language writing to the effect that the reader constructs meaning of the text, Rankine suggests through her use of image that we as readers construct meanings around society whether we are conscious of our process or not. Not only is there a world beyond the text, Rankine suggests, but in our shared recognition of it and in the decisions we make to receive or contest its products we are participants in and coproducers of this material real.

Meditating on the theme of death in contemporary American culture as both literal and metaphorical, private and visually spectacular (as in "televised"), Rankine's speaker turns over many stones in her search for ways of representing pain and loss in a degraded material present, laying bare in the process the ways in which language always fall short of communicating to another the essential loneliness of the autonomous American individual in a profoundly alienating media-saturated culture. Throughout the poem and in clear prose, Rankine moves through consideration of loss on very personal terms (the lyric speaker up late at night, thinking about death, suicide, and depression) and on public/political terms (the text reproducing a laundry list of major pharmaceutical companies who have lobbied the South African government for the withholding of generic AIDS antiretroviral medication). The poem gives an account of the speaker visiting a friend with Alzheimer's who has lost his ability to communicate clearly, requiring the speaker's concentrated attention in order for her to make out what he means to say (and what he means to say turns out to be a reference to a popular television show), as well as another account of the speaker visiting a friend dying of cancer whose hospital room is dominated by the widely recognized DNR ("do not resuscitate") sign, a signifier of the omnipresence of death if ever there was one. Perhaps most personally (but, as Rankine has pointed out, fictively), the speaker's sister has lost her husband and children in a car accident and must assemble evidence of her children's lives so that the insurance company can adequately reimburse the bereaved based on her children's estimated future worth. In each of these cases, the distance between the speaker and another in a visual/capitalist culture, and the inadequacy of language to close that gap, produce comfort, or pass on love is pronounced. Language fails, as numerous of the visual images serve only to emphasize (for example, the baldly impersonal "Funeral No Parking" sign in a parking lot that follows the speaker's mention of her sister's loss), even as the dominant culture in the form of medicine, insurance companies, and suicide hotlines attempts to organize human experience into bland officialdom through normatizing language practices. In foregrounding the workings of mainstream culture as promulgated in the subtly coercive languages of the state, Rankine writes in the spirit of John Ashbery, who in her own estimating creates "meander[ing] sentences ... [that] ask us to have looser expectations" of the language that is given to us in the everyday.[37] Departing from Ashbery's syntactical play while retaining Ashbery's attention to resignifying on the American mainstream, Rankine constructs a bulwark of subjective affective response and refusal, insisting that the individual speaking subject has a role to play in gathering the shards and bearing witness to the suffering of others, and—ultimately—a role to play in reforming this society in which we find ourselves.

The poem's many and varied meditations on the politics of death, grief, and mourning are folded into a narrative that includes the speaker's quest to understand her own particular place as a racialized citizen in the twenty-first century. Following the sections on visiting ill friends and in concert with these prose-lyric sections, the text also reproduces media images that recount major instances of racial violence in recent American history, including the dragging-death murder of James Byrd, Jr. in Texas in 1998 (the legal punishments for which George Bush couldn't seem to remember), the brutal police rape of Abner Louima in New York City in 1997, the police murder of an unarmed Amadou Diallo in 1999, and the tragic case of Lionel Tate, the fourteen-year-old boy who in 2001 entered the prison system as a convicted murderer, having been tried as an adult for the death of another child whom he killed while imitating professional wrestling as seen on TV. Each of these cases is represented visually and linguistically, photos taken from these events framed in TV sets and followed by the speaker's anomie-laden meditations on their meanings as Rankine attempts to organize and make sense of the senseless. Making reference to her own body as it responds physically to news of Byrd's murder, Rankine writes in a poetics statement that appears in Ann Keniston and Jeffrey Gray's *The New American Poetry of Engagement*:

> When I first read the account of James Byrd, Jr.'s death in June of 1998 I was sickened. I am not being hyperbolic—whatever was in my stomach was regurgitated. It was as if my body could not accept his life as he was dragged behind the pickup until his arms and legs were severed. . . . The sorrow was deep, it was recognized, and the arbitrariness of the murder made me fearful of the pervasiveness of racism, but that might be a definition of being black in America.[38]

A comparison of this poetics statement to the speaker's reflection on Byrd's death in *Don't Let Me Be Lonely* points up the degree to which the *I* of the poem draws heavily upon the affective experience of the poet herself. Here is a passage from the text in which the speaker connects Cornel West's claim of nihilism in the black community with her own response to both the murder of Byrd and to George W. Bush's ignorance of the meting out of punishment in the legal aftermath. Beginning with an accusation of then president Bush, the speaker says,

> *You don't know because you don't bloody care. Do you?* I forget things, too. It makes me sad. Or it makes me the saddest. The sadness is not really about George W. or our American optimism; the sadness lives in the recognition that a life can not matter. Or, as there are billions of lives, my sadness is alive alongside the recognition that billions of lives never mattered. . . . Cornel West says this is what is wrong with black people today—too nihilistic. Too scarred by hope to hope, too experienced to experience, too close to dead is what I think. (22–23)

Having said that in *Don't Let Me Be Lonely*, she finally had the "tools to address race and the space around what it means to be human, such as our responsibility to society,"[39] Rankine links the lyric subject of the poem to both her own physical body and to the material world beyond the text, bearing witness in the space opened by this triangle to a painful point of broken connection between the Levinasian subject and the other who is obliterated, no longer there ("my body could not accept his life") to be recognized as human.

As counterpoint to the sections on Byrd, Louima, Diallo, and Tate, Rankine adds a section on Timothy McVeigh, executed for the bombing of the Alfred P. Murrah Federal Building in Oklahoma City. Rather than show an image of McVeigh, Rankine opts to include an image of an empty execution chair, above which she writes "Timothy McVeigh died at 7:14 a.m. and a news reporter asks relatives of his 168 victims if they have forgiven him. Perhaps because McVeigh is visually the American boy next door, this is yet another attempt by the media to immunize him from his actions" (47). In the same poetics statement cited above, Rankine says that in following the news coverage of the Oklahoma City bombing she was impressed by the fact that this catastrophic event was originally thought to be a plot by Muslims, the media promulgating this allegation. Once it was discovered that it was a crime committed by white Americans, and that McVeigh was "visually the American boy next door," the tenor of the media coverage shifted from overtones of hatred and fear to sad musings on the possibility of forgiveness of this white native son. Considered in this light, the empty execution chair stands not for the state-sanctioned murder of one convicted of capital crimes (Rankine's speaker displays no remorse about this), but rather for the status of the racialized as always the presumed suspect. In other words, Americans were far better prepared for a racially marked body in that chair, and the fact that it was a white body produces a profound and bewildered silence surrounding an image marked by absence.

In yet another displacement of the racially marked body, Rankine includes mention of the death of Princess Diana in 1997, providing an image of the vast outlay of flowers and condolence cards in front of Buckingham Palace, a sea of love graced with a portrait of the angelic Diana, her diamond-studded tiara serving now as halo. This leads to the speaker's mention of the Museum of Emotions in London, where the speaker has taken part in a survey that asked about her feelings surrounding the death of Diana. On stating that she didn't feel grief over this loss, she is ejected from the survey. To not care about Diana, a fantasy white woman, is to be wrong, this experience reveals, at the same time that we are encouraged to receive news of violence against black people in the United States as commonplace and easily forgotten.

Although Rankine has spoken directly to the social significance of several of these instances, that is, their significance beyond any representation, it is not surprising—given the text's heavy use of the visual image—that critics have tended to read *Don't Let Me Be Lonely* as a critique of the process and politics of visual mediation, that is, of the ubiquity and power of the American mass media to frame information and delimit experience. Linking the text's motifs of loneliness and death to the subject's position within a deadening media mass culture, Kevin Bell has argued that *Don't Let Me Be Lonely* examines the ways in which American media technologies function to delimit and control the social subject at every level. Bell sees Rankine's manipulation of images as a means to alerting the reader of one's own imbrication in this system:

> The words that appear on the narrator's television screen, and which re-surface inside the lids of her closed eyes, are the living fabric of a spectacular haunting in which we cannot help but be disturbed by our very awareness of the completeness with which our thoughts, anxieties and desires have been created almost entirely by what we have absorbed passively. Part of what is arrested in the frozenness of the photographic TV image is the falsity of its intelligibility—or rather the falsity of this intelligibility's self-evident immediacy.[40]

In a similar vein, with particular attention to the mediated discourses of fear following the events of September 11, 2001, Emma Kimberley argues that *Don't Let Me Be Lonely* makes visible the ways in which the transparent language of mainstream culture "so efficiently fulfills its task of conveying meaning that we become accustomed to seeing the process of verbal communication as a direct and unmediated transmission of information; we pay attention to the message without looking closely at the medium through which we receive it."[41] Moreover, Kimberley argues that "[l]ike many of her contemporaries, Rankine chooses to foreground visual and narrative frames as a comment on the fact that all representations, whether they acknowledge it or not, are framed."[42] For both Bell and Kimberley, the power of *Don't Let Me Be Lonely* resides in its ability to make visible what has come to be invisible—the ideology undergirding the means of media production and dissemination in our own time.

Bell's and Kimberley's readings are useful in interpreting one facet of *Don't Let Me Be Lonely*, but both critics fail to take into consideration the larger shape and scope of Rankine's long and layered work. Of course it is true—as Rankine herself has averred[43]—that the text has something important to say about American media culture, but it is precisely its interpenetration of lyric and visual, its holistic vision of our current historical moment as mediated along multiple axes and in multiple registers, that renders this text beyond the reach of such arguments. Indeed, insightful as Bell and Kimberley both are on the subject of the image, their readings are symptomatic of a certain myopia in contemporary criticism, in which complicated texts are reduced to the interpretation of but a single facet—in this case, analysis of the image. For as I am arguing here, *Don't Let Me Be Lonely* is as much about the long poem tradition, the power of the epiphanic lyric, the hybridization of form, the spatial turn to materiality, the politics of social subjectivity, and the reach toward connection with the other as it is about dissemination of the image in a media age. Moreover, if we were going to venture to select one unifying element to this intricately complex poem, it could not finally be a point of technique or technology; rather, the unifying principle to this complicated whole—and a principle that informs Rankine's oeuvre—is the abiding importance of emotion and affective response as a tool of understanding and social connectivity with others.

But Rankine moves past a mere aesthetics of indecision and into a more sweeping humanist claim to the presence and power of the socially aware human subject situated in the text. In a 1999 interview in *VERSE* magazine—and well before publication of *Don't Let Me Be Lonely*—Rankine repeatedly returns to emotion and subjective experience as a fundamental concern in her work. Commenting on *The End of the Alphabet* (1998), her second book, Rankine says that she was in that linguistically disjunctive work "experimenting with the idea that emotion could generate language. I wanted to create a 'language self,' that was built up from her insides, from her pulse and breath. I wanted to enter her subjectivity in such a way that the resulting text was ultimately the experience of her fundamental humanity."[44] Rankine adds that she aims to create "a feeling of feelings (a core sense of basic humility) that is capable of taking into account a knowledge (including its chaos) of thought," and says that "[t]he stories of our lives are so similar and repetitive that it seems to me that the moment when we are able to intersect into another's consciousness happens when we are allowed into the process, the flux of feeling and thought."[45] Notable here—and resonant throughout *Don't Let Me Be Lonely*—is Rankine's stated belief that "our lives are so similar," an ostensibly facile yet in fact deeply radical claim that flies in the face of much of the critical thinking emergent in the second half of the twentieth century, from that of civil rights to second-wave feminism to Language writing to multiculturalism to third-wave feminism to the current moment. The claim crosses theory, social spaces, and political discourses to assert, finally, the fundamental obligation of one human being to another, and it is a claim—harking back to the values of an earlier age—that perhaps can prove useful in a global climate of sectarian warfare and an American culture of military aggression and imperialism. Indeed, inheriting from the searching poetics of Stevens, the dreams of Miłosz, and the ethics of Celan, Rankine continues to work toward that which will suffice in our own complicated time.

But if there is a single poet whose work most informs *Don't Let Me Be Lonely*, it is perhaps Francophone poet Aimé Césaire, whose *Notebook of a Return to the Native Land* is predicated on the demand for witness to suffering in his homeland of Martinique. Rankine's American lyric opens with a quote from Césaire's revolutionary surrealist long poem: "And most of all beware, even in thought, of assuming the sterile attitude of the spectator, for life is not a spectacle, a sea of grief is not a proscenium, a man who wails is not a dancing bear."[46] The significance of Césaire to Rankine's poem is manifold, for like Césaire, Rankine has written a lyrical long poem of many formal parts throughout which a single note of despair and hope can be heard. In Césaire, these notes range from private familial sadness ("a cruel little house whose demands panic the ends of our months and my temperamental father gnawed by one persistent ache"[47]) to the layering of grief, confusion, and political rage ("but *can* one kill Remorse, perfect as the stupefied face of an English lady discovering a Hottentot skull in her soup tureen?"[48]) to consideration of death as both personal and—often for the black subject in particular—political,

> What is mine
> a lone man imprisoned in whiteness
> a lone man defying the white screams of white death
> (TOUSSAINT, TOUSSAINT L'OUVERTURE)
> a man who mesmerizes the white sparrow hawk of white death
> a man alone in the sterile sea of white sand
> a coon grown old standing up to the waters of the sky
> Death traces a shining circle above this man
> death stars softly above his head
> death breathes, crazed, in the ripened cane field of his arms
> death gallops in the prison like a white horse
> death gleams in the dark like the eyes of a cat.[49]

Admittedly, Rankine's work is realist rather than surrealist, materially situated rather than imagistically abstract; nevertheless, like the Martiniquan Césaire, Rankine, who was born in Jamaica, struggles with the legacy of racism and emotional poverty as these structure her American homeland, and too, Rankine's lyric language and intimate tone create a series of moments impelling readers' affective identification. Both poets meditate on the state of their respective lands and both sing for an audience they implore to be newly aware and sympathetic, even as each outlines the terms of national oppression: colonialism on the one hand, and the products of global multinational capitalism on the other. Césaire and Rankine conclude their long lyric works with a cry for healing and societal change, but, most pronouncedly, it is echoes of the *spiritual* cadence of Césaire that can be heard in the searching voice of Rankine's lyric speaker as she explores the rank detritus of our own shared culture, seeking to ward off an elemental loneliness and to contest the many social deaths past, present, and future through emotional connection with another.

In all, Rankine's return to the poetry of Aimé Césaire, Wallace Stevens, Czeslaw Miłosz, and Paul Celan is part of her search for a new lyric language of the imagination that can lift us out of the misery of our material historical moment while mirroring back to us that in which we are embedded but which we have been unable to fully see. In this way, Rankine is also returning to the modernist belief that an aesthetic *as aesthetic* carries salvific potential and humanist value. Indeed, Rankine is revivifying and enacting in a new key the search for forms adequate to a supremely difficult task; in this, and in implicating all readers in this American society of suffering, *Don't Let Me Be Lonely* issues an open call to all readers to *feel*, while offering the possibility that the lessons of humanity to be found in art have the potential to bring us together as a culture once again. At the same time, and in a timely way, the poem's unique hybrid structure makes an argument for the role of the redesigned long poem form, suggesting that the grand lyric, revised, is rescuable from the margins established by earlier avant-garde.

Moreover, as an important part of Rankine's measured critique of linguistic abstraction for its own sake, the poem also insists that an aesthetics of affect and emotional communication is vitally necessary in our current moment; yet at the same time, in her many engagements with the stuff of material mass culture, she is able to reveal at key moments what Johanna Drucker asserts is our collective inability to perceive the constructedness of the world we inhabit.[50] In several crucial ways, then, *Don't Let Me Be Lonely* sits at the crossroads of the reinvigorated debate surrounding modernism and postmodernism, sharing features of both movements and insisting on the futility of attempts to establish firm categories. For indeed, at the dawn of an age defined by new forms of global catastrophe and a long, painful human history of oppression, Rankine's return to and revisions of the long poem makes a compelling argument for the cultural value of narratives of human suffering, even as her revolutionary work challenges the way we conceive of the sufferer as separate—or not separate—from ourselves.

In "On the Lyric As Experimental Possibility," Mark Wallace writes,

> No statement about the final value of a form or genre of poetry can possibly be true.... It always remains possible to test the value of a form or genre again, to see what use might be made in the present moment of its historically determinable characteristics, or to alter, recombine, or change those characteristics to redefine possibilities in the present moment. One interesting possibility, for instance, would be to combine elements of another form, thus distorting both forms to create new hybrids. In any case, while the value of a form or genre can be determined partly by looking at all the uses that have been made of it, that determination can never be complete, not only because new readings of old uses of that form or genre can always take place, but also because the value of the forms and genres can and will be changed by any new uses made of it.[51]

Wallace's open call for new hybrids resonates strongly in my reading of Rankine's new lyric, even as we see Rankine—as well as the other poets discussed in this study—eluding through formal innovation those forces of control and containment that hover ever at the site of the new, forces that work insidiously to co-opt new art forms and fold them back into the workings of official or mass-mediated culture. Indeed, Wallace warns that "[t]he 'new' itself is fraught with contradictions, and is easily co-opted by the forces of capitalism and imperialism, which are both interested in extending themselves into the terrain of the 'new' in order to expand their resources and control."[52] Such are the very doubts and fears shared by those aligned with our contemporary avant-garde who see the encroachment of the hybrid as necessarily a regressive move toward cooptation of art for capitalist means, and in fact it is true that recent marketers of poetic hybrids do seem to be targeting a mainstream audience, though whether this necessarily foretells the death of intelligent political poetry is an open question. For, as this study has shown, and as critics as diverse as Lauren Berlant, Johanna Drucker, Andreas Huyssen, and Susan Rubin Suleiman have argued or suggested elsewhere, the use of mainstream mass culture against itself can be the site of trenchant social critique that includes always a critical awareness of its own form, even as the collisions among pulp narrative, the languages of film and marketing, televised "news," and linguistic/formal experimentation produce new compositions, heretofore impossible, that demand our attention even as they invite our participation. In borrowing from the Language movement's radically democratic ethos of reader involvement in the making of meaning while foregrounding the tendency toward closure endemic to popular media and/or established forms, the poets studied here forge new paths in our own thinking about our imbrication in a material present constituted in many instances by the detritus of mainstream mass culture. At the same time, in remaking these forms and offering them back to a public that is indeed increasingly mainstream, these poets are expanding the community of an intellectually and critically attuned readership to include a readership that emerges from a wider variety of intellectual communities and cultural contexts. In other words, in the texts studied herein, that radically democratic ethos of reader participation assumes and applies to all comers in ways that previous works of avant-garde poetry did not, could not, or would not accommodate, a point made by Johanna Drucker in relation to visual art that I take up above. Finally, after all, in prying open these genres and media discourses such that their inner workings are simultaneously boldly manifest and thoroughly disrupted, these poets—Gertrude Stein, Laura Mullen, Alice Notley, Harryette Mullen, and Claudia Rankine—have made possible new and various modes of creative resistance to those banal yet relentlessly effective forces of consumer capitalist ideology that infiltrate our collective and uniquely American-made unconscious, forces that show no sign of abating as we wade into the twenty-first century.

Notes

Introduction

1. Stephen Burt, "*Fence*, or the Happy Return of the Modernist Alligator," in *A Best of Fence*, vol. 1, ed. Rebecca Wolff et al. (Albany, NY: Fence Press, 2009), 15.

2. David St. John, introduction to *American Hybrid*, ed. Cole Swensen and David St. John (New York: Norton, 2009), xxv–xxvi.

3. Cole Swensen, introduction to *American Hybrid*, xxi.

4. St. John, *American Hybrid*, xxviii.

5. In a fair congruence, *Fence* magazine's *A Best of Fence* vol. 1: *The First Nine Years*, includes work by Lee Ann Brown, Harryette Mullen, Rae Armantrout, Lyn Hejinian, Ann Lauterbach, Eileen Myles, Fanny Howe, and Alice Notley, among others.

6. Swensen, *American Hybrid*, xviii–xix.

7. Ibid., xxii.

8. Laura Mullen, unpublished interview with author, March 3, 2012.

9. Swensen, *American Hybrid*, xxi.

10. Cole Swensen, "Response to 'Hybrid Aesthetics and Its Discontents,'" in *The Monkey and the Wrench: Essays into Contemporary Poetics*, ed. Mary Biddinger and John Gallaher (Akron, OH: University of Akron Press, 2011), 148–53.

11. Ron Silliman, *Ron Silliman's Blog*, April 2, 2009, accessed March 26, 2013, http://ronsilliman.blogspot.com/search?q=post+avant.

12. Steve Evans, "The Resistible Rise of Fence Enterprises," *Third Factory Notes*, January 2001, accessed March 27, 2013, http://www.thirdfactory.net/resistible.html.

13. Mary Biddinger and John Gallaher, eds., *The Monkey and Wrench: Essays into Contemporary Poetics* (Akron, OH: University of Akron Press, 2011).

14. Craig Santos Perez, "Whitewashing American Hybrid Aesthetics," in *Monkey and the Wrench*, 139.

15. Ibid., 140.

16. Burt, "*Fence*, or the Happy Return," 20.

17. Cole Swensen, "The Hybrid: The Meeting of American Poetry's Extremes," *Etudes Anglaises* 61, no. 2 (Apr./June 2008): 141.

18. See Fredric Jameson, *Postmodernism, Or, The Cultural Logic of Late Capitalism* (Durham, NC: Duke University Press, 1991), 1–54. See also Marjorie Perloff's critique of Jameson in *Poetry On and Off the Page: Essays for Emergent Occasions* (Evanston, IL: Northwestern University Press, 1998), 19–21.

19. Johanna Drucker, *Sweet Dreams: Contemporary Art and Complicity* (Chicago: University of Chicago Press, 2005), 8.

20. Ibid., 1–3. In her discussion of Gregory Crewdson's photographic art, Drucker shows how Crewdson borrows from mass culture and the world of technology without any overt political agenda but rather in a "pure" aesthetic move to create the beautiful out of the detritus of the everyday. In Drucker's view, what constitutes the political in such art is precisely its ability to refract our unconscious, unexamined desires.

21. Susan Rubin Suleiman, *Subversive Intent: Gender, Politics, and the Avant-Garde* (Cambridge, MA: Harvard University Press, 1990), 199.

22. Ibid.

23. Andreas Huyssen, *After the Great Divide: Modernism, Mass Culture, Postmodernism* (Bloomington: Indiana University Press, 1986).

24. Elisabeth A. Frost, *The Feminist Avant-Garde in American Poetry* (Iowa City: University of Iowa Press, 2005). Claudia Rankine and Juliana Spahr, eds., *American Women Poets in the Twenty-First Century: Where Lyric Meets Language* (Middletown, CT: Wesleyan University Press, 2005).

25. Linda Kinnahan, *Lyric Interventions: Feminism, Experimental Poetry, and Contemporary Discourse* (Iowa City: University of Iowa Press, 2004). Lynn Keller, *Forms of Expansion: Recent Long Poems by Women* (Chicago: University of Chicago Press, 1997).

26. Joan Retallack, *The Poethical Wager* (Berkeley: University of California Press, 2003).

27. Caroline Bergvall, "The Conceptual Twist: A Forward," in *I'll Drown My Book: Conceptual Writing by Women*, ed. Bergvall et al. (Los Angeles: Les Figues, 2012), 18.

28. Amy Moorman Robbins, "Alice Notley's Post-Confessional I: Toward a Poetics of Postmodern Witness," *Pacific Coast Philology* 41 (2006): 76–90.

29. Holly Iglesias, *Boxing Inside the Box: Women's Prose Poetry* (Florence, MA: Quale Press, 2005).

30. Elisabeth Frost has outlined what she terms "hybrid traditions" in Mullen's work prior to *Sleeping with the Dictionary*. See *The Feminist Avant-Garde in American Poetry* (Iowa City: University of Iowa Press, 2003), 136–64.

31. Kathleen Stewart, *Ordinary Affects* (Durham, NC: Duke University Press, 2007), 61.

1 / Gertrude Stein's *Blood on the Dining-Room Floor*

1. Gertrude Stein, "Reflection on the Atomic Bomb" (1946), in vol. 1 of *The Previously Uncollected Writings of Gertrude Stein*, ed. Robert Bartlett Haas (Los Angeles: Black Sparrow Press, 1973), 161.

2. See Janet Malcolm, *Two Lives: Gertrude and Alice* (New Haven: Yale University Press, 2007); and Barbara Will, *Unlikely Collaboration: Gertrude Stein, Bernard Faÿ, and the Vichy Dilemma* (New York: Columbia University Press, 2011).

3. As but one example of recent allegations that Stein was apolitical or even reactionary, Alan Dershowitz wrote a scathing rebuke of the Metropolitan Museum of Art in New York when the museum mounted *The Steins Collect*, an exhibit of Stein's art collection. In his essay "Suppressing Ugly Truth for Beautiful Art," published in the *Huffington Post* in May 2012, Dershowitz writes, "Anyone walking through this beautiful exhibit of the Stein family's exquisite tastes in art would learn nothing about Gertrude Stein's horrible taste in politics and friends"; available at http://www.huffingtonpost.com/alan-dershowitz/met-gertrude-stein-collaborator_b_1467174.html. Allegations such as Malcolm's, Will's, and Dershowitz's have prompted numerous Stein scholars to vehemently protest claims regarding Stein's alleged sympathies with the Vichy regime, pointing to her vulnerable position as an elderly lesbian Jew who had made her home in France prior to the war, and pointing also to the deep ironies in Stein's statements regarding Hitler and fascism. For a fair-minded discussion of Stein's complicated position during World War II, see Charles Bernstein, "Gertrude Stein's War Years: Setting the Record Straight: A Dossier," in *Jacket 2*, accessed December 16, 2013, https://jacket2.org/feature/gertrude-steins-war-years-setting-record-straight. Edward Burns, Ulla Dydo, Joan Retallack, Renate Stendhal, and Marjorie Perloff also weigh in on this issue in the *Jacket 2* dossier.

4. Kirk Curnutt writes of Stein's uneasy transition from unknown artist to a name-in-lights celebrity in "Inside and Outside: Gertrude Stein on Identity, Celebrity, and Authenticity," *Journal of Modern Literature* 23, no. 2 (Winter 1999): 291–308.

5. Gertrude Stein, "What Are Master-pieces and Why Are There So Few of Them" 1936, in *Gertrude Stein: Selections*, ed. Joan Retallack (Berkeley: University of California Press, 2008), 312.

6. Gertrude Stein, *Everybody's Autobiography* (1937; reprint, Cambridge: Exact Change, 1993), 2.

7. Lyn Hejinian attributes Stein's interest in detective stories to an interest in the arrangement of details such that criminality is buried. I return to Hejinian's argument later in this chapter. See Hejinian, "Two Stein Talks," in *The Rejection of Closure* (Berkeley: University of California Press, 2000), 91.

8. Brooks Landon, "'Not Solve It But Be In It': Gertrude Stein's Detective Stories and the Mystery of Creativity," *American Literature* 53, no. 3 (Nov. 1981): 487–98.

9. For a discussion of this, see Susanne Rohr, "'Everybody Sees, and Everybody Says They Do': Another Guess at Gertrude Stein's Blood on the Dining-Room Floor," *Amerikastudien/American Studies* 41, no. 4 (1996): 594.

10. Stein, "Why I Like Detective Stories" (1937), in *How Writing Is Written*, vol. 2 of *The Previously Uncollected Writings of Gertrude Stein*, ed. Robert Haas (Los Angeles: Black Sparrow, 1974), 148–49.

11. Joan Retallack, introduction to *Gertrude Stein: Selections*, ed. Joan Retallack (Berkeley: University of California Press, 2008), 29–30.

12. Gertrude Stein, "And Now" (1934), in *How Writing Is Written*, 64.

13. Kirk Curnutt, "Inside and Outside," 291–308. See also Susanne Rohr, "'Everybody Sees, and Everybody Says They Do.'" Rohr analyses the text for the ways it produces what she terms a "semiotic undercurrent," arguing that the novel "explains the process of reality formation as a distinct guessing process," 593. Rohr's analysis is indeed provocative, yet she doesn't deal directly with Stein's use of the genre to investigate worldly politics.

14. James R. Mellow, *Charmed Circle: Gertrude Stein Company* (Boston: Houghton Mifflin, 1974).

15. Ulla Dydo with William Rice, *Gertrude Stein: The Language That Rises, 1923–1934* (Evanston, IL: Northwestern University Press, 2003), 568.

16. See Elisabeth A. Frost, *The Feminist Avant-Garde in American Poetry* (Iowa City: University of Iowa Press, 2003); Rebecca Scherr, "Tactile Erotics: Gertrude Stein and the Aesthetics of Touch," *LIT: Literary Interpretation Theory* 18, no. 3 (2007); Joan Retallack, *The Poethical Wager* (Berkeley: University of California Press, 2003).

17. Detective novelist and critic James Ellroy writes, "*The Dain Curse* is all grotesquerie. It lacks context. The colourful geography and a few pithy characters fail to eclipse the what's-going-on-here?, was-this-book-written-on-booze? questions." *The Guardian*, September 28, 2007, accessed September 16, 2013, http://www.theguardian.com/books/2007/sep/29/crime.fiction.

18. See Catherine Ross Nickerson's *The Web of Iniquity: Early Detective Fiction by American Women* (Durham, NC: Duke University Press, 1998) for an excellent discussion of the turn-of-the-century women's detective genre and the prevalent use of gothic conventions to foreground domestic and psychological insecurity. Nickerson offers a lucid and compelling reading of late nineteenth—and early twentieth-century domestic detective fiction as emerging out of the gothic tradition and illuminating in more modern ways the cultural anxieties surrounding changing roles for women—particularly single women—during this period.

19. Stanley Orr, *Darkly Perfect World: Colonial Adventure, Postmodernism, and American Noir* (Oxford: Ohio State University Press, 2010).

20. Mark McGurl, "Making 'Literature' of It: Hammett and High Culture," *American Literary History* 9, no. 4 (Winter 1997): 706.

21. See Stein, "What Are Master-pieces," and McGurl, "Making 'Literature' of It," 712–13.

22. Nickerson, *Web of Iniquity*, 7–8.

23. Eve Sedgwick, *The Coherence of Gothic Convention* (New York: Routledge, 1986), 13.

24. Nickerson, *Web of Iniquity*, 8.

25. Huyssen, *After the Great Divide: Modernism, Mass Culture, Postmodernism* (Bloomington: Indiana University Press, 1986), 46.

26. Ibid., 46.

27. Ibid. Quote from Christa Wolf, *Cassandra: A Novel and Four Essays* (New York, Farrar, Strauss, Giroux, 1984), 300f.

28. Gertrude Stein, "American Crimes and How They Matter" (1935) in *How Writing Is Written*, 103.

29. Stein, "Why I Like Detective Stories," 148–49.

30. See Linda Wagner-Martin, *Favored Strangers: Gertrude Stein and Her Family* (New Brunswick, NJ: Rutgers University Press, 1995), 195.

31. Stein, "Why I Like Detective Stories," 148–49.

32. Retallack argues for a reading of *Blood* as a "fractal model," a text that stages an ethical and investigative poetics in the disruption of received form. My own argument turns to develop in greater detail the implications of Stein's formal combinations and what I see as the primary social critique emergent out of this clearly investigative text.

See Retallack, *The Poethical Wager* (Berkeley: University of California Press, 2003), 145–53.

33. Stein, *The Making of Americans*, 1925 (Normal, IL: Dalkey Archive, 1995), 152.

34. Stein, *Blood on the Dining-Room Floor*, 1933 (New York: Dover, 1982), 3–4. All subsequent references will be noted in the text with page numbers.

35. Orr, *Darkly Perfect World*, 5–6.

36. Stein, *Three Lives*, 1909 (New York: Norton, 2006), 19.

37. Eve Sedgwick, *The Coherence of Gothic Convention* (New York: Routledge, 1986), xi–xviii.

38. Nickerson, *Web of Iniquity*, 160.

39. Ibid., 172.

40. Stein, "American Crimes," 103.

41. Stein, *Tender Buttons*, 1914, in *Selected Writings of Gertrude Stein*, ed. Carl Van Vechten (New York: Vintage, 1990), 477.

42. Stein, "Sacred Emily," 1922, in *Geography and Plays* (New York: Dover, 1999), 178.

43. Stein, *Autobiography of Alice B. Toklas*, 14.

44. Stein, *Making of Americans*, 204–36.

45. Ibid., 212.

46. See Linda Wagner-Martin's discussion of this affair in *Favored Strangers: Gertrude Stein and Her Family* (New Brunswick, NJ: Rutgers University Press, 1995), 57–58.

47. See Elisabeth A. Frost, *Feminist Avant-Garde*, 21. Frost quotes William Gass in making this point.

48. Stein, *Everybody's Autobiography*, 63.

49. Stein, *Tender Buttons*, 471.

50. Stein, *Everybody's Autobiography*, 85.

51. Ibid.

52. See Eric Haralson, "Rereading Gertrude Stein Rereading Henry James (After a Fashion)," *The Henry James Review* 2, no. 5 (2004): 243.

53. Sedgwick, *Coherence of Gothic Convention*, 5.

54. Hejinian, "Two Stein Talks," 91.

55. Stein, "Merry Nettie," in *Gertrude Stein: Writings 1903–1932*, ed. Catharine Stimpson and Harriett Chessman (New York: The Library of America by Penguin, 1998), 459–64.

56. Stein, "American Crimes," 102.

2 / Laura Mullen's *Murmur*

1. Gertrude Stein, "Marry Nettie," in *Gertrude Stein: Selected Writings 1903–1932*, ed. Catharine Stimpson and Harriett Chessman (New York: Library of America by Penguin, 1998), 459.

2. Laura Mullen, Robbins interview with author, March 3, 2012. Not paginated. Hereafter referred to as "Robbins interview."

3. Alice Notley, *Disobedience* (New York: Penguin, 2001), 110.

4. Robbins interview.

5. Gertrude Stein, "What Are Master-pieces and Why Are There So Few of Them," in *Gertrude Stein: Selections*, ed. Joan Retallack (Berkeley: California University Press, 2008), 312.

6. Andreas Huyssen, "Mass Culture as Woman," in *After the Great Divide: Modernism, Mass Culture, Postmodernism* (Bloomington: Indiana University Press, 1987), 44–62.

7. Caroline Bergvall, "The Conceptual Twist: A Foreword," in *I'll Drown My Book: Conceptual Writing by Women*, ed. Bergvall et al. (Los Angeles: Les Figues, 2012), 18.

8. Quoted in Edward Howe, "An Interview with Susan Howe," *Talisman: A Journal of Contemporary Poetry and Poetics* 4 (1990): 14–38.

9. Quoted in Laura Mullen, *Murmur*, n.p. Wilkie Collins, *The Law and the Lady* (1875) (New York: Penguin, 1999).

10. Mullen, *Murmur*, section not paginated. Hereafter all quotes from *Murmur* will be noted in line with the page number or with "n.p." ("not paginated").

11. Marsha Bryant offers a brilliant discussion of women poets, particularly Plath, who rewrote domestic ideology. See Bryant, *Women's Poetry and Popular Culture* (New York: Palgrave Macmillan, 2011), 121–48.

12. Gregory J. Siegworth and Melissa Gregg, "An Inventory of Shimmers," in *The Affect Theory Reader*, ed. Siegworth and Gregg (Durham, NC: Duke University Press, 2010), 1.

13. Robbins interview. Mullen avers, "While in a free verse lyric-slash-language poem . . . because you don't know what will happen . . . you don't come to it thinking 'well this *has to* happen,' and so you don't have the same opportunity to notice the mistake, to borrow Gertrude Stein's wonderful word." Mullen refers to Stein's "Poetry and Grammar," in which Stein writes, "It is wonderful the number of mistakes a verb can make." See Gertrude Stein, "Poetry and Grammar" (1934), in *Lectures in America* (Boston: Beacon Press, 1985).

14. Rebecca Scherr, "Tactile Erotics: Gertrude Stein and the Aesthetics of Touch," *Literature Interpretation Theory* 18, no. 3 (July/Sept 2007): 193–212.

15. Charles Altieri, *The Particulars of Rapture: An Aesthetics of the Affects* (Ithaca, NY: Cornell University Press, 2003), 2.

16. Ibid., 235.

17. Ibid., 2.

18. Charles Altieri, "Reading for Affect in the Lyric: From Modern to Contemporary," in *Poetry and Pedagogy: The Challenge of the Contemporary*, ed. Joan Retallack and Juliana Spahr (New York: Palgrave Macmillan, 2006), 54.

19. Ibid., 53.

20. For examples of this image, see *Annunciation* by Rubens (1628), *Annunciation* by Murillo (1655), and *Annunciation* by Paolo de Matteis (1720). For a general discussion of the white bird as traditionally representative of "soul" in iconography of the Annunciation, see Herbert Friedman, "Giovanni del Biondo and the Iconography of the Annunciation," *Simiolus, Netherlands Quarterly for the History of Art* 3, no. 1 (1968–69): 6–15, accessed June 14, 2012, http://www.jstor.org/stable/3780470?&Search=yes&searchText=bird&searchText=annunciation&list=hide&searchUri=%2Faction%2FdoBasicSearch%3FQuery%3D%2528%2528annunciation%2529%2BAND%2B%2528bird%2529%2529%26gw%3Djtx%26acc%3Don%26prq%3D%2528%2528annunciation%2529%2BAND%2B%2528white%2Bbird%2529%2529%26Search%3DSearch%2

6hp%3D25%26wc%3Don&prevSearch=&item=4&ttl=1500&returnArticleService=showFullText.

21. Robbins interview. Mullen says, "I exposed or exhibited her in *Murmur* as a woman who is both the consumer of the book that is being written and the dead body at its center," 12.

22. Robert Coover, *Gerald's Party* (New York: Grove Press, 1997). Laura Mullen points to this connection in a discussion with the author.

23. Kathleen Stewart, *Ordinary Affects* (Durham, NC: Duke University Press, 2007), 5–6.

24. Lauren Berlant, *Cruel Optimism* (Durham, NC: Duke University Press, 2011). Berlant writes, "A relation of cruel optimism exists when something you desire is actually an obstacle to your flourishing," 1.

25. Robbins interview.

26. Hal Foster, "Obscene, Abject, Traumatic," *October* 78 (Autumn 1996): 110, emphasis in original.

27. Leonardo da Vinci, *Thoughts on Art and Life*, trans. Maurice Baring, e-book, accessed September 16, 2013, http://www.gutenberg.org/files/29904/29904-h/29904-h.htm.

28. Sylvia Plath, "Lady Lazarus" (1962) in *The Norton Anthology of Modern and Contemporary Poetry*, vol. 3, 3rd ed., ed. Ramazani et al. (New York: Norton, 2003), 612–14.

29. Colin Davis, "Psychoanalysis, Detection, and Fiction: Julia Kristeva's Detective Novels," *Journal of Twentieth Century Contemporary French Studies* 6, no. 2 (Fall 2002): 295.

30. Ibid., 298.

31. Marsha Bryant, *Women's Poetry and Popular Culture* (New York: Palgrave Macmillan, 2011), 149–73.

32. Joan Retallack, *The Poethical Wager* (Berkeley: University of California Press, 2003), 9. See Pierre Bourdieu, *The Logic of Practice*, trans. Richard Nice (Stanford, CA: Stanford University Press, 1995).

3 / Alice Notley's *Disobedience*

1. See Maggie Nelson's chapter on Notley in *Women, the New York School, and Other True Abstractions* (Iowa City: University of Iowa Press, 2007). Nelson conducts an in-depth analysis of Notley's work in the context of New York School poetics.

2. Alice Notley, "Dr. Williams' Heiresses: A Lecture Delivered at 80 Langton Street in San Francisco, February 12, 1980," *Tuumba Press* 28 (July 1980).

3. See Ann Vickery, *Leaving Lines of Gender: A Feminist Genealogy of Language Writing* (Hanover, NH: University Press of New England for Wesleyan University Press, 2000).

4. Juliana Spahr and Stephanie Young, "Numbers Trouble," *Chicago Review* (August 2007): 88–111.

5. Romana Huk, "The Progress of the Avant-Garde: Reading/Writing Race and Culture According to Universal Systems of Value," in *Poetry and Contemporary Culture: The Question of Value*, ed. Andrew Michael Roberts and Johnathan Allison (Edinburgh: Edinburgh University Press, 2002), 141–64.

6. Ron Silliman and Leslie Scalapino, "What/Person: An Exchange," *Poetics Journal* 9 (1988–89): 51–68.
7. Alice Notley, "The Poetics of Disobedience," *Electronic Poetry Center*, accessed June 15, 2013, http://epc.buffalo.edu/authors/notley/disob.html.
8. Linda Kinnahan, *Lyric Interventions: Feminism, Experimental Poetry, and Contemporary Discourse* (Iowa City: University of Iowa Press, 2004), xiii.
9. Alice Notley, "Voice," *Coming After* (Ann Arbor: University of Michigan Press, 2005), 152.
10. Ibid., 148.
11. Alice Notley, *Mysteries of Small Houses* (New York: Penguin, 1998), 5.
12. Alice Notley, *Selected Poems* (Hoboken, NJ: Talisman House, 1973), 13–19.
13. T. S. Eliot, "Preludes," in *The Norton Anthology of Modern and Contemporary Poetry*. vol. 1, 3rd ed., ed. Ramazani et al. (New York: Norton, 2003), 466–67.
14. Notley, *Selected Poems*, 62.
15. Interview conducted by Judith Goldman, *Poetry Project Newsletter* 164 (Feb.–Mar. 1997): 8.
16. Sylvia Plath, "Lady Lazarus," in *Norton Anthology of Modern and Contemporary Poetry*, vol. 1, 614.
17. Notley, "Poetics of Disobedience," 1.
18. Eileen Myles, "Being Female," *Vidaweb*, accessed May 31, 2013, http://www.vidaweb.org/being-female.
19. Notley, *Selected Poems*, 7.
20. See Robert Lowell's "Commander Lowell" for the first quote, and his "Memories of West Street and Lepke" for the second, this latter being taken by Lowell from Henry James's writing about the street on which Lowell's family would eventually live. *Robert Lowell: Collected Poems*, ed. Frank Bidart and David Gewanter (New York: Farrar, Straus & Giroux, 2003), 172–74, 187–88.
21. Jed Rasula, *Syncopations: The Stress of Innovation in Contemporary American Poetry* (Tuscaloosa: University of Alabama Press, 2004), 180.
22. Kathleen Fraser, "Partial Local Coherence," *Translating the Unspeakable: Poetry and the Innovative Necessity* (Tuscaloosa, University of Alabama Press, 2000), 76.
23. Notley, "Poetics of Disobedience," 2.
24. See Amy Robbins, "Alice Notley's Post-Confessional I: Toward a Poetics of Postmodern Witness," *Pacific Coast Philology* 41 (Fall 2006): 76–90, for my previous analysis of Notley's innovation in the lyric.
25. Marjorie Perloff, "Language Poetry and the Lyric Subject: Ron Silliman's Albany, Susan Howe's Buffalo," *Critical Inquiry* 25 (Spring 1999): 405–34.
26. Notley, *Mysteries of Small Houses*, 57.
27. Ibid., 101–3, emphasis in original.
28. See Silliman and Scalapino, "What/Person: An Exchange," 54.
29. Alice Notley, "A Conversation," interview with Claudia Keelan, *The American Poetry Review* (May/June 2004): 15–19.
30. Notley, *Coming After*, 172.
31. Ibid., 177.
32. Susan Stanford Friedman, "Craving Stories: Narrative and Lyric in Contemporary Theory and Women's Long Poems," in *Feminist Measures: Soundings in Poetry and Theory*, ed. Lynn Keller and Christanne Miller (Ann Arbor: University of Michigan Press, 1994), 24.

33. Page duBois, "'An Especially Peculiar Undertaking': Alice Notley's Epic," *differences* 12, no. 2 (2001): 95.

34. Along similar lines, Susan McCabe has argued that Notley undertakes the writing of a feminist epic both philosophical and ludic, a long poem enacting the search for new ways of being through a rewriting of Western tradition on feminist terms. See Susan McCabe, "Alice Notley's Experimental Epic: 'An Ecstasy of Finding Another Way of Being,'" in *We Who Love to Be Astonished: Experimental Women's Writing and Performance Poetics*, ed. Laura Hinton and Rachel Blau DuPlessis (Tuscaloosa: University of Alabama Press, 2002), 41–53.

35. Lynn Keller, *Forms of Expansion: Recent Long Poems by Women* (Chicago: University of Chicago Press, 1997), 2.

36. Brian Kim Stefans, interview with Alice Notley, *Jacket 15*, accessed January 8, 2003, http://www.jacket.zip.com.au/jacket15/stef-iv-not.html,1.

37. Alice Notley, *Disobedience* (New York: Penguin, 2001), 3. All subsequent references will be noted in the text with page numbers.

38. Nelson, *Women*, 163.

39. Ibid., 165.

40. Marjorie Perloff, introduction, *Gunslinger*, by Ed Dorn (Durham, NC: Duke University Press, 1989), xi.

41. Ibid., vi–vii.

42. Ibid., xvii

43. Patricia Waugh, excerpt from *Modernism, Postmodernism, Feminism: Gender and Autonomy Theory*, in *Postmodernism: A Reader*, ed. Patricia Waugh (London: Edward Arnold, 1992), 191–92.

44. Marjorie Perloff, *The Dance of the Intellect: Studies of Poetry of the Pound Tradition* (Evanston, IL: Northwestern University Press, 1985), 161, emphasis in original.

45. Brian McHale, "Telling Stories Again: On the Replenishment of Narrative in the Postmodern Long Poem," *The Yearbook of English Studies* 30 (2000): 250–62.

46. Alice Notley, "The 'Feminine' Epic," *Coming After* (Ann Arbor: University of Michigan Press, 2005), 180.

47. Timothy Melley, *Empire of Conspiracy: The Culture of Paranoia in Postwar America* (Ithaca, NY: Cornell University Press, 2000), 32–34.

48. Ibid., 107–32.

49. Sianne Ngai, *Ugly Feelings* (Cambridge, MA: Harvard University Press, 2005), 301.

50. Ibid., 9–15.

51. Alice Notley, *Tell Me Again*, unpublished manuscript, not paginated, emphasis in original.

52. Notley, "Poetics of Disobedience," 2.

53. James Naremore, *More Than Night: Film Noir in Its Contexts* (Berkeley: University of California Press, 1998), 19, 22.

54. Jennifer Fay and Justus Nieland, eds., *Film Noir: Hard-Boiled Modernity and the Cultures of Globalization* (London: Routledge, 2009), 21, emphasis in original.

55. Ibid., 39.

56. Ibid., 41.

57. Ngai, *Ugly Feelings*, 298–331.

4 / Harryette Mullen's Poetics in Prose

1. For Nielsen's argument regarding cannibalism, an argument I address more thoroughly later in this chapter, see Aldon Lynn Nielsen, *Reading Race in American Poetry: "An Area of Act"* (Urbana: University of Illinois Press, 2000).

2. Jonathan Monroe, *A Poverty of Objects: The Prose Poem and the Politics of Genre* (Ithaca: Cornell University Press, 1987), 95–96.

3. Andreas Huyssen makes this argument in *After the Great Divide: Modernism, Mass Culture, Postmodenism*. (Bloomington: Indiana University Press, 1986), 46.

4. Margueritte Murphy, *A Tradition of Subversion: The Prose Poem in English from Wilde to Ashbery* (Amherst: University of Massachusetts Press, 1992), 1.

5. Although critics have identified Maurice de Guerin's *Le Centaure*, Aloyisus Bertrand's *Gaspard de la nuit*, and the work of Edgar Allan Poe and Thomas De Quincey as Baudelaire's early influences, it is generally accepted that Baudelaire's prose poetry is in the end a new form unto itself. See Michael Hamburger's introduction to Charles Baudelaire, *Twenty Prose Poems (Petits poèmes en prose)*, translated by Michael Hamburger (San Francisco: City Lights, 1988), 2.

6. Michel Delville writes that "the history of the contemporary prose poem in English is, to a large extent, the history of the successive attempts by poets to redefine the parameters governing our expectations of what a poem (or a prose poem) should look or sound like." See Delville, *The American Prose Poem: Poetic Form and the Boundaries of Genre* (Gainesville: University Press of Florida, 1998), 2. Refusing to firmly fix the genre of the prose poem in normative terms while insisting upon the role of reading in determining what a prose poem may be, Steven Monte writes that "understanding prose poetry as a genre means exploring the interpretive consequences of reading what has been called the *poème en prose*, or prose poem, as if it were a genre. In other words, I am interested more in what prose poetry is or has been in specific historical and cultural contexts than in what prose poetry is in a normative sense." See Stephen Monte, *Invisible Fences: Prose Poetry as a Genre in French and American Literature* (Lincoln: University of Nebraska Press, 2000), 1–2.

7. David Lehman, introduction to *Great American Prose Poems: From Poe to the Present* (New York: Scribner, 2003), 13, emphasis in original.

8. Holly Iglesias, *Boxing Inside the Box: Women's Prose Poetry* (Niantic, CT: Quale Press, 2004), 14. Iglesias quotes Robert Pinsky and Peter Johnson.

9. This trend is evident in David Lehman's anthology as well as in the critical work done by Stephen Monte and Margueritte Murphy. See Monte, *Invisible Fences*, and Murphy, *Tradition of Subversion*.

10. Iglesias, *Boxing Inside the Box*, 3–4.

11. Paul Naylor, *Poetic Investigations: Singing the Holes in History* (Evanston, IL: Northwestern University Press, 1999).

12. Maxine Chernoff quoted in Holly Iglesias, *Boxing Inside the Box*, 98.

13. Charles Baudelaire, *Les Fleurs du mal*, translated by Keith Waldrop (Middletown, CT: Wesleyan University Press, 2006). Waldrop cites this poem as 28 in *Les Fleurs du mal*, whereas in Richard Howard's translation, this is poem 29, "As If a Serpent Danced." *Les Fleurs du mal*, translated by Richard Howard (Jaffrey, NH: Godine Press, 1982), 33.

14. Michael North, *The Dialect of Modernism: Race, Language, and Twentieth-Century Literature* (New York: Oxford University Press, 1994).

15. See Nathaniel Mackey, *Discrepant Engagement: Dissonance, Cross-Culturality, and Experimental Writing* (Tuscaloosa: University of Alabama Press, 1993), 18.

16. Harryette Mullen, "Imagining the Unimagined Reader: Writing to the Unborn and Including the Excluded," reprinted in *The Cracks Between What We Are and What We Are Supposed to Be* (Tuscaloosa: University of Alabama Press, 2012), 6–7.

17. Ibid., 7

18. Evie Shockley, *Renegade Poetics: Black Aesthetics and Formal Innovation in African American Poetry* (Iowa City: University of Iowa Press, 2011), 7.

19. Ibid., 19.

20. Meta DuEwa Jones, *The Muse Is Music: Jazz Poetry from the Harlem Renaissance to the Spoken Word* (Chicago: University of Illinois Press, 2011).

21. Robin Tremblay-McGaw, "Enclosure and Run: The Fugitive Recyclopedia of Harryette Mullen's Writing," *MELUS* 35, no. 2 (Summer 2010): 71–94.

22. Amy Moorman Robbins, "Harryette Mullen and Race in Language/Writing," *Contemporary Literature* 51, no. 2 (Summer 2010): 341–70.

23. Gertrude Stein, *Tender Buttons* (1914), in *Selected Writings of Gertrude Stein*, ed. Carl Van Vechten (New York: Vintage, 1990), 471

24. Harryette Mullen, *Trimmings* (Providence, RI: Tender Buttons Press, 1991), 15.

25. Elisabeth A. Frost, *The Feminist Avant-Garde in American Poetry* (Iowa City: University of Iowa Press, 2000), 153.

26. Deborah Mix, "Tender Revisions: Harryette Mullen's *Trimmings* and *S*PeRM**K*T*," *American Literature* 77, no. 1 (Mar. 2005): 65–92.

27. North, *Dialect of Modernism*, 32.

28. Ibid., 27.

29. Nielsen, *Reading Race in American Poetry*, 7.

30. See Andreas Huyssen, *After the Great Divide: Modernism, Mass Culture, Postmodernism* (Bloomington: Indiana University Press, 1986), 46. This process echoes the process of white cooptation of African American culture and African symbolism that Michael North explores in *The Dialect of Modernism*. See also North, *The Dialect of Modernism*.

31. Rebecca Munford, "Re-Presenting Charles Baudelaire/Re-Presencing Jeanne Duval: Transformations of the Muse in Angela Carter's 'Black Venus,'" *Forum for Modern Language Studies* 40, no. 1 (Jan. 2004): 1–13. See Nicole Ward Jouve, *Baudelaire: A Fire to Conquer Darkness* (New York: Palgrave Macmillan, 1980), 157.

32. Poem 25 (untitled), in *Les Fleurs du mal*, trans. Waldrop, 38.

33. Poem 23, "Hair," in Baudelaire, *Les Fleurs du mal* (Waldrop trans.), 35.

34. Carol Clark and Robert Sykes, introduction to *Baudelaire in English*, trans. John Ashbery et al. (New York, Penguin, 1997), xxii.

35. Gayatri Chakravorty Spivak, "Imperialism and Sexual Difference," *Oxford Literary Review* 8, nos. 1–2 (1988): 229.

36. Charles Baudelaire, "Un hémisphère dans une chevelure," translated by Michael Hamburger (San Francisco: City Lights Books, 1988), 31.

37. Nielsen, *Reading Race in American Poetry*, 3–4.

38. Ibid., 4.

39. Ibid., 9. See Patricia Turner, *I Heard It Through the Grapevine: Rumor in African-American Culture* (Berkeley, University of California Press, 1993), 25.

40. Quoted in Nielsen, *Reading Race in American Poetry*, 6.

41. Hortense J. Spillers, "Mama's Baby, Papa's Maybe: An American Grammar Book," in *Feminisms: An Anthology of Literary Theory and Criticism*, ed. Robyn R. Warhol and Diane Price Herndl (New Brunswick, NJ: Rutgers University Press, 1997), 384.

42. Patricia Hill Collins, *Fighting Words: Black Women and the Search for Justice* (Minneapolis: University of Minnesota Press, 1998).

43. Ibid., 51.

44. Griselda Pollock, *Vision and Difference: Femininity, Feminism, and the History of Art* (New York, Routledge, 2003). Quoted in Munford, "Re-Presenting Charles Baudelaire," 2.

45. Interview with Barbara Henning in *Looking Up Harryette Mullen: Interviews on Sleeping with the Dictionary and Other Works* (New York: Belladonna, 2011), 55.

46. Harryette Mullen, *S*PeRM**K*T* (Philadelphia: Singing Horse Press, 1992). Reprinted in *Recylocopedia: S*PeRM**K*T, and Muse & Drudge* (St. Paul, MN: Graywolf, 2006), 74.

47. Nielsen, *Reading Race in American Poetry*, 5.

48. *Recyclopedia*, 82.

49. Mullen says that "Bleeding Hearts" was a specific response to the way black neighborhoods are portrayed in the media. Henning, *Looking Up Harryette Mullen*, 55.

50. Harryette Mullen, *Sleeping with the Dictionary* (Berkeley: University of California Press, 2002), 14. All subsequent references will be noted in the text with page numbers.

51. Henning, *Looking Up Harryette Mullen*, 56.

52. Ibid., 59.

53. Poem 28, "Dancing Serpent," in Baudelaire, *Les Fleurs du mal* (Waldrop trans.), 41.

54. Therese Dolan, "Manet's Portrait of Baudelaire's Mistress, Reclining," *The Art Bulletin* 79, no. 4 (Dec. 1997): 615.

55. Edgar Allan Poe, *The Philosophy of Composition*, 1846. Reprint in *The New Anthology of American Poetry*, vol. 1, ed. Axelrod et al. (New Brunswick, NJ: Rutgers University Press, 2003), 324.

56. Dolan, "Manet's Portrait," 615.

57. Poem 29, "Carrion," Baudelaire, *Les Fleurs du mal* (Waldrop trans.), 42.

5 / Claudia Rankine's *Don't Let Me Be Lonely*

1. Joan Retallack, *The Poethical Wager* (Berkeley: University of California Press, 2003).

2. Elaine Scarry, *The Body in Pain* (New York: Oxford University Press, 1985), 14.

3. Jennifer Ashton, *From Modernism to Postmodernism: American Poetry and Theory in the Twentieth Century* (Cambridge: Cambridge University Press, 2005). Ashton argues that despite the New Critical insistence upon the affective fallacy as being detrimental to any understanding of the autonomous text, these critics' simultaneous insistence upon a close reading and sounding out of the poem invites an affective response. According to Ashton, some of the major works of modernism are

participatory "open texts" much in the same way postmodern poems privileging indeterminacy are.

4. Jennifer Flescher and Robert N. Casper, interview with Claudia Rankine, *jubilat* 12 (July 2006): 2, accessed January 15, 2013, http://poems.com/special_features/prose/essay_rankine.php.

5. Mark Nowak, *Shut Up Shut Down* (Minneapolis: Coffee House Press, 2008).

6. Charles Olson, "Projective Verse," in *Postmodern American Poetry: A Norton Anthology*, ed. Paul Hoover (New York: Norton, 1994), 614.

7. Flescher and Casper interview, 6.

8. Marjorie Perloff and Brian McHale are but two contemporary critics debating the legacy of modernism and the originality or lack of originality in postmodernism. See Perloff, *Twenty-First Century Modernisms* (London: Blackwell, 2005), and McHale, *The Obligation Toward the Difficult Whole* (Tuscaloosa: University of Alabama Press, 2004).

9. Flescher and Casper interview, 1.

10. Ezra Pound, *The ABC of Reading* (1934) (New York: New Directions, 2010).

11. Susan Stanford Friedman, "When a 'Long' Poem Is a 'Big' Poem: Self-Authorizing Strategies in Women's Twentieth-Century 'Long' Poems," in *Feminisms: An Anthology of Literary Theory and Criticism*, ed. Robyn Warhol and Diane Price Herndl (New Brunswick, NJ: Rutgers University Press, 1997), 721–38.

12. Ibid., 722–23.

13. Ibid., 725. As examples of each of the four strategies she outlines, Friedman analyzes the work of Mina Loy, Alicia Ostriker, Judy Grahn, and Betsy Warland.

14. Ibid., 724.

15. Ibid., 722.

16. Ibid.

17. Lynn Keller, *Forms of Expansion: Recent Long Poems by Women* (Chicago: University of Chicago Press, 1997).

18. Ibid., 2.

19. Ibid., 16.

20. Keller considers the work of Sharon Doubiago, Judy Grahn, Rita Dove, Marie Osbey, Marilyn Hacker, Susan Howe, and Rachel Blau DuPlessis.

21. Retallack, *Poethical Wager*, 112.

22. Ibid., 90–101.

23. Flescher and Casper interview, 4.

24. Alicia Suskind Ostriker, "Beyond Confession: The Poetics of Postmodern Witness," *The American Poetry Review* 30, no. 2 (2001): 35–39. Ostriker's term constituted her concerned response to the Language movement's disparagement of the lyric mode.

25. Muriel Rukeyser, "Note" at the end of *U.S. 1* (New York: Covici and Friede, 1938). Quoted in Flescher and Casper interview, 4.

26. Katy Lederer, interview with Claudia Rankine, *Verse* 8, 2–3, reprinted in *The Verse Book of Interviews*, ed. Brian Henry and Andrew Zawacki (Amherst, MA: Verse Press, 2005), 147–51.

27. Ibid., 147.

28. In her interview with Flescher and Casper, Rankine cites Joan Didion as one of her many influences.

29. Emmanuel Levinas, "The Transcendence of Words" (1949), in *The Levinas Reader*, ed. Séan Hand (Oxford: Blackwell, 1989), 144–49. Quoted in Claudia Rankine, *Don't Let Me Be Lonely* (Minneapolis: Graywolf, 2004), 120.

30. Flescher and Casper interview, 4.

31. Lederer interview, 150.

32. Clair Wills, "Contemporary Women's Poetry: Experimentalism and the Expressive Voice," *Critical Inquiry* 36, no. 3 (Autumn 1994): 41–42. Quoted in Linda Kinnahan, *Lyric Interventions: Feminism, Experimental Poetry, and Contemporary Discourse* (Iowa City: University of Iowa Press, 2004), 22.

33. Flescher and Casper interview, 8.

34. Brian McHale, *The Obligation Toward the Difficult Whole* (Tuscaloosa: University of Alabama Press, 2004), 258–61. In presenting a set of features that he sees as characterizing the postmodernist long poem, McHale is arguing against Marjorie Perloff's recent attempts to show that postmodernism is but an extension of modernism, the latter being the determining aesthetic.

35. Wallace Stevens, "Of Modern Poetry," in *The Norton Anthology of Modern Poetry*, vol. 1, 3rd ed., ed. Ramazani et al. (New York, Norton, 2003), 255.

36. Alan Gilbert, "The Ethics of Language," *Boston Review*, February/March 2005, accessed January 15, 2013, bostonreview.net/BR30.1/gilbert.php.

37. Flescher and Casper interview, 5.

38. Poetics statement in *The New American Poetry of Engagement*, ed. Ann Keniston and Jeffrey Gray (Jefferson, NC: McFarland, 2012), 245–46.

39. Ibid., 2.

40. Kevin Bell, "Unheard Writing in the Climate of Spectacular Noise: Claudia Rankine on TV," *The Global South* 3, no. 1 (Spring 2009): 98.

41. Emma Kimberley, "Politics and Poetics of Fear After 9/11: Claudia Rankine's *Don't Let Me Be Lonely*," *Journal of American Studies* 45, no. 4 (2011): 778.

42. Ibid., 782.

43. Flescher and Casper interview.

44. Lederer interview, 148.

45. Ibid., 149–50.

46. Aimé Césaire, *Notebook of a Return to the Native Land* (1947), trans. Clayton Eshelman and ed. Annette Smith (Middletown, CT: Wesleyan University Press, 2001).

47. Ibid., 10.

48. Ibid., 12.

49. Ibid., 16.

50. Drucker, *Sweet Dreams*, 8.

51. Mark Wallace, "On the Lyric as Experimental Possibility," *Electronic Poetry Center*, accessed December 17, 2013, http://wings.buffalo.edu/epc/authors/wallace/lyric.html.

52. Ibid.

Index

abject, the, 16, 61–64, 122, 123
affect: in films of 1950s and 1960s, 62; in Laura Mullen's *Murmur*, 16, 47, 50–53, 55, 57, 60, 64, 69; in noir, 93, 96; in Notley's work, 81, 82, 87; in Rankine's *Don't Let Me Be Lonely*, 135, 141, 142, 145, 147
African Americans: African American blues epic, 107; Black Arts movement, 108, 112–13, 114; criticism of literature of, 105; marginality of, 109; in Harryette Mullen's work, 115–23; as other, 110; violence against, 142–43. *See also* black women
Altieri, Charles, 52–53, 54, 55
"American Crimes and How They Matter" (Stein), 22, 36–37, 42
American Hybrid (Swensen and St. John), 1, 3, 4–10
American Women Poets in the Twenty-First Century: Where Lyric Meets Language (Rankine and Spahr), 13, 152n24
Armantrout, Rae, 4, 5, 151n5
Ashbery, John, 10, 76, 101, 102, 136, 141
At Night the States (Notley), 71
Autobiography of Alice B. Toklas, The (Stein), 23, 43
avant-garde community: aporias in aesthetics of, 106; author signature in works of, 80; Baudelaire's *Les Fleurs du Mal* and, 100; gender politics in, 13, 72;

and high-low divide, 13, 27; and hybrid poetics, 1–2, 4, 7, 11, 12–13, 14, 80, 85; on the lyric, 79; mandate to renew of, 6, 7; marginality associated with, 109; masculinist dogma of, 2, 28, 85; Stein's *Blood on the Dining-Room Floor* and, 29; as white dominated, 9

Baudelaire, Charles: black women in poems of, 104–5, 110–12; flâneur of, 17, 71, 74, 104, 110, 114; *Les Fleurs du Mal*, 46, 100, 104, 110–11, 120–23, 126, 160n5; prose poem invented by, 17, 100, 101, 160n5; "Sed Non Satiata," 117
Bell, Kevin, 144–45
Bergvall, Caroline, 16, 47
Berlant, Lauren, 60, 70, 149, 157n24
Bidart, Frank, 47, 56
Biddinger, Mary, 8
Black Arts movement, 108, 112–13, 114
black women: in Baudelaire's poems, 104–5, 110–12; black female body in early prose poetry, 17, 105; as desired and discarded, 122; Manet and, 108, 109, 120–21; Harryette Mullen and, 100, 105, 106–7, 109, 113, 114, 116–20, 121; objectified in modern poetry, 101, 105, 112; in subject position, 131
Blood on the Dining-Room Floor (Stein), 20–43; Lizzie Borden in, 15, 29–30, 36, 37–39; critical reception of, 14, 23,

24, 26, 28, 31; dead Englishwoman in, 41–42; death in the village hotel, 22, 32, 39; desire for closure frustrated in, 15, 26, 30, 41; as detective story, 14, 15, 23, 24, 26, 29, 30–31, 41, 43, 44; domesticity critiqued in, 15, 29, 30, 31–33, 35, 36, 37, 40–41, 42; as genre fiction, 14, 153n13; gothic conventions in, 15, 26, 29, 31, 32, 35, 41–42, 43, 44; Hammett's *The Dain Curse* compared with, 25–26; as "just conversation, 22, 30, 31, 36; lesbian sexuality in, 15, 29, 30–31, 32, 33, 34, 39, 42; Laura Mullen's *Murmur* compared with, 16, 44, 56; narrator of, 15, 22, 31, 35–36, 37; new servants arrive, 22, 31–32, 37, 40–41; patriarchy critiqued in, 15, 29, 34, 35, 41, 42; plotting of, 23, 30, 31, 33, 42; "read the beginning again," 27, 34; references to other Stein works in, 22, 29, 40, 42; as social critique, 154n32; as textual hybrid, 22–23, 24, 29, 43
Borden, Lizzie, 15, 29–30, 36–39, 40
Bryant, Marsha, 49, 68–69
Burt, Stephen, 3–4, 5, 9–10, 102
"But He Says I Misunderstood" (Notley), 78–79

cannibalism, 100, 111–17
capitalism: consumer, 12; in established criticism, 11; loss of vocabulary for talking about, 93; mass-market fiction as revelatory of structure of, 44; Harryette Mullen in context of international, 106; noir in export of, 95–96; Notley's *Disobedience* on, 16–17, 87, 99; Rankine's *Don't Let Me Be Lonely* on, 138, 141; Stein's *Blood on the Dining-Room Floor* on, 41
Celan, Paul, 124, 134–35, 146, 147
Césaire, Aimé, 18, 124, 146–47
Cha, Theresa, 3, 127, 136
Close to Me and Closer (Notley), 71
Clover, Joshua, 7–8
Collins, Patricia Hill, 17, 113–14
Coming After (Notley), 75
Confessionalism, 77, 78
consumerism: consumer capitalism, 12; consumer culture, 2, 13, 18; demand for female corpses, 44; Harryette Mullen's *S*PeRM**K*T* on, 114–15; Laura Mullen's *Murmur* on, 49; in Notley's *Disobedience*, 88, 95–96; racism in popular consumer culture, 18
Curnutt, Kirk, 23, 153n4

Dain Curse, The (Hammett), 14, 15, 24–26, 154n17
Descent of Alette, The (Notley), 16, 83–84
detective fiction: as about details, 42; domestic, 26, 27, 31, 35, 37, 41, 43; hard-boiled, 25, 26, 87, 88–89, 95; of Kristeva, 64–65; logos-driven male detective in, 36; Laura Mullen's *Murmur* reworks genre, 15–16, 48, 55, 56, 64, 65–68, 69; Notley's *Disobedience* as, 85, 87–89, 90, 91; Notley's *The Descent of Alette* as, 83; politics of class and ethnicity in, 32; Stein on, 20, 21–22, 25–26, 46, 153n7; Stein's *Blood on the Dining-Room Floor* as, 14, 15, 23, 24, 26, 29, 30–31, 35, 41, 43, 44; women's, 15, 25, 26–27, 154n18
Didion, Joan, 133, 137
Disobedience (Notley), 85–99; agency as uncertain in, 88, 91–93; as detective fiction, 85, 87–89, 90, 91; as epic, 16, 85, 87, 92, 99; feminism of, 16, 86–87, 93, 94; lyric subject in, 46, 85–87, 91; as multisited critique of late capitalism, 16–17; paranoia in, 17, 92–94, 97–98; on plot, 71, 87, 88
domesticity: domestic detective fiction, 26, 27, 31, 35, 37, 41, 43; frustrated, 49; in Hammett's *The Dain Curse*, 25; as isolating force, 50; lesbian, 15, 29, 39, 41, 108; in Harryette Mullen's in *S*PeRM**K*T*, 116; in Notley's work, 76–77, 78, 80–81; Stein's *Blood on the Dining-Room Floor* critiques, 15, 29, 30, 31–33, 35, 36, 37, 40–41, 42
Don't Let Me Be Lonely: An American Lyric (Rankine), 124–49; affect in, 135, 141, 142, 145, 147; Césaire and, 18, 124, 146–47; endnotes in, 124, 125, 127; as hybrid, 124, 127, 136, 145, 147; influences on, 124, 126–27, 146–47; layered structure of, 125, 126, 127, 144; as long poem, 124, 125, 126, 127, 128, 130–31, 136, 145, 146; as lyric, 125, 126, 127, 131–35, 145, 147; speaking subject of, 131, 132–39, 147
Dorn, Ed, 89–90

Drucker, Johanna, 11–12, 147, 149, 152n20
Dydo, Ulla, 14, 23, 24

Eliot, T. S.: as consumer of African peoples, 112; in long poem tradition, 128; "The Love Song of J. Alfred Prufrock," 52, 67, 126; on marginality and the avant-garde, 109; "Preludes," 46, 76; prose poetry of, 101; *The Waste Land*, 26, 46, 60
End of the Alphabet, The (Rankine), 145
Enduring Freedom: A Little Book of Mechanical Brides (Mullen), 47
epic: African American blues, 107; feminist, 16, 73–74, 83, 84, 159n34; Notley in reinventing of, 16, 73–74, 83, 84, 85, 91; Notley's *Disobedience* as, 16, 85, 87, 92, 99
Evans, Steve, 7
Everybody's Autobiography (Stein), 21, 32, 41, 43

female body: as abject, 62–63; black female body in Baudelaire's poems, 104–5, 110–12; black female body in early prose poetry, 17, 105; Harryette Mullen on black women, 100, 105; in Harryette Mullen's *Sleeping with the Dictionary*, 116–20; in Laura Mullen's *Murmur*, 16, 44, 55–56, 57–59, 62–63, 69; mutilated, 16, 44, 55–56, 57–59, 62–63, 69, 117; in Notley's "The Trouble with You Girls," 81; in Rankine's *Don't Let Me Be Lonely*, 125–26; sexualized, 58, 116, 128
"'Feminine Epic,' The" (Notley), 91
feminism: Confessionalism, 77; feminist avant-garde, 13; feminist epic, 16, 73–74, 83, 84, 159n34; feminist subject, 81, 87; hybrid poetics foments feminist, populist avant-gardism, 11, 12–13; in long poems, 129; Mullen's *Murmur* reworks detective fiction genre in terms of, 16, 66; Notley and, 16, 76, 77–78, 80, 84, 86–87, 93, 94; paranoia as feminist response, 94, 97; in radical art, 85
Fence (magazine), 1, 3, 7–8, 9, 10, 151n5
flâneur/flâneuse: of Baudelaire, 17, 71, 74, 104, 110, 114; as disembodied, 115; gaze of, 111, 114, 122; of Harryette Mullen, 17, 123; of Notley, 74, 81, 87, 96
Flaubert, Gustave, 16, 27–28, 100–101, 109

Fleurs du Mal, Les (Baudelaire), 46, 100, 104, 110–11, 120–23, 126, 160n5
Fraser, Kathleen, 5, 9, 28, 79
Friedman, Susan Stanford, 84, 128–29, 130
Frost, Elisabeth A., 13, 15, 24, 40, 108, 152n230

Gallaher, John, 8
gaze, 58, 61–62, 104, 111, 114, 120, 122, 123
gender: artistic production and consumption as gendered, 27–29; codes in literary devices, 15; gendered subject, 13, 48, 80, 82, 97, 103–4; ideology, 99; imbalance, 78, 80–81; long poems as gendered, 128, 130; masculinist dogma of avant-garde community, 2, 28, 85; mass culture associated with low feminine, 10, 14, 27; modernism–mass culture binary as gendered, 24; modernist values as gendered, 2; in Laura Mullen's work, 47, 67–68; noir's hypermasculinity, 16, 17; poetry teachers as male, 8; and power, 32, 34, 44, 65, 76, 78; schools and camps dominated by male poets, 1. *See also* patriarchy; women
genre fiction: closure underpins, 99; as feminized, 47; gaps between genres, 54; mixing avant-garde art with, 14; Mullen on crossing genres, 45; Notley's *Disobedience* uses conventions of, 87; politics of, 129; postmodern undercuts genres, 90; ready-made affective atmospheres in, 53; redefining possibilities of, 148; Retallack on, 31; Stein's *Blood on the Dining-Room Floor* as, 14, 153n13. *See also* detective fiction; gothic fiction
"Gentle Lena, The" (Stein), 33
"Good Anna, The" (Stein), 33
gothic fiction: as feminized, 35, 47; Hammett's *The Dain Curse* as, 14, 24, 25, 26; Mullen's *The Tales of Horror* as, 47; Sedgwick's model of, 26, 27, 35, 41; the spinster in, 36; Stein's *Blood on the Dining-Room Floor* as, 15, 26, 29, 31, 32, 35, 41–42, 43, 44; by women, 26–27, 129

Hammett, Dashiell: *The Dain Curse*, 14, 15, 24–26, 154n17; Stein on, 14, 21, 24; urban spaces of alienation in, 46

hard-boiled detective fiction, 25, 26, 87, 88–89, 95
Hejinian, Lyn, 5, 7, 42, 53, 72–73, 101, 151n5, 153n7
Howe, Susan, 5, 7, 48, 72–73, 103
"How Spring Comes" (Notley), 77
Huyssen, Andreas, 10, 13, 14, 16, 21, 23, 27–28, 47, 109, 149
hybrid poetics: avant-garde community and, 1–2, 4, 7, 11, 12–13, 14, 80, 85; as both on the rise and under fire, 19; as complicit in mass culture, 10–11, 12, 13; defined, 1; high and low mixed in, 2, 10, 11, 12; Language writing and, 4, 5, 8, 10, 53–54; of long poems, 85, 129, 130; of Harryette Mullen, 10, 101, 152n30; Laura Mullen's *Murmur* as hybrid, 16, 44, 45, 54; newness attributed to, 1, 3–7; of Notley, 10, 74, 78, 79, 85; politics of, 1, 2, 5, 7–10; prose poetry as hybrid, 17, 102; Rankine's *Don't Let Me Be Lonely* as hybrid, 124, 127, 136, 145, 147; Stein and, 3, 14, 22–23, 24, 29, 30, 43; women writers, 2, 5, 8

Iglesias, Holly, 17, 102–3, 104, 108, 121
"Imagining the Unimagined Reader" (Mullen), 100, 106

"January" (Notley), 76–77

Keller, Lynn, 13, 84–85, 129–30
Kim, Myung Mi, 5, 124
Kimberley, Emma, 144–45
Kinnahan, Linda, 13, 74
Kristeva, Julia, 64–65, 129

Language writing: avant-garde aesthetics influences, 106; collective fear of being wrong about politics as legacy of, 9; democratic ethos of reader participation of, 149; Dorn's *Gunslinger* and, 89; hybrid poetics and, 4, 5, 8, 10, 53–54; influence declines, 19; lyric versus, 4, 5, 6, 7, 13, 45, 72–73, 79, 136; mass culture rejected by, 11; Harryette Mullen and, 105–8; Notley associated with, 71, 80; Post-Language, 1; prose poetry, 101; Rankine's *Don't Let Me Be Lonely* and, 125, 127, 132, 140; Vietnam War and, 82; women and, 53, 72, 73

lesbian sexuality: the "mannish lesbian," 36; in Stein's *Blood on the Dining-Room Floor*, 15, 29–34, 39, 41, 42; in Stein's "Sacred Emily," 40; and Stein's *Tender Buttons*, 15, 108
Levinas, Emmanuel, 124, 132, 143
Long Gay Book, A (Stein), 29, 39
long poems: Dorn's *Gunslinger* as, 89; as hybrid, 85, 129, 130; modernist, 60, 125; postmodernist, 90, 136–37; Rankine's *Don't Let Me Be Lonely* as, 124, 125, 126, 127, 128, 130–31, 136, 145, 146; by women, 13, 84–85, 128–30
lyric, the: affect's relation to lyric poetry, 52–53; "coming to voice" in, 114; frustrated domesticity in women's lyric poetry, 49; Language writing versus, 4, 5, 6, 7, 13, 45, 72–73, 79, 136; lyric subject, 18, 46, 53, 72–76, 78, 79–83, 85–87, 89–90, 91, 97–98, 125, 131–38, 142; in Laura Mullen's *Murmur*, 16, 44, 45, 53–54; in Notley's work, 16, 17, 73–74, 75; in Rankine's *Don't Let Me Be Lonely*, 125, 126, 127, 131–43, 145, 147

Mackey, Nathaniel, 105
Making of Americans, The (Stein), 29, 40
Manet, Edouard, 108, 109, 120–21
"Marry Netti" (Stein), 42, 155n1
mass culture: flâneur observes, 114; hybrid poetics' complicit attitude toward, 10–11, 12, 13; low feminine associated with, 10, 14, 27, 47; modernism versus, 10, 23–24, 25; in Harryette Mullen's work, 18; in Laura Mullen's hybrid works, 45, 54; Notley's work and, 74, 98–99; in Rankine's *Don't Let Me Be Lonely*, 127, 144, 147; as site of social critique, 149; Stein's *Blood on the Dining-Room Floor* and, 22, 28, 43; women's consumption of mass-market fiction, 16, 26–28, 62, 109. *See also* popular literature
Melley, Timothy, 92–93
Milosz, Czeslaw, 124, 138–39, 146, 147
misogyny, 47, 61, 70, 101
modernism: black female body in, 105, 109–10, 112; on form, 134, 136; gendered values of, 2; Hammett as modernist novelist, 14, 24; on high-low divide, 10, 13; long poems, 60, 125; mass culture versus, 10, 23–24, 25; noir

compared with, 46; on primitivism, 105, 108, 109, 112; prose poetry, 17, 101; Rankine's *Don't Let Me Be Lonely* and, 147, 148; split with neo-Romanticism, 5–6; Stein and, 22, 27, 28, 29, 30, 43

Mullen, Harryette, 100–123; in *American Hybrid* anthology, 5; Baudelaire as influence on, 17, 100, 101; in *A Best of Fence*, volume 1, 151n5; on black women, 100, 105, 106–7, 109, 113, 114, 121; Burt's view of hybrid poetics and, 4; Frost on, 13; fugitive poetics of, 107; high art and mass culture mixed in work of, 18; hybrid traditions in work of, 10, 101, 152n30; "Imagining the Unimagined Reader," 100, 106; implicit political strategy of, 2; and Language writing, 105–8; *Muse & Drudge*, 17, 105, 106, 107, 114; on noir, 104–5; prose poetry of, 17–18, 100, 105, 106, 108, 114, 121; Rankine compared with, 131–132; "Resistance is Fertile," 118; *Trimmings*, 105, 108, 116, 120–21; "Wino Rhino," 122–23. *See also Sleeping with the Dictionary*; *S*PeRM**K*T*

Mullen, Laura: in *American Hybrid* anthology, 5; *Enduring Freedom: A Little Book of Mechanical Brides*, 47; on the I, 46; implicit political strategy of, 2, 45; as marginal to experimental community, 16; on mistakes in poetry, 156n13; mixture of forms and modes in, 10; on not having to choose, 6; *The Tales of Horror*, 47; on thought and feeling, 44. *See also Murmur*

Murmur (Mullen), 44–70; the abject in, 16, 61–64; activated spaces produced by, 45–46, 70; affect in, 16, 47, 50–53, 55, 57, 60, 64, 69; "L'Aura" section, 68; "Beginning Again & Again" section, 55–57; "Chewed *Vague*" section, 57–58; dedication to The Audience, 48–51; "Demonstrating Bodies" section, 58–59; detective genre reworked by, 15–16, 48, 55, 56, 64, 65–68; footnotes in, 60–61; "Forensics" section, 59–62; "Gravida Loca" section, 62–63; as hybrid, 16, 44, 54; "I Shadow (Private)" section, 65–68; "The Killer Confesses to Unspeakable Acts" section, 68–69; lyric in, 16, 44, 53–54; mutilated female corpse in, 16, 45, 55–56, 57–59, 62–63; noir compared with, 16, 46, 47–48, 50, 55, 62, 67; "A Nouns Meant" section, 54–55, 157n21; precursor texts, 47; Stein's *Blood on the Dining-Room Floor* compared with, 16, 44, 56

Muse & Drudge (Mullen), 17, 105, 106, 107, 114

Myles, Eileen, 78, 151n5

Mysteries of Small Houses (Notley): alternative aesthetics in, 78; as feminist intervention, 80; "I'm Just Rigid Enough," 75; lyric subject in, 79–83, 85; poetics of witness in, 16; "Sept 17 / Aug 29, '88," 82–83; "The Trouble with You Girls," 80–81

New American Poetry (Allen), 6
New York School, 16, 71, 87
Ngai, Sianne, 93, 97
Nickerson, Catherine Ross, 26–27, 36, 154n18
Nielsen, Aldon Lynn, 17, 100, 109, 111–12, 115
noir, 95–96; Hammett's *The Dain Curse* as, 14; hypermasculinity in, 16, 17; Harryette Mullen and, 104–5; Laura Mullen's *Murmur* compared with, 16, 46, 47–48, 50, 55, 62, 67; Notley's *Disobedience* and, 85, 87–89, 90, 94–98; paranoia associated with, 17, 90, 95; Stein's *Blood on the Dining-Room Floor* and, 30

Notley, Alice, 71–99; alternative aesthetics of, 78–79; in *A Best of Fence*, volume 1, 151n5; critical neglect of, 72, 74, 85; epic reinvented by, 16, 73–74, 83, 84, 85, 91; hybridity of work of, 10, 74, 78, 79, 85; implicit political strategy of, 2; Language writing associations of, 71, 80; in long poem tradition, 128; lyric subject in work of, 74, 78, 81; on male dominance, 77–78; New York School associations of, 16, 71, 87. *See also Disobedience*; *Mysteries of Small Houses*

Nowak, Mark, 126–27

O'Hara, Frank, 71, 76, 77, 81, 86, 99
Olson, Charles, 6, 126–27, 128, 136
"open form" poets, 136

Patriarchal Poetry (Stein), 30, 65
patriarchy: Borden as victim of, 30; loss of vocabulary for talking about, 93; the "mannish lesbian" as threat to, 36; Mullen's *Murmur* critiques, 44; Stein's *Blood on the Dining-Room Floor* critiques, 15, 29, 34, 35, 41, 42
Perloff, Marjorie, 7, 14, 73, 80, 85, 89, 90, 163n8
"PETTICOAT, A" (Stein), 108
Plath, Sylvia, 49, 63, 72, 77
"Poetics of Disobedience, The" (Notley), 77
"Poetry and Grammar" (Stein), 156n13
popular literature: academic bias against, 23; masculinist pulp sensibility, 93; mass-market fiction, 16, 20, 21, 27, 28–29, 42–43, 44, 46, 47, 62, 64, 70; Laura Mullen's *Murmur* engages, 47, 45–46, 47, 59–61; Notley's *Disobedience* uses conventions of, 16, 87; saccharine narratives common to, 95; the spinster/lesbian in, 36; Stein and, 20, 22–23. *See also* detective fiction; gothic fiction
postmodernism: flâneur and mass culture of, 114, 115; interested social critique lacking in, 10, 13; long poems, 90, 136–37; male nostalgia for universal subject in, 91, 93; Laura Mullen's *Murmur* and, 44, 47, 66; Notley's postmodern poetics, 16, 87; paranoia associated with, 92, 93; pastiche in, 10, 66, 90; postmodern subject, 75, 78, 91; prose poetry, 101; Rankine's *Don't Let Me Be Lonely* and, 125, 126, 127, 135, 148
poststructuralism, 89, 91, 92, 136
Pound, Ezra, 71, 105, 109, 128
primitivism, 105, 108, 109, 112
prose poetry, 101–4; of Harryette Mullen, 17–18, 100, 105, 106, 108, 114, 121; in Rankine's *Don't Let Me Be Lonely*, 125, 139; by women, 102–3

Q.E.D. (Stein), 40

race: appearing and disappearing at will, 109; essentialism, 107; mark on the body, 113; racialized body, 115, 143; in Rankine's *Don't Let Me Be Lonely*, 124, 141–43; white anthologies, 8–9. *See also* African Americans; racism
racism, 18, 88, 117, 142, 147

Rankine, Claudia: *The End of the Alphabet*, 145; implicit political strategy of, 2; lyric subject of, 18; mixture of forms and modes in, 10; *Nothing in Nature Is Private*, 131; on similarity of our lives, 145–46. *See also Don't Let Me Be Lonely: An American Lyric*
"Reflection on the Atomic Bomb" (Stein), 20–21, 22
Retallack, Joan, 14, 22–23, 24, 28, 31, 70, 130, 154n32
Rohr, Susanne, 23, 153n13
Rukeyser, Muriel, 3, 9, 128, 130

"Sacred Emily" (Stein), 29, 40
St. John, David, 4–5, 7, 9
Scalapino, Leslie, 53, 73
Scherr, Rebecca, 15, 24, 52
Sedgwick, Eve, 26, 27, 35, 41
"Sept 17 / Aug 29, '88" (Notley), 82–83
Sexton, Anne, 49, 72
Shockley, Evie, 106–7
Silliman, Ron, 7, 9, 73
"Sitwell Edith Sitwell" (Stein), 40
Sleeping with the Dictionary (Mullen), 116–20; "Bleeding Hearts," 117; "Daisy Pearl," 117–18; "Free Radicals," 118; "The Gene for Music," 118–20, 121; new version of flâneur in, 17, 123; on representing black body, 105; "Resistance is Fertile," 118; tropes of cannibalism and eating in, 113; on white desire for black body, 100; "Wino Rhino," 122–23
Spahr, Juliana, 4, 5, 7, 13, 72, 93, 97, 136, 152n24
S*PeRM**K*T (Mullen), 114–16; new version of flâneur in, 17, 114; Rankine's *Don't Let Me Be Lonely* compared with, 132; on representing black body, 105; on white desire for black body, 100
Stanzas in Meditation (Stein), 51
Stein, Gertrude: "American Crimes and How They Matter," 22, 36–37, 42; artistic status as uncertain, 21, 23, 28; *The Autobiography of Alice B. Toklas*, 23, 43; criticism of politics of, 20–21, 153n3; on detective fiction, 20, 21–22, 25–26, 46, 153n7; events of summer 1933 and Stein/Toklas household, 22, 32, 33, 34, 37;

Everybody's Autobiography, 21, 32, 41, 43; experimental feminine of, 130; in gendered terrain of artistic production and consumption, 27–29; "The Gentle Lena," 33; "The Good Anna," 33; on Hammett, 14, 21, 24; hybrid aesthetics of, 3, 10, 30; implicit political strategy of, 2; legacy for mixed-genre poetics in work of, 9, 43; *A Long Gay Book,* 29, 39; in long poem tradition, 128; *The Making of Americans,* 29, 40; on marginality and the avant-garde, 109; "Marry Netti," 42, 155n1; *Melanctha,* 108; in Notley's literary ancestry, 71; *Patriarchal Poetry,* 30, 65; permanence of relationship with Toklas, 41; "A PETTICOAT," 108; "Poetry and Grammar," 156n13; as precursor of Laura Mullen's *Murmur,* 47, 51, 68; and primitivism, 105; prose poetry of, 17, 101, 103; *Q.E.D.,* 40; Rankine's *Don't Let Me Be Lonely* influenced by, 124; "Reflection on the Atomic Bomb," 20–21, 22; "Sacred Emily," 29, 40; "Sitwell Edith Sitwell," 40; *Stanzas in Meditation,* 51; "Subject-Cases: The Background of a Detective Story," 22; sudden celebrity of, 21, 23, 153n4; "There is no such thing as being good to your wife," 44, 68; *Three Lives,* 29, 33, 42; "What Are Master-pieces and Why Are There So Few of Them," 21; "Why I Like Detective Stories," 22, 30; writer's block of, 23; on writing for God versus writing for Mammom, 25. *See also Blood on the Dining-Room Floor; Tender Buttons*
Stevens, Wallace, 124, 128, 136–37, 146, 147
subject: agency as uncertain in Notley's *Disobedience,* 88, 91–93; embodied, 73, 74, 82, 108, 126, 140; erasure of woman as, 109; gendered, 13, 48, 80, 82, 97, 103–4; integral, 91–94, 135; Levinasian, 143; lyric, 18, 46, 53, 72–76, 78, 79–83, 85–87, 89–90, 91, 97–98, 125, 131–38, 142; position, 16, 45, 78, 79, 108, 131–33; postmodern, 75, 78, 91; social, 114, 126, 133, 134, 135, 140, 145; speaking, 73, 74, 81, 92, 97, 131–43, 147
"Subject-Cases: The Background of a Detective Story" (Stein), 22

Suleiman, Susan Rubin, 12–13, 149
Swensen, Cole, 4–7, 8, 9, 10, 102

Tales of Horror, The (Mullen), 47
Tell Me Again (Notley), 94
Tender Buttons (Stein): female intimacy in, 39; idea of containment in, 103; lesbian sexuality and, 15, 108; Harryette Mullen's *Trimmings* influenced by, 108, 120; pleasures of intimacy and privacy in, 42; "rosy charm" in, 41; and Stein's *Blood on the Dining-Room Floor,* 29; tactile erotics in, 52; "This is the dress, Aider" section, 40
Three Lives (Stein), 29, 33, 42
Toklas, Alice B.: events of summer 1933 and Stein/Toklas household, 22, 32, 33, 34, 37; permanence of relationship with Stein, 41; privacy guarded by, 42; sits with the wives at salon, 40; Stein's *Blood on the Dining-Room Floor* preserved by, 14; Stein's *The Autobiography of Alice B. Toklas,* 23, 43
Tremblay-McGaw, Robin, 107
Trimmings (Mullen), 105, 108, 116, 120–21

Waldrop, Keith, 104, 111
Wallace, Mark, 8, 148
Waugh, Patricia, 90, 91
"What Are Master-pieces and Why Are There So Few of Them" (Stein), 21
Whitman, Walt, 126, 128
"Why I Like Detective Stories" (Stein), 22, 30
Williams, William Carlos: hybrid aesthetics of, 3; legacy for mixed-genre poetics in work of, 9–10; in long poem tradition, 128; Notley influenced by, 71, 76, 77; *Paterson,* 9, 60, 128; as precursor of Laura Mullen's *Murmur,* 47; prose poetry of, 101; "Red Wheelbarrow," 61; "Spring and All," 77; "The Young Housewife," 52, 55
"Wino Rhino" (Mullen), 122–23
Wolff, Rebecca, 7–8
women: artists considered inferior, 28, 30; consumption of mass-market fiction by, 16, 21, 26–28, 62, 109; in dedication to Laura Mullen's *Murmur,* 48–51; detective fiction by, 15, 25, 26–27, 154n18; double consciousness of, 78;

erasure in American culture, 66, 109; erasure of women poets, 2, 8, 9, 19, 92; experimentally feminine texts, 24; fear of feminization in postmodern fiction, 92–93; gothic fiction as feminized, 35, 47; gothic fiction by, 26–27, 129; hybrid poetics of, 2, 5, 8; Language poetry and, 53, 72, 73; long poems by, 13, 84–85, 128–30; lyric subject in poetry of, 79; mass culture associated with low feminine, 10, 14, 27, 47; misogyny, 47, 61, 70, 101; in New York School, 87; paranoia in texts by, 93–94; prose poetry by, 102–3; reading woman in Laura Mullen's *Murmur,* 54–55, 157n21; restrictive place in middle-class heteronormative family, 37; as at some distance from avant-garde's center, 29; spinsters, 36, 40; Stein's feminine aesthetics, 24; in Williams's "The Young Housewife," 52, 55. *See also* black women; female body; lesbian sexuality

Young, Stephanie, 72

About the Author

Amy Moorman Robbins is an assistant professor of English at Hunter College, CUNY, where she specializes in modern and contemporary American poetry.

www.ingramcontent.com/pod-product-compliance
Ingram Content Group UK Ltd.
Pitfield, Milton Keynes, MK11 3LW, UK
UKHW041305180426
11947UKWH00009B/700